Pop It in the Toaster Oven

Pop It IN THE Toaster Oven

*From Entrées to Desserts,
More Than 250
Delectable, Healthy,
and Convenient Recipes*

Lois DeWitt

THREE RIVERS PRESS
NEW YORK

Copyright © 2002 by Lois DeWitt

Published by Three Rivers Press, New York, New York.
Member of the Crown Publishing Group, a division of Random House, Inc.
www.randomhouse.com

THREE RIVERS PRESS and the Tugboat design are registered trademarks of Random House, Inc.

Printed in the United States of America

Design by Susan Hood

Library of Congress Cataloging-in-Publication Data
DeWitt, Lois.
    Pop it in the toaster oven : from entrées to desserts, more than 250 delectable, healthy, and convenient recipes/Lois DeWitt.—1st ed.
        p. cm.
    1. Toaster oven cookery.   I. Title.
    TX840.T63 D48 2002
    641.5'89—dc21   2002018122

ISBN 0-609-80768-4

10 9 8 7 6 5

First Edition

My gratitude to Catherine Houck, who initiated the writing of this book, and to Samantha DeWitt for providing inspiration and support.

Contents

Introduction

You may be asking, "What can my toaster oven *really* do?" Perhaps you think that a toaster oven cookbook consists of nothing more than a hundred dreary variations on toasted cheese sandwiches. But you'd be mistaken! The toaster oven can go far beyond just "toasting." The BROIL function can caramelize sugar, sauté onions and peppers, and produce stir-fries, crisp hash browns, and quick cake layers for a torte. The BAKE function makes perfectly cooked grains, soups, and casseroles. And because all the uncooked ingredients are combined in a baking dish and baked to completion, there's the added advantage of no "watched pot." The TOAST function produces excellent sunny-side up eggs and omelets. In fact, an awesome variety of healthy meals can be created in a toaster oven via one or more of the standard functions and using only one third to one half the energy required by a full-size oven!

The recipes included in this book need *only* a toaster oven and call for a minimum of procedures, utensils, and dishes. Most require just one dish or pan for baking, broiling, or toasting to completion. Reliably, the results are delicious. By baking and broiling, nutrients are retained and flavors concentrated. Using the toaster oven functions, it's easy to make low-fat meals, sophisticated in taste and texture, using herbs and spices for flavoring instead of fats, oils, rich gravies, and sauces. Soon you'll be asking yourself, "What *can't* my toaster oven do?"

Choosing a Toaster Oven

There are dozens of brands and models priced from $30 to $300. I recommend choosing a well-known brand. They have a better warranty, are easier to use, and have more updated safety features than inexpensive, lesser-known brands.

Consider doing a little research before you browse the stores. If you do a search of toaster ovens on the Web, you will be amazed at the wealth of consumer information that is available. There are several websites that inform consumers on toaster oven safety and hazard alerts, such as UL.com (Underwriters Laboratories Inc.), WRAL.com, and the *Consumer Reports* website (consumerreports.org). Current consumer buying guides can also be a good source of the latest documented reviews of toaster oven brands and models. When narrowing down your choices, consider not only the prices, but also the wide range of features, such as:

Capacity: This refers to the interior size, measured by cubic feet (length by width by height in inches) or by how many slices of bread you can toast at once.

Cool-touch exterior: The exterior is made of a heat-resistant material that inhibits exterior radiation of heat.

Advancing oven rack: The oven rack automatically comes forward when you open the toaster oven door.

Removable crumb tray: With a nonstick coating, it should be easily accessible and slide out for convenient cleaning.

Keep-warm cycle: This refers to a postbaking function that keeps food warm for a limited amount of time.

Broiler function: Most medium- to large-size toaster ovens have this function. Research the features of several toaster ovens to compare the broiling range temperatures.

Thermostat temperature: Some models have a 450°F. limit, while others go up to 500°F.

Easy-cleaning interior: The interior is coated with a nonstick material that facilitates cleaning.

Convection feature: A fan circulates air during baking or broiling, reducing cooking time.

Accessories: Most toaster ovens come equipped with at least a broiling rack or tray that fits into a baking pan.

Timer: This comes with a bell or chime to announce the end of toasting, baking, or broiling time.

Size: Choose a model that fits the space where you plan to put it. A four- to six-slice toaster oven will give you the best options, from toasting bread and bagels to roasting a 3½-pound chicken *and* for trying all of the wonderful recipes in this cookbook without having to downsize the proportions!

Toaster oven sizes and capacities vary depending upon the make and model. As a frame of reference for proportioning the recipes, I used a medium-size, moderately-priced four- to six-slice-capacity toaster oven with an interior measuring 11 inches wide × 5½ inches high × 5¼ inches deep. Its functions included: timed TOAST, BAKE to 450°F., and BROIL. If you have a smaller toaster oven, it may be necessary to reduce the quantities of ingredients by one half. For instance, if the recipe calls for 1 cup of flour, reduce the quantity to ½ cup, making sure to reduce all of the ingredients by the same standard of one half. Baking or broiling times will be shorter, but not necessarily half of the given time. Calculate about three quarters of the time and note the actual cooking completion time on the recipe page. If you have a larger toaster oven, you can expand the recipes to whatever you need as long as the total portions still fit your toaster oven. With an increased quantity, you may want to slightly increase baking or broiling times as well. By using your toaster oven frequently, you will get a feeling for its capacity and cooking times.

A Brief Toaster Oven History

The toaster, invented in 1909, was originally an appliance with a wire heating element and trays that could hold bread slices upright for browning. Ten years later, the pop-up toaster, with its slots and timer, became popular. The earliest model toaster ovens, on store shelves in the late 1950s, were no more than toasters with a horizontal ovenlike rack that held two to four slices of bread. Some models had one or two low baking temperature options and, being poorly insulated, they radiated a tremendous amount of heat during baking.

Over the years, the insulation, capacity, BAKE, and BROIL functions improved, addressing the needs of a growing market. Today's toaster ovens are vastly improved in performance, with all sorts of features, including cool-touch exteriors, nonstick interiors, interiors that can be removed for easy cleaning, nonstick removable crumb trays, touch-pad controls, dual racks, defrosting and light pastry options, timer controls, auto off, and even bread-making capabilities. These new features have created a more versatile appliance that not only toasts bread and bagels, but can bake or broil just about anything a large oven can without heating up the kitchen or escalating the electric bill.

Keep in mind that toaster ovens are essentially small ovens. They are not, however, to be confused with microwaves, even though they are about the same size. A baked potato still takes forty or fifty minutes to bake in a toaster oven as it does in a regular oven and a casserole still requires thirty to forty minutes. What then, you may ask, are the benefits of baking or broiling in the toaster oven? The first benefit is the flavor. A baked potato is much tastier than a microwaved potato and baked vegetables are more flavorful and have a better texture than the bland taste and rubbery texture that microwaving, boiling, or steaming often produces. This is because baking allows moisture within the food to slowly evaporate, concentrating flavors within the fiber of the food itself. The high direct heat of broiling seals the surface of the food, creating a browned, crusted surface while the center is flavorfully moist. The second advantage is minimal involvement. Once you have prepared the food, you can let your toaster oven do the rest. In less than one hour your low-fat, highly flavorful meal is ready!

Toaster Oven Utensils and Bakeware

Most 1-quart-capacity baking dishes will fit a midsize toaster oven, but their domed lids are usually too high. Use aluminum foil for covering 1-quart baking dishes instead. Keep in mind that toaster ovens require the same ovenproof bakeware as a regular oven, such as Pyrex oven-safe glass, Nordic Ware, Corning, Anchor Hocking bakeware, Mirro, and Wearever aluminum and stainless steel baking pans. Or you can try the wide variety of aluminum foil baking ware that's available in most supermarkets. The majority of these lightweight, inexpensive containers of heavy molded aluminum foil are scaled for toaster ovens and come in a wide variety of shapes: muffin tins, loaf pans, pie pans, and baking pans.

Remember that plastic containers, wax paper, plastic wrap, paper plates, or paper towels that might be acceptable in a microwave will be inflammable or will melt in your toaster oven. When precooking food in your microwave and transferring it to your toaster oven, use baking and broiling dishes (Corning Ware, Pyrex ovenware, and ceramic bakeware) that are compatible with both appliances.

Here is an index for the utensils and bakeware you will need for this cookbook. They are based on a midsize average toaster oven's requirements. These are also specified in each recipe as needed.

Bakeware / Utensil	*Dimensions: Width / Length / Height*	*Material*
Small loaf pan	$3\frac{1}{2}$" × $7\frac{1}{2}$" × $2\frac{1}{4}$"	Aluminum, preferably nonstick
Regular-size loaf pan	$4\frac{1}{2}$" × $8\frac{1}{2}$" × $2\frac{1}{4}$"	Aluminum, preferably nonstick
Baking sheet	$6\frac{1}{2}$" × 10"	Aluminum, preferably nonstick
Cake pan (square)	$8\frac{1}{2}$" × $8\frac{1}{2}$" × 2"	Aluminum, preferably nonstick
All-purpose pan (square)	$6\frac{1}{2}$" × $9\frac{1}{4}$" × 2"	Aluminum, preferably nonstick
Six-muffin tin	7" × 10" × $1\frac{1}{2}$"	Aluminum, preferably nonstick
Pie pan (round)	$9\frac{3}{4}$" diameter	Aluminum, preferably nonstick
Cake pan (round)	$9\frac{1}{2}$" diameter	Aluminum, preferably nonstick

Bakeware/ Utensil	Dimensions— Width/Length/Height	Material
1-quart baking dish	$8\frac{1}{2}$" $\times$ $8\frac{1}{2}$" $\times$ 4"	Ovenproof: Corning, Pyrex, etc.
1-cup ovenproof dish	Any size or shape	Ovenproof: Corning, Pyrex, etc.
1-quart baking dish (round)	$8\frac{3}{4}$" diameter $\times$ 3"	Ovenproof: Corning, Pyrex, etc.
1-cup baking dish	Round or square	Ovenproof: Corning, Pyrex, etc.
Oven mitts (1 or 2 pair)	$5\frac{1}{2}$" $\times$ 11" (over the wrist)	Cotton, cotton/polyester with cotton or polyester insulation
Trivet (1 or 2)	6" or 8" square or diameter	Heat/flameproof
Whisk	$9\frac{1}{2}$"	Steel, aluminum
Large spoon	2" $\times$ 11" (approximately)	Stainless steel, wooden, enamel
Tongs	9" (approximately)	Aluminum, stainless steel, wooden

Where to Put Your Toaster Oven

You will want to choose a space in your kitchen where your toaster oven will be easily accessible (parents might want to give special attention to placing the toaster oven well out of reach of inquiring little fingers). Even the cool-touch models radiate heat. Make sure there are four to six inches of space surrounding the back and sides of the oven, six to twelve inches at the top. There should be ample counter space in front of it to accommodate opening and closing the oven door and moving dishes in and out of the oven. Curtains, tieback sashes, blind cords, and any other potentially flammable material should not be near the oven. Toaster ovens require a regular three-prong plug. Check the receptacle you are going to use to see if it is in good working order. Allocate a place for oven mitts, trivets, and tongs within easy reach.

Rediscovering Your Toaster Oven

Perhaps you have a toaster oven and use it for breakfast toast, bagels, and an occasional toasted cheese sandwich. If you have a package of chicken breasts or catfish fillets, your first impulse may be to reach for the skillet. Or, if you have fresh broccoli or carrots, you may automatically start your preparation by grabbing the saucepan. It may not have occurred to you that the chicken breasts or catfish fillets could be broiled in your toaster oven and be ready to serve in fifteen minutes. Or that the broccoli could be stir-fried under the broiler with a tablespoon of vegetable oil and a teaspoon of Chinese five-spice powder and be ready for the table in twenty minutes.

Maybe it's time to see what your toaster oven can really do. Once you get started, I suspect that you'll come to use your toaster oven daily. For example, it can toast your bagels in the morning, melt cheese and tomato on whole wheat bread for lunch, and broil chicken breast filets and skewered veggies for supper. Ironically, most preparation instructions on any given food product do not include the toaster oven. A best-kept secret is that frozen vegetables taste great broiled in a toaster oven, personal-size pizzas are an ideal toaster oven candidate, and packaged rice, grains, and cereals can also be easily cooked in a toaster oven, with excellent results.

A Word About Cleaning

Consult your toaster oven manual for specific instructions for cleaning the interior and exterior. Always unplug the appliance before cleaning. Do not use oven cleaner and do not attempt to clean the elements with water, which can damage the electric connections. Empty and clean the crumb tray regularly and wipe up food spatters after baking when the oven is cool and unplugged, so they do not bake on the next time you use the oven.

Toaster Oven Functions

THAWING

Some toaster ovens have settings for defrosting, but even without a special setting, a low baking temperature will accomplish the thawing process. Place unwrapped, separated pieces in an ovenproof dish at 200° F. or 250° F. and monitor the thawing, poking the food periodically with a fork, to know when the food has gone from thawing to cooking so you can gauge your cooking time accordingly. *Note:* If you are planning to freeze fresh meat or fish, remove it from the store package, rinse, pat with paper towels, trim off any fat, cut into portions, and place each portion in a resealable plastic bag. This will make thawing much easier. Immersing a resealable plastic bag of frozen food in warm water for a minute or two will aid in removing the food from the bag. *Note:* If you thaw meat or poultry in the toaster oven, be sure to continue to cook it to completion. Thawing by this heating method and delaying cooking or refreezing can encourage the growth of harmful bacteria in the food.

TOASTING

Most toaster ovens have a setting for lightness and darkness of toast. This is a helpful gauge for toasting bagels, heating pastries and leftover pizza, crisping breads, chips, or nachos, and cooking sunny-side up eggs and omelets. Recipes in this cookbook that refer to the TOAST function are gauged for a medium toast setting. Basically, TOAST is simply a timed bake with the lower and upper elements active at a high temperature for a short period of time. This is why toasting once or twice will cook a two-egg omelet, crepes, or a cake layer for a torte.

BAKING

For top performance, preheat the toaster oven for five to ten minutes. Avoid opening the oven door frequently while cooking, to avoid heat loss. Baking heat should be even. If the muffins on one side of the tin are browned and those on the other side are not, there could be a problem with the elements. Of course, toaster oven models vary and so do their baking times. It might be necessary to adjust the baking time required by this cookbook for your toaster oven. If the variation is more than five or ten minutes, the elements of your toaster oven may be malfunctioning. Most toaster oven manuals have a basic index for cooking times that you can use as a gauge to determine whether the elements are in good working order.

BROILING

The broiling rack should be placed four inches beneath the upper elements and food items should be at least two inches from the elements. Because only the top elements are active in the broiling feature, all cooking is done on the top surface of the food. Broiling is excellent for items of uniform thickness and with high moisture content, like steaks, fish, chicken, and vegetables, as well as pancakes, French toast, and crepes. The broiling feature also works well for browning food and bread crumb toppings, melting cheese toppings, melting margarine and baking chocolate, precooking vegetables and meat for soups, stews, and casseroles, and roasting.

KEEPING FOOD WARM

A toaster oven can keep prepared food warm while you finish cooking the rest of the meal. A low baking temperature of 200° F. will keep most food adequately warm before serving. Whether in the toaster oven or under heat lamps at a restaurant, a certain degree of continued cooking occurs whenever palatable warmth must be maintained. Good candidates for keeping warm are items less sensitive to continued cooking—breads, rolls, pies, casseroles, soups, and stews. Dishes that will be compromised and more than likely overcooked by continued warming would be fish fillets, steaks, skewered meat and vegetables, and baked eggs.

About the Recipes

Most of the recipes in this cookbook have an average preparation time of fifteen minutes and an average cooking time of twenty-five minutes. The majority of ingredients required are fresh or minimally processed foods for nutritious, healthy eating, with an emphasis on textures, flavors from seasonings and herbs, and low- or reduced-fat options. The following ingredients used in the recipes in this cookbook are low-fat alternatives that replace traditional high-fat ingredients. Here is my chart of traditional ingredients and their low-fat substitutions, most of which are used in the recipes:

If you usually use	*Replace with*
Cream	Fat-free half-and-half, evaporated skim milk
Butter	Nonhydrogenated margarine, margarine
Oil	Canola or olive oil
Sugar	Honey, raw or brown sugar, maple syrup
Cheese	Part-skim, low-moisture mozzarella, low-fat shredded or brick cheeses, tofu
Cream cheese	Neufchâtel, nonfat cream cheese, yogurt cheese, or farmer (pot) cheese
Egg	Egg whites (2 to 1 egg), egg substitute
Mayonnaise	Low-fat or fat-free mayonnaise, one-half the required amount, mixed with one-half plain yogurt
Bacon	Low-fat turkey bacon
Chicken broth	Reduced-fat, fat-free, low-sodium, or homemade broth
Ground beef	Lean ground round or sirloin
Chicken	Skinless, boneless thighs or breasts
Baking chocolate 1 square	3 tablespoons dry cocoa, 2 teaspoons sugar, and 1 tablespoon water
Nuts	Half the amount required, toasted
Sour cream	Nonfat sour cream, plain nonfat yogurt, yogurt cheese
Whole milk ricotta	1% cottage cheese, part-skim ricotta
Bread crumbs	Homemade or natural, herbal commercial bread crumbs

Herbs and Spices

The shelf life of most commercial seasonings is about six months, so if your spices are older, increase the quantity to make up for lost flavor. You can reawaken their flavor by placing them in a baking pan and TOASTing once or twice. Whole spices, of course, assure freshness and strength of flavor. Just grind what you need in the blender. Common spices that are used in the recipes in this cookbook are cinnamon, salt, freshly ground pepper, butcher's pepper, cayenne pepper, white pepper, cumin, paprika, lemon zest, nutmeg, cardamom, ginger, garlic powder, chili powder, five-spice powder, and ground bay leaves.

One teaspoon of dried herbs is equal to one tablespoon of fresh. But keep in mind that it's easy to overcook fresh herbs. For many fresh herbs, the longer the cooking time, the less flavor. Dried herbs can be enhanced by combining them with lemon zest (grated lemon rind) or steeping them in a small amount of hot water prior to adding them to other ingredients. Or you can try growing your own herbs. With adequate watering and a sunny windowsill, most herbs in a pot do very well. Also, most fresh herbs freeze well. Prepare them by rinsing them well, patting them dry with paper towels, separating the leaves from the stems, then chopping them if desired, placing them in resealable plastic bags, and pressing the air out before sealing. Be sure to label the bags to identify the herbs, since they can all look pretty much the same in the freezer. Some herbs that can grow easily are basil, bay leaves, chives, cilantro, dill, marjoram, mint, oregano, parsley, rosemary, sage, savory, tarragon, and thyme.

Indexes for Toaster Oven Baking and Broiling Times

These charts will give you a general idea of how long it will take to toast, bake, or broil a particular food item. *Note:* Some of these items may have food processor or microwave shortcuts written into the recipes. For most of us, time is of the essence and the emphasis these days is on how quickly a meal can be prepared, often at the expense of nutrition. Consider what you can do while your nutritious meal is baking in your toaster oven. You can take a bath, read a magazine, work out, help the kids with their homework, or do any number of things you've been wanting to do. Replace a fast-food mentality with a good-food mentality and make low-fat, nutritious meals in your toaster oven!

Estimated Toaster Oven Baking Times

Food Item	*Temp F.*	*Time*
Four chicken thighs (skinless, boneless)— covered or with sauce	400	30 minutes
Two chicken breasts (skinless, boneless)— covered or with sauce	350	50 minutes
Two pork chops (approx. ¾" thick)— covered or with sauce	350	50 minutes
Homemade pizza (single or personal size)	400	25 minutes
Two fish fillets (perch, flounder, scrod)— covered or with sauce	400	20 minutes
Two fish steaks (swordfish, salmon)— covered or with sauce	350	25 minutes
Meat loaf	400	35 minutes
Split game hen	400	25 minutes
Whole game hens (2)	350	45 minutes
2 cups vegetables in foil packet	400	25 minutes
Four potatoes	450	60 minutes
Four sweet potatoes	425	35 minutes
Casserole (in 1-quart baking dish)	375	40 minutes
Six muffins (in a muffin pan)	425	15 minutes
Two apples (cored and filled)	375	30 minutes
Two acorn squash (4 halves)	400	25 minutes
Cake (8 × 8" cake pan)	350	30 minutes
Pumpkin pie	400	35 minutes
Soup (in 1-quart baking dish)	350	25 minutes
Meatballs (1 pound ground beef)	350	25 minutes

Estimated Toaster Oven Broiling Times

Food Item	*Time*
Two beef steaks—¾" thickness (add 2 minutes for 1" thickness)	8 minutes
Rare—turn after 3 to 4 minutes	6–8 minutes
Medium—turn after 5 to 6 minutes	10–12 minutes
Well done—turn after 7 to 8 minutes	14–16 minutes
Lamb chops—¾" thickness (add 2 minutes for 1" thickness)	10 minutes
Medium—turn after 5 to 6 minutes	10–12 minutes
Well done—turn after 7 to 8 minutes	14–16 minutes
Two pork chops—¾" thickness (add 2 minutes for 1" thickness)	8 minutes
Medium—turn after 6 minutes	12 minutes
Well done—turn after 7 minutes	15 minutes
Two hamburgers—¾" thickness	15 minutes
Medium—turn after 5 minutes	10 minutes
Well done—turn after 6 minutes	12 minutes
Four chicken thighs (skinless, boneless)—turn after 10 minutes	20 minutes
Two chicken breasts (skinless, boneless)—turn after 10 minutes	20 minutes
Two fish fillets—½" to ¾" thickness	5 minutes
Two fish steaks—1" thickness	10 minutes
Four 9" skewers of vegetables/meat	16 minutes
Shrimp (1 lb.)	6 minutes
Scallops (1 lb.)	3 minutes
Stir-fry vegetables and meat	30 minutes

Chapter 1

Breakfasts

It's obvious that toaster ovens make great toast. Before I started experimenting with the toaster oven, I thought that was basically all I could make—toast. And, indeed, I started with toast, then went to bagels, English muffins, and muffins. Then one morning, after I'd made my toast, I decided to try cooking my eggs in the toaster oven. So I whisked two eggs together with a bit of milk, salt, and pepper and poured the mixture into a small, oiled loaf pan. Then I put it in my toaster oven and put the setting on TOAST. I was surprised when I removed the pan after the toast bell rang. I had a perfectly done omelet! I went on to experiment with other recipes, many of which are in this chapter, including pancakes, French toast, baked eggs, breakfast pita, buttermilk biscuits, hash brown potatoes, and granolas. That was just the beginning. With each chapter I discovered new toaster oven capabilities and began creating new recipes for the toaster oven. But I must confess it all started here, at breakfast!

Breakfast Banana Bread

Freshly baked banana bread, still warm from the oven and spread with butter or margarine, makes a healthy breakfast or snack. The aroma brings to my mind the wintry Minnesota late afternoons of my childhood, the warm kitchen and just-baked banana bread. Big ovens may be great for warming up a kitchen in the winter, but should that keep you from baking banana bread (or anything else, for that matter) in the summer? No. And this is where the toaster oven comes in. Bake or broil anything, anytime without heating up the kitchen. This is the freedom and flexibility the toaster oven provides.

For this recipe, my trail mix consists of sunflower seeds, raisins, pecans, and walnuts. You can substitute the trail mix for chopped nuts or omit that option altogether. Note:

On the grocery shelves these days, there are great dried fruit medleys that are a tasty alternative to nuts.

2 ripe bananas	1 cup unbleached flour
1 egg	¾ cup chopped trail mix
½ cup skim milk	1 teaspoon baking powder
2 tablespoons honey	Salt
1 tablespoon vegetable oil	

PREHEAT the toaster oven to 400° F.

PROCESS the bananas, egg, milk, honey, and oil in a blender or food processor until smooth and transfer to a mixing bowl.

ADD the flour and trail mix, stirring to mix well. Add the baking powder and stir just enough to blend it into the batter. Add salt to taste. Pour the mixture into an oiled or nonstick 4½ × 8½ × 2¼-inch loaf pan.

BAKE for 40 minutes, or until a toothpick inserted in the center comes out clean.

Prep: 10 minutes
Total time: 50 minutes
Serves 6

Cinnamon Rolls

Land O Lakes makes an absolutely wonderful fat-free half-and-half, which is available in supermarkets.

Buttermilk Biscuit dough (page 14)

Cinnamon mixture:
3 tablespoons dark brown sugar
3 tablespoons chopped pecans
2 tablespoons margarine
1 teaspoon ground cinnamon
Salt to taste

Icing:
1 cup confectioners' sugar, sifted
1 tablespoon fat-free half-and-half
½ teaspoon vanilla extract
Salt to taste

PREHEAT the toaster oven to 400° F.
MAKE the buttermilk biscuit dough.

Continued

ROLL out or pat the dough to $\frac{1}{2}$ inch thick. In a small bowl, combine the cinnamon mixture ingredients. Spread the dough evenly with the cinnamon mixture and roll up like a jelly roll. With a sharp knife, cut the roll into 1-inch slices. Place on an oiled or nonstick $6\frac{1}{2} \times 10$-inch baking sheet.

BAKE for 15 minutes, or until lightly browned. Let cool before frosting.

COMBINE the icing ingredients in a small bowl, adding more half-and-half or confectioners' sugar until the consistency is like thick cream. Drizzle over the tops of the cinnamon rolls and serve.

> *Prep:* 25 minutes
> *Total time:* 35 minutes
> Makes approximately 12 rolls and $\frac{1}{2}$ cup icing

Buttermilk Biscuits

Most toaster oven baking sheets accommodate six biscuits, so for a dozen, bake them in two batches. These biscuits are easy to make and have many variations, including Cinnamon Rolls (preceding recipe) and shortcake for strawberries (page 190).

2 cups unbleached flour	3 tablespoons margarine, at room
1 tablespoon baking powder	temperature
$\frac{1}{2}$ teaspoon baking soda	1 cup low-fat buttermilk
Salt	Vegetable oil

PREHEAT the toaster oven to 400° F.

COMBINE the flour, baking powder, baking soda, and salt to taste in a medium bowl. Cut in the margarine with 2 knives or a pastry blender until the mixture is crumbly.

STIR in the buttermilk, adding just enough so the dough will stay together when pinched.

KNEAD the dough on a floured surface for one minute, then pat or roll out the dough to $\frac{3}{4}$ inch thick. Cut out biscuit rounds with a $2\frac{1}{2}$-inch biscuit cutter. Place the rounds on an oiled or nonstick $6\frac{1}{2} \times 10$-inch baking sheet.

BAKE for 15 minutes, or until golden brown.

> *Prep:* 15 minutes
> *Total time:* 30 minutes
> Makes approximately 12 biscuits

Breakfast Bars

No time for breakfast? Need to grab something fast as you head out of the door? Breakfast bars are perfect! Wrap the squares in foil or plastic wrap and store them in the refrigerator, ready to toss into your briefcase or lunch bag or to eat in the car en route. They are easy to make, nutritious, great for instant energy, and cheaper than "health bars" available in the supermarket and health food stores. Breakfast bars are my mainstay when my schedule is fast and furious.

1 cup unsweetened applesauce
1 carrot, peeled and grated
$\frac{1}{2}$ cup raisins
1 egg
1 tablespoon vegetable oil
2 tablespoons molasses
2 tablespoons brown sugar

$\frac{1}{4}$ cup chopped walnuts
2 cups rolled oats
2 tablespoons sesame seeds
1 teaspoon ground cinnamon
$\frac{1}{4}$ teaspoon grated nutmeg
$\frac{1}{4}$ teaspoon ground ginger
Salt to taste

PREHEAT the toaster oven to 375° F.

COMBINE all the ingredients in a bowl, stirring well to blend. Press the mixture into an oiled or nonstick $8\frac{1}{2} \times 8\frac{1}{2} \times 2$-inch square baking (cake) pan.

BAKE for 35 minutes, or until golden brown. Cool and cut into squares.

Prep: 15 minutes
Total time: 50 minutes
Makes 6 bars

Coffee Cake

This is a rich-tasting cake that rivals in flavor high-fat store-bought cakes. Simple and quick to make, it has a spicy, cinnamon/nutmeg aroma that smells wonderful during baking! If it's Saturday morning and you feel like having coffee cake for breakfast, why not make something that tastes good but still allows you to live with yourself? In thirteen minutes you can make a delicious coffee cake and put it in the toaster oven to bake. In forty minutes you have a kitchen that smells wonderful and a great homemade coffee cake, without all the fat, chemicals, and sodium.

Continued

Cake:
2 cups unbleached flour
2 teaspoons baking powder
2 tablespoons vegetable oil
1 egg
1¼ cups skim milk

Topping:
½ cup brown sugar
1 tablespoon margarine, at room
  temperature
1 teaspoon ground cinnamon
⅛ teaspoon grated nutmeg
¼ cup chopped pecans
Salt to taste

PREHEAT the toaster oven to 375° F.

COMBINE the ingredients for the cake in a medium bowl and mix thoroughly. Pour the batter into an oiled or 8½ × 8½ × 2-inch square baking (cake) pan and set aside.

COMBINE the topping ingredients in a small bowl, mashing the margarine into the dry ingredients with a fork until the mixture is crumbly. Sprinkle evenly on top of the batter.

BAKE for 40 minutes, or until a toothpick inserted in the center comes out clean. Cool and cut into squares.

Prep: 13 minutes
Total time: 53 minutes
Serves 6

Bagel Melt

The advantage of the slices being horizontal in a toaster oven instead of vertical as in a toaster leads to all kinds of wonderful bagel topping creations. Here are two delectable breakfast bagel recipes that demonstrate this advantage.

1 bagel, split
4 slices Swiss cheese

4 strips lean turkey bacon, cut in
  half

LAYER the bagel halves with 2 slices of Swiss cheese and 4 half strips of turkey bacon each.

TOAST once on the oven rack.

Prep: 2 minutes
Total time: 5 minutes
Serves 1 or 2

Classic Breakfast Bagel

Try these "schmears" or be inspired and custom make your own homemade spread to have on hand, ready for a breakfast bagel. Spreads can be stored in the refrigerator for one week. Try Yogurt Cheese Spread (page 32) also.

NY Schmear

2 tablespoons reduced-fat cream cheese
2 tablespoons farmer or yogurt cheese
1 tablespoon grated celery
1 tablespoon grated carrot
1 teaspoon plain fat-free yogurt
Salt and freshly ground black pepper to taste

COMBINE all ingredients in a small bowl, mixing well.

Florida Schmear

2 tablespoons reduced-fat cream cheese
2 tablespoons farmer or yogurt cheese
1 tablespoon finely chopped pecans
1 tablespoon finely chopped fresh pineapple or mango, drained
1 teaspoon orange juice
Pinch of lemon zest

COMBINE all ingredients in a small bowl, mixing well.

Fancy Toasted Bagels

2 bagels, cut in half
4 tablespoons grated Parmesan cheese
Paprika

Spread:
4 tablespoons low-fat cream cheese
2 tablespoons chopped pimientos
1 tablespoon chopped scallions
1 tablespoon chopped fresh parsley
$1/4$ teaspoon Worcestershire sauce
$1/2$ teaspoon garlic powder
Salt and freshly ground black pepper to taste

Continued

SPRINKLE each bagel slice with 2 tablespoons Parmesan cheese and paprika to taste.

TOAST once on the oven rack.

COMBINE the ingredients for the spread, mixing well. Adjust the seasonings to taste. Spread the mixture in equal portions on the toasted bagel slices and serve.

> *Prep:* 10 minutes
> *Total time:* 12 minutes
> Serves 2

Portable Omelet

I invented this portable egg, bacon, and cheese sandwich as a healthy alternative to high-fat, high-sodium fast-food offerings. Options such as chopped black olives, onions, tomatoes, peppers, and mushrooms can be used in place of bacon. In a scant nine minutes you can have a great breakfast sandwich to take to work or eat while inching along on the expressway. Making this quick omelet takes less time than it does to go through the drive-through.

2 slices multigrain bread	2 strips turkey bacon
2 eggs	2 tablespoons shredded low-
1 tablespoon plain nonfat yogurt	moisture, part-skim mozzarella
Salt and freshly ground black pepper	cheese

TOAST the bread slices and set aside.

WHISK together the eggs and yogurt in a small bowl and season with salt and pepper to taste.

LAYER bacon strips in a small 4 × 8 × 2¼-inch loaf pan. Pour the egg mixture on top and sprinkle with the cheese.

TOAST once, or until the egg is done to your preference. Cut the omelet into toast-size squares and place between the 2 slices of toast to make a sandwich. (**TOAST** takes 2 to 3 minutes.)

> *Prep:* 5 minutes
> *Total time:* 9 minutes
> Serves 1

Breakfast Pita

Toasted whole wheat pita loaves are excellent for breakfast and have only 2 percent fat content. I created this recipe as a low-fat alternative to a fried egg and toast. Lay the pita flat when cutting out the top layer and be careful not to cut through both layers. Use the concave side for making the cut—the pita shape should resemble a little dish.

1 5-inch whole wheat pita loaf
1 teaspoon olive oil
1 egg, well beaten
2 tablespoons shredded low-fat
  mozzarella cheese

Garlic powder
Salt and freshly ground black pepper

CUT a circle out of the top layer of one pita bread loaf and remove the disk-shaped layer, leaving the bottom intact. Brush the pita loaf with the olive oil. Carefully pour the beaten egg into the cavity. Sprinkle with cheese and season with garlic powder and salt and pepper to taste.

TOAST once on the oven rack, or until the egg is cooked thoroughly and the cheese is lightly browned.

Prep: 7 minutes
Total time: 10 minutes
Serves 2

Gypsy Lights

When we were kids, my twin brother and I made Gypsy Lights frequently. This method of egg/toast preparation probably has many other names. I often wondered how it was so lyrically named: perhaps by the same person who dubbed that famous graham cracker/Hershey bar/toasted marshmallow trio S'mores. A young person making a Gypsy Light learns a lesson in resourcefulness. Why waste that little circle of bread that is cut out of the bread slice? Sprinkle it with Parmesan cheese and bake it along with the slices. They are smaller and finish sooner, which means you can have a little appetizer before your main Gypsy Light entrée.

1 slice multigrain bread
1 teaspoon vegetable oil

1 egg
Salt and freshly ground black pepper

Continued

BRUSH both sides of bread with the oil and place in a $6\frac{1}{2} \times 6\frac{1}{2} \times 2$-inch square (cake) pan. Cut or tear a circle of bread out of the center (the circle should be about $1\frac{1}{2}$ inches across). Place the circle in the pan also.

POUR the egg into the cavity in the center of the bread. Season to taste with salt and pepper.

TOAST twice, or until the egg is done to your preference.

Prep: 6 minutes
Total time: 10 minutes
Serves 1

Sunny-side Up Eggs

Eggs "fried" in a toaster oven look regal. The whites are firm and glossy and the yolks a perfect golden dome. TOAST*ing once makes a perfect sunny-side up egg. Try it!*

2 large eggs
Salt and freshly ground black pepper

CRACK the eggs into an oiled or nonstick small $4 \times 8 \times 2\frac{1}{4}$-inch loaf pan. Sprinkle with salt and pepper to taste.

TOAST once, or until the eggs are done to your preference.

Prep: 3 minutes
Total time: 6 minutes
Serves 2

Baked Parmesan Eggs

It's easy to make individualized Baked Parmesan Eggs. Additions of crumbled lean turkey bacon, Worcestershire sauce, chopped Spanish olives, chopped peppers and onions, shredded low-fat cheese, salsa, and the like can be added as your guests or family desires. Custom-made baked eggs for everyone!

4 large eggs, each cracked into a
small 1-cup baking dish
4 tablespoons grated Parmesan cheese

4 tablespoons fat-free half-and-half
Salt and freshly ground black pepper

PREHEAT the toaster oven to 400° F.

TOP each egg with 1 tablespoon Parmesan cheese and 1 tablespoon half-and-half. Season to taste with salt and pepper and add any preferred additions.

BAKE for 10 minutes, or to your preference, testing the eggs by touching the surface with a spoon for the desired firmness after 5 minutes.

Prep: 10 minutes
Total time: 20 minutes
Serves 4

Heavenly Hash Browns

Hash browns are an excellent vehicle for hot sauce, ketchup, or barbecue sauce. The broiling time in this recipe will produce hash browns that are moderately crisp and brown. Increase the broiling time by two or three minutes to produce very crisp hash browns. Make a double recipe and store baked hash browns in the freezer, wrapped individually in plastic wrap or in separate resealable plastic bags. On Sunday morning, it's a snap to unwrap them, place them on the broiling rack, and TOAST twice. They'll taste as if you just made them.

Shortcut: Grating potatoes and onions in a food processor shortens prep time to approximately 8 minutes.

2 cups raw, peeled potatoes, grated	1 teaspoon garlic powder
2 tablespoons vegetable oil	1 teaspoon paprika
½ cup grated onion	Salt and butcher's pepper to taste

COMBINE all the ingredients in a small bowl, mixing well. Spread the potato mixture evenly in an oiled or nonstick 6½ × 6½ × 2-inch square baking (cake) pan.

BROIL for 30 minutes. Remove the pan from the oven and, with a spatula, cut the potatoes into squares and carefully turn them over. Broil for another 20 minutes, or until browned and crisped to your preference.

Prep: 20 minutes
Total time: 1 hour and 10 minutes
Serves 4

French Toast

French toast is easy to make in a toaster oven. Just soak the bread slices in the egg mixture, put in a baking pan, and BROIL *'em! Less fat is used in broiling French toast than the traditional method of frying. Because of the egg content of the French toast mixture, liberally brush a regular or nonstick pan with vegetable oil. This will eliminate potential sticking and make cleanup easy.*

2 eggs	Salt
1 cup skim milk or low-fat soy milk	4 slices multigrain bread
1 tablespoon honey	Vegetable oil

WHISK together the eggs, milk, honey, and salt to taste in a shallow bowl. Add a bread slice to the mixture and let it soak for one minute. Carefully turn it over and let the liquid saturate the other side. With a spatula, place the bread slice in an oiled $6\frac{1}{2} \times 6\frac{1}{2} \times 2$-inch square (cake) pan.

BROIL for 5 minutes, then turn carefully with a spatula and broil for another 5 minutes, or until golden brown. Repeat the soaking and broiling procedure for the remaining slices.

Prep: 5 minutes
Total time: 45 minutes
Serves 4

Cinnamon Toast

Who doesn't have tender childhood memories of cinnamon toast? With a toaster oven you can spread the cinnamon, sugar, and margarine mixture on the bread and then TOAST. *What's the difference? You'll be pleasantly surprised!*

1 tablespoon brown sugar	$\frac{1}{4}$ teaspoon ground cinnamon
2 teaspoons margarine, at room temperature	2 slices whole wheat or multigrain bread

COMBINE the sugar, margarine, and cinnamon in a small bowl with a fork until well blended. Spread each bread slice with equal portions of the mixture.

TOAST once, or until the sugar is melted and the bread is browned to your preference.

Prep: 5 minutes
Total time: 7 minutes (Toasting: approximately 2 minutes)
Serves 2

Buttermilk Pancakes

Pancakes made in a toaster oven? Of course! Instead of frying the pancakes in a skillet, BROIL *them. The consistency of the batter in this recipe produces pancakes of approximately ¹/₈-inch thickness. If you like thinner pancakes, increase the amount of buttermilk by teaspoonfuls to thin the batter. The olive oil imparts a very rich flavor to the pancakes. Try it and see!*

Batter:
1 cup low-fat buttermilk
1 egg
1 cup unbleached flour
3 tablespoons wheat germ
1 tablespoon honey
1 tablespoon olive oil
Salt to taste

1 teaspoon baking powder
1 tablespoon olive oil for brushing
    pan

Honey, maple syrup, or molasses

BLEND the batter ingredients in a food processor or blender until smooth. Stir in the baking powder. Pour enough batter into an oiled or nonstick 9¹/₂-inch-diameter round cake pan to make the size pancake you prefer.

BROIL 5 minutes, or until the batter pulls away from the sides and starts browning. Remove the pan from the oven and, with a spatula, turn the pancake over.

BROIL again for 5 minutes, or until the pancake is lightly browned. Transfer to a plate and repeat the broiling steps for the remaining batter. Serve with honey, maple syrup, or molasses.

Prep: 10 minutes
Total time: 30 minutes
Serves 4

Blueberry Muffins

This recipe is scaled for toaster ovens that can accommodate only a six-muffin tin. To make a dozen, double the recipe and bake the muffins in two batches. Many commercially made muffins have a very high fat content. Place a purchased muffin on a paper towel or napkin and leave it there for at least 15 minutes. The size of the grease stain will give you an idea of how much fat is in the muffin. Then do the same to one of these blueberry muffins you've made. Dare to compare!

1 cup fresh or frozen blueberries	1 egg
1 cup unbleached flour	1/4 cup low-fat buttermilk
1 tablespoon vegetable oil	1/2 teaspoon vanilla extract
1/4 cup sugar	Salt to taste
1 teaspoon baking powder	

PREHEAT the toaster oven to 350° F.

COMBINE all the ingredients in a bowl, blending well. In a six-muffin 7 × 10 × 1 1/2-inch tin, brush the pans with vegetable oil or use baking cups. Fill the pans or cups three-fourths full with batter.

BAKE for 25 minutes, or until golden brown.

Prep: 10 minutes
Total time: 35 minutes
Makes 6 muffins

Sam's Maple Raisin Bran Muffins

My daughter modified this recipe by adding more raisins and using low-fat soy milk, whole eggs, and maple syrup. Most toaster ovens accommodate a six-muffin tin only, so do the muffins in two batches if you want to make a dozen. The second batch might be slightly lighter and fluffier because the baking powder in the batter has been given 15 minutes to do its work. I like using the paper or foil baking cups, which are inexpensive and make removing the first batch of muffins quick and easy so that the second batch can go in right away. They can be found in the baking section of the supermarket.

2 cups oat bran

2 teaspoons baking powder

2 eggs

1¼ cups low-fat soy milk

¾ cup raisins

3 tablespoons maple syrup

2 tablespoons vegetable oil

Pinch of salt (optional)

PREHEAT toaster oven to 425° F.

COMBINE all the ingredients in a bowl and stir until well blended. In a six-muffin 7 × 10 × 1½-inch tin, brush the pans with vegetable oil or use baking cups. Fill the pans or cups three-fourths full with batter.

BAKE for 15 minutes, or until a toothpick inserted in the center of a muffin comes out clean.

Prep: 10 minutes

Total time: 25 minutes

Makes 12 muffins

English Muffins

Toaster ovens can hold four to eight English muffin halves, depending on the model and capacity. When you've got a crowd at breakfast, everyone can order a muffin custom-made with the topping(s) of their choice (see options for suggestions). For starters, here is a quick and nourishing breakfast that you can wrap up and take with you to work or eat in the car en route.

1 English muffin, split

1 plum tomato, chopped

2 slices reduced-fat or low-fat cheese

2 slices reduced-fat honey ham

1 tablespoon chopped fresh parsley

LAYER each muffin half with equal portions of tomato, cheese, and ham. Place on a broiling rack with a pan underneath.

TOAST once.

GARNISH each with equal portions of chopped parsley.

Prep: 5 minutes

Total time: 9 minutes

Serves 2

Suggested English muffin toppings

SPREAD each muffin half with $1/2$ teaspoon spicy brown mustard, then layer with 1 slice reduced-fat Cheddar cheese and $1/2$ strip lean turkey bacon.
TOAST once on the oven rack.

SPREAD each muffin half with margarine and marmalade.
TOAST once on the oven rack.

SPREAD each muffin half with 1 tablespoon reduced-fat peanut butter and 1 tablespoon jam or jelly.
TOAST once on the oven rack.

WHISK 1 egg, seasoning to taste with salt and freshly ground black pepper. Make a depression in each muffin half by pressing into it with your fingers. Pour half the beaten egg mixture into the depression of each half.
TOAST once on the oven rack.

Homemade Granola

Make your own granola in the toaster oven! Change the proportions and the ingredients to fit your preference. Instead of nuts add more fruit, or increase the wheat germ and lessen the amount of rolled oats. Presto, you have your own custom-made granola! I have created some great granolas from things I had in my pantry that I wanted to use up: a box of cereal with two tablespoons left, $1/4$ package dried apricots, 2 packets of instant rolled oats, a few pine nuts, the remaining tablespoon of molasses, and an overripe banana. The quantities of these granola recipes, between 3 and 4 cups, are large enough to have an ample supply on hand, stored in the refrigerator.

Granola:
1 cup uncooked rolled oats
$1/2$ cup oat bran
$1/2$ cup wheat germ
$1/4$ cup chopped walnuts or pecans
$1/4$ cup honey or maple syrup

$1/2$ cup unsweetened applesauce
1 teaspoon vanilla extract
$1/4$ teaspoon sea salt
$1/2$ teaspoon ground cinnamon
$1/4$ cup chopped dried fruit

PREHEAT the toaster oven to 375°F.
COMBINE all the granola ingredients in a medium bowl, mixing well. Spread the mixture in an oiled or nonstick $6^{1}/_{2} \times 6^{1}/_{2} \times 2$-inch square (cake) pan.

BAKE for 20 minutes, turning the ingredients every 5 minutes with tongs until uniformly toasted. When cooled, add the dried fruit and stir to mix well. Store in an airtight container in the refrigerator.

Prep: 15 minutes
Total time: 35 minutes
Makes 3 cups

Flaky Granola

¼ cup rolled oats
½ cup wheat flakes
½ cup bran flakes
¼ cup wheat germ
2 tablespoons sesame seeds
¼ cup unsweetened shredded
   coconut

½ cup chopped almonds, walnuts,
   or pecans
2 tablespoons chopped pumpkin
   seeds
½ cup honey or molasses
2 tablespoons vegetable oil
Salt to taste

PREHEAT the toaster oven to 375°F.
COMBINE all the ingredients in a medium bowl, stirring to mix well.
SPREAD the mixture in an oiled or nonstick 6½ × 6½ × 2-inch square (cake) pan.
BAKE for 20 minutes, turning with tongs every 5 minutes to toast evenly. Cool and store in an airtight container in the refrigerator.

Prep: 12 minutes
Total time: 32 minutes
Makes approximately 3¾ cups

Granola with Sesame and Sunflower Seeds

2 cups rolled oats
$\frac{1}{2}$ cup sunflower seeds
$\frac{1}{2}$ cup sesame seeds
$\frac{1}{2}$ cup unsweetened shredded
  coconut
$\frac{1}{2}$ cup slivered almonds

$\frac{1}{2}$ cup honey
1 tablespoon vegetable oil
1 teaspoon toasted sesame oil
1 teaspoon ground cinnamon
Pinch of grated nutmeg
Salt to taste

PREHEAT the toaster oven to 375°F.

COMBINE all the granola ingredients in a large bowl, mixing well.

SPREAD the mixture evenly in an oiled or nonstick $6\frac{1}{2} \times 6\frac{1}{2} \times 2$-inch square (cake) pan.

BAKE for 20 minutes, turning the ingredients every 5 minutes with tongs to toast evenly. Cool and store in an airtight container in the refrigerator.

Prep: 15 minutes
Total time: 35 minutes
Makes 4 cups

Chapter 2

Sandwiches

The most obvious use of the toaster oven is for toast and sandwiches, and for many people, that is its prime function. In compiling the recipes for this chapter, I expanded the variety of sandwiches to include nachos, tortillas, burritos, picnic loaf, melts, and broilers, as well as burgers and sandwiches, to offer a broad selection of sandwich options and to showcase the toaster oven's capabilities. The ultimate in sandwich creativity is Dagwood Bumstead in the *Blondie* comic strip and, in homage, I created the sandwich recipe on page 31. If you choose to accept the mission of making this sandwich, you will not be disappointed! If you crave something delicious but less rigorous, read on. This chapter offers something for everyone!

Cheese and Sun-Dried Tomato Sandwiches

Sun-dried tomatoes and two cheeses mingle as they melt and the result is delicious! Sun-dried Tomato Spread produces a large enough quantity so you will have some on hand for a sandwich spread or a dip for tortillas.

4 slices multigrain bread
2 tablespoons reduced-fat mayonnaise
4 slices reduced-fat Swiss cheese

4 slices reduced-fat Cheddar cheese
4 tablespoons Sun-Dried Tomato
  Spread (recipe follows)

SPREAD the bread slices with the mayonnaise. Layer 2 of the bread slices with 2 slices each of Swiss cheese, Cheddar cheese, and 2 tablespoons Sun-Dried Tomato Spread. Top with the remaining slices.

Continued

29

TOAST twice on a broiling rack with a pan underneath, or until the cheese is melted and lightly browned. Cut into quarters.

Prep: 5 minutes
Total time: 8 minutes
Serves 2

Sun-Dried Tomato Spread

½ cup minced sun-dried tomatoes
3 tablespoons olive oil
2 tablespoons grated Parmesan cheese
1 teaspoon dried oregano or 1 tablespoon chopped fresh oregano

3 tablespoons chopped pecans or walnuts
2 garlic cloves, chopped
Salt and freshly ground black pepper to taste

COMBINE the sun-dried tomatoes and ⅔ cup water in an oiled or nonstick 8½ × 8½ × 2-inch baking (cake) pan.

BROIL for 4 minutes, or until the tomatoes are softened. Remove from the oven and transfer the tomatoes with the liquid to a bowl. Add all the other ingredients and mix well.

PROCESS the mixture in a blender or food processor until smooth. Adjust the seasonings.

Prep: 10 minutes
Total time: 14 minutes
Makes approximately 1¾ cups

Tomato Mozzarella Sandwiches

Vidalia onions are milder and sweeter than other onions. TOAST*ing does not cook the onion, but heats it enough to blend the flavors with all of the other sandwich ingredients. It's a matter of personal preference how thick the onion slices should be. If you prefer the onions fully cooked, slice the onions very thin and* TOAST *two or three times or* BROIL *for 6 minutes until the onions are well done. Serve as open-faced sandwiches or combine slices for sandwiches and slice in half diagonally.*

4 slices multigrain or sprouted grain
  bread
1 tablespoon olive oil
2 tablespoons Dijon mustard
4 tablespoons shredded low-fat
  mozzarella cheese

2 Vidalia onion slices
1 plum tomato, chopped
2 tablespoons chopped fresh parsley
Paprika
Garlic powder
Salt and freshly ground black pepper

BRUSH the bread slices with olive oil on both sides.

SPREAD the bread on one side with equal portions of mustard, cheese, onion, tomato, and parsley. Season to taste with paprika, garlic powder, and salt and pepper. Place on a broiling rack with a pan underneath.

TOAST twice, or until the cheese is melted and the onions cooked to your preference.

Prep: 7 minutes
Total time: 12 minutes
Serves 2

Grilled Dagwood

Assembling this sandwich is a challenge, but the rewards are great! Putting it all together is even more fun if it is a team effort. Make the Yogurt Cheese Spread beforehand.

4 slices whole wheat or multigrain
  bread
1 tablespoon Dijon mustard
2 tablespoons fresh or canned bean
  sprouts, washed and well drained
2 tablespoons chopped watercress
2 tablespoons chopped roasted
  pimientos
3 slices reduced-fat Swiss cheese
2 slices low-fat honey ham

2 tablespoons garlic hummus
6 slices sweet pickle
4 slices low-fat smoked turkey
1 tablespoon Yogurt Cheese Spread
  (recipe follows)
1 tablespoon chopped Vidalia onion
1 tablespoon ketchup
1 tablespoon pitted and chopped
  black olives

PREHEAT the toaster oven to 350°F.

SPREAD the first bread slice with $\frac{1}{2}$ tablespoon Dijon mustard. Add 1 tablespoon

Continued

sprouts, 1 tablespoon watercress, 1 tablespoon pimientos, 1 slice Swiss cheese, and 1 slice honey ham.

SPREAD the second bread slice with ½ tablespoon Dijon mustard, turn it over, and lay it on top of the first. Spread the other side of the second slice with 1 table-spoon hummus, 1 slice honey ham, 3 pickle slices, 1 tablespoon watercress, and 2 slices smoked turkey.

SPREAD the third bread slice with the Yogurt Cheese Spread, turn it over, and lay it on top of the second slice of bread. Spread the other side of the third slice with 1 tablespoon hummus and add the chopped onion, 1 tablespoon pimientos, 3 pickle slices, 1 slice Swiss cheese, and 2 slices smoked turkey.

SPREAD the fourth bread slice with the ketchup and add 1 tablespoon sprouts, 1 tablespoon pimientos, 1 slice Swiss cheese, and the black olives. Lift up all the other bread slices together and place this one on the bottom. Then put the slices together and wrap in aluminum foil so that the seam is on the top of the slices. Open the seam to expose the tops of the slices and place on the rack in the toaster oven, seam side up.

BAKE 20 minutes, or until the top is lightly browned and the cheese is melted.

Prep: 20 minutes
Total time: 40 minutes
Serves 4

Yogurt Cheese Spread

Here's a lovely smooth spread that is literally fat free. Put the yogurt and coffee filters in the fridge in the morning—when you come home at night, the yogurt cheese will be ready! Additions of fresh chopped herbs, onions, and seasonings to this plain cheese produce a tasty, aromatic spread for sandwiches.

1 cup plain yogurt (without starch, gum, or gelatin added)

Seasonings:
1 tablespoon olive oil
1 teaspoon chopped fresh chives
Salt and butcher's pepper or freshly ground black pepper to taste

PLACE 2 coffee filters in a sieve over a bowl. Spoon the yogurt into the filters and place in the refrigerator for 6 to 8 hours, or until most of the moisture is drained from the yogurt and it is firm. Changing coffee filters several times during draining will expedite the process. Transfer the yogurt cheese to a bowl and add the oil, chives, and seasonings. Blend well and adjust the seasonings to taste.

Prep: 5 minutes (Drain: 6 hours)
Total time: 6 hours and 5 minutes
Makes 1 cup

Brunch Burritos

Why go to the drive-through when you can make a much less fattening (and more delicious) burrito in your toaster oven? To make tortillas pliable so they can be rolled, place them on the toaster oven rack and broil for 1 or 2 minutes.

Egg mixture:
4 medium eggs, lightly beaten
3 tablespoons finely chopped bell pepper
2 tablespoons finely chopped onion
4 strips lean turkey bacon, uncooked and cut into small $1/4 \times 1/4$-inch pieces
1 tablespoon chopped fresh cilantro

$1/2$ teaspoon ground cumin
$1/2$ teaspoon chili powder
Salt and red pepper flakes to taste

4 6-inch flour tortillas
4 tablespoons salsa
4 tablespoons shredded part-skim, low-moisture mozzarella

COMBINE the egg mixture ingredients in an oiled or nonstick $8^{1}/_{2} \times 8^{1}/_{2} \times 2$-inch square baking (cake) pan.

TOAST twice, or until the mixture is firm and cooked.

SPOON the egg mixture in equal portions onto the center of each tortilla. Add 1 tablespoon salsa and 1 tablespoon mozzarella cheese to each. Roll each tortilla around the filling and lay, seam side down, in an oiled or nonstick $8^{1}/_{2} \times 8^{1}/_{2} \times 2$-inch square baking (cake) pan.

BROIL for 8 minutes, or until lightly browned.

Prep: 10 minutes
Total time: 24 minutes
Serves 4

Cheddar Bacon Broiler

A great, sumptuous open-faced sandwich with a painterlike assemblage of colors, flavors, and textures.

4 slices pumpernickel bread
4 strips lean turkey bacon, cut in half
4 tablespoons shredded Cheddar cheese
4 tablespoons grated Parmesan cheese

4 tablespoons finely chopped bell pepper
1 medium tomato, chopped
2 tablespoons finely chopped onion
Salt and freshly ground black pepper
2 tablespoons chopped fresh parsley or cilantro

LAYER the bread slices with 2 half strips turkey bacon and 1 tablespoon each Cheddar cheese, Parmesan cheese, and bell pepper. Sprinkle each with equal portions of tomato and onion. Season to taste with salt and pepper.

BROIL on a broiling rack with a pan underneath for 8 minutes, or until the cheese is well melted. Before serving, sprinkle with parsley or cilantro.

Prep: 10 minutes
Total time: 18 minutes
Serves 4

Honey Ham and Swiss Broiler

Two broiled slices can be put together to make a sandwich, or the slices can be served as open-faced sandwiches. Most packaged sandwich ham, chicken, and turkey are low in fat content (2 or 3 percent). Read the "Food Facts" on the packages to find the slices with the least fat.

4 slices pumpernickel bread
1 tablespoon olive oil
1 tablespoon spicy brown mustard
1 tablespoon horseradish

4 slices reduced-fat honey ham
4 slices reduced-fat Swiss cheese
2 tablespoons finely chopped fresh parsley

BRUSH one side of the 4 bread slices with oil and lay, oil side down, in an oiled or nonstick $8^{1}/_{2} \times 8^{1}/_{2} \times 2$-inch square baking (cake) pan.

SPREAD 2 slices with mustard and 2 slices with horseradish.

LAYER each with 1 slice honey ham and 1 slice Swiss cheese.

BROIL for 5 minutes, or until the cheese is melted. Sprinkle with equal portions of parsley and serve.

Prep: 8 minutes
Total time: 13 minutes
Serves 2

Tomato and Artichoke Broiler

Serve this sandwich cut into quarters with pasta and a small salad. This broiler also makes a great appetizer. Cut the loaf of French bread in half lengthwise (do not quarter it). Scoop out some of the bread in the middle and add the sandwich mixture. Broil as directed, then cut the halves into 1-inch slices. If your toaster oven cannot accommodate four French bread quarters, broil them in two batches.

1 small loaf Italian or French bread, sliced in half lengthwise, then quartered

Filling:
2 plum tomatoes, chopped
1 5-ounce jar artichokes, drained and chopped
2 tablespoons chopped black olives

2 tablespoons chopped onion
2 garlic cloves, minced
2 tablespoons olive oil
Salt and freshly ground black pepper to taste

4 tablespoons grated Parmesan cheese

REMOVE enough bread from each quarter to make a small cavity for the sandwich mixture.

COMBINE the filling ingredients and spoon the mixture in equal portions into each of the bread quarter cavities. Sprinkle each quarter with 1 tablespoon Parmesan cheese.

BROIL on a broiling rack with a pan underneath for 10 minutes, or until the bread is lightly browned. Slice and serve.

Prep: 10 minutes
Total time: 20 minutes
Serves 4

Savory Salsa Cheese Rounds

Use your favorite brand of salsa or make your own. Do two batches of six rounds each in a square baking pan.

1 French baguette, cut to make 12
  1-inch slices (rounds)
¼ cup olive oil
1 cup Tomato Salsa (recipe follows)

½ cup shredded low-fat mozzarella
2 tablespoons finely chopped fresh
  cilantro

BRUSH both sides of each round with olive oil.

SPREAD one side of each slice with salsa and sprinkle each with mozzarella. Place the rounds in an oiled or nonstick 8½ × 8½ × 2-inch square baking (cake) pan.

BROIL for 6 minutes, or until the cheese is melted and the rounds are lightly browned. Garnish with the chopped cilantro and serve.

Prep: 5 minutes
Total time: 11 minutes
Makes 12 slices

Tomato Salsa

½ cup chopped sun-dried tomatoes
½ cup boiling water
1 8-ounce can tomato sauce
1 jalapeño pepper, seeded and
  chopped (Wear protective latex
  gloves when handling to avoid
  skin irritation.)
2 tablespoons chopped onion
2 tablespoons chopped bell pepper

2 tablespoons olive oil
½ cup pitted Spanish olives
2 tablespoons diced pimiento
2 tablespoons chopped fresh cilantro
½ teaspoon garlic powder
1 teaspoon chili powder
1 teaspoon lemon juice
Salt and freshly ground black pepper
  to taste

COMBINE the sun-dried tomatoes and the boiling water in a small bowl and let sit for 10 minutes, or until the tomatoes are softened. Drain in a sieve. Add all the remaining ingredients, mixing well. Adjust the seasonings. Chill for 3 hours before serving.

Total time: 10 minutes
Makes 1½ cups

Ham and Swiss Melts

This melt is ideal for a concert on the lawn, a picnic, a soccer game, or brunch at the beach. Just assemble, broil, cool, reassemble into original loaf form, and wrap well. Or, if you prefer, cut into slices and wrap individually.

Spread:
2 scallions, finely chopped
2 tablespoons finely chopped radishes
2 tablespoons brown mustard
1 teaspoon Worcestershire sauce
2 tablespoons low-fat mayonnaise

4 slices low-fat Swiss cheese
4 slices lean baked ham

2 6-inch submarine rolls, cut in half
   lengthwise

COMBINE the spread ingredients in a small bowl and spread in equal portions on the flat side of the bread halves. Add 2 slices of cheese and ham per each, folding to fit, if necessary. Place on an oiled or nonstick $6^1/_2 \times 10$-inch baking sheet.

BROIL for 8 minutes, or until the cheese is melted and browned lightly.

Prep: 10 minutes
Total time: 18 minutes
Serves 2

Turkey and Tuna Melt

Any reduced-fat cheese can be used, but I like Monterey Jack the best. Packaged low-fat turkey slices are good, and deli sliced turkey is better, but the most delicious is baked turkey breast slices. Fresh turkey breast is available in the supermarket in a variety of sizes: breast quarters, breast halves, or the whole breast. Consider buying one of these convenient sizes and baking it in your toaster oven! One quarter of a breast baked (covered) at 400° F. will take about 25 minutes. A half breast will take about 40 minutes and a whole breast about an hour.

4 slices multigrain bread
Spicy brown mustard
1 6-ounce can tuna in water, drained
   well and crumbled

$1/_4$ pound thinly sliced turkey breast
4 slices low-fat Monterey Jack cheese
2 tablespoons finely chopped scallions
Salt and freshly ground black pepper

Continued

SPREAD one side of each bread slice with mustard and place on an oiled or nonstick 6$\frac{1}{2}$ × 10-inch baking sheet.

LAYER 2 slices with equal portions of tuna, turkey, cheese, and scallion. Season to taste with salt and pepper.

TOAST twice, or until the cheese is melted.

Prep: 8 minutes
Total time: 12 minutes
Serves 2

Zucchini Melt

The sandwich ingredients are roasted under the broiler to speed up prep time and give the bread filling a depth of flavor and texture. Topped with melted cheese, this open-faced sandwich is definitely "hearty vegetarian."

Sandwich mixture:
1 small zucchini, chopped
1 plum tomato, chopped
2 tablespoons chopped scallions
$\frac{1}{4}$ cup sliced mushrooms
1 bell pepper, seeded and chopped
1 tablespoon olive oil
2 tablespoons minced pimientos
1 teaspoon dried oregano

$\frac{1}{2}$ teaspoon dried basil
1 teaspoon minced garlic

6 slices multigrain or rye bread
$\frac{1}{2}$ cup shredded low-fat mozzarella cheese
2 tablespoons grated Parmesan cheese

COMBINE the sandwich mixture ingredients in a medium bowl, mixing well. Transfer to an oiled or nonstick 8$\frac{1}{2}$ × 8$\frac{1}{2}$ × 2-inch square baking (cake) pan.

BROIL for 10 minutes, or until the zucchini and scallions are tender.

SPOON the mixture onto each slice of bread in equal portions. Sprinkle each slice with equal portions of the cheeses. Place the bread slices on a broiling rack with a pan underneath.

BROIL for 6 minutes, or until the cheese is melted.

Prep: 10 minutes
Total time: 26 minutes
Serves 6

Beef and Bean Quesadillas

The steak strips, jalapeño pepper, onion, and tomato are roasted under the toaster oven broiler, then the beans and cilantro are added, as well as the cheese, to make the filling. To make tortillas pliable so that they can be rolled, heat on the oven rack under the broiler for 1 or 2 minutes, or until pliable. Serve with dollops of low-fat or fat-free sour cream.

Quesadilla filling:
1 8-ounce flank steak, trimmed and cut into thin $1/8 \times 2$-inch strips
1 jalapeño pepper, seeded and minced
2 plum tomatoes, chopped
1 small onion, cut into thin strips
1 bell pepper, seeded and cut into thin strips
2 garlic cloves, minced

1 15-ounce can black beans, rinsed and drained
2 tablespoons chopped fresh cilantro
$1/2$ cup reduced-fat Monterey Jack cheese
4 6-inch flour tortillas
Low-fat or fat-free sour cream

COMBINE the filling ingredients in an oiled or nonstick $8^{1}/_{2} \times 8^{1}/_{2} \times 2$-inch square baking (cake) pan, mixing well to blend.

BROIL for 10 minutes, remove from the oven, and turn the pieces with tongs. Broil for 10 minutes, or until the pepper, onion, and beef are cooked and tender. Remove from the oven and transfer to a bowl. Add the beans and cilantro and mix well.

SPREAD one quarter of the tortilla mixture in the center of each tortilla. Sprinkle each tortilla with 2 tablespoons cheese. Roll up the edges and lay each, seam side down, in the pan.

BROIL for 10 minutes, or until the tortillas are lightly browned and the cheese is melted. Serve with sour cream.

Prep: 15 minutes
Total time: 45 minutes
Serves 2

Spicy Beef Fajitas

The fajita ingredients are all easily precooked under the broiler of the toaster oven. Snip away any fat deposits on the flank steak with scissors before you cut it into strips. After broiling, press the fajita mixture between several layers of paper towels to extract any excess fat or moisture before filling the tortillas. You will have all of the flavor but none of the fat!

Mixture:
1 pound flank steak, cut into thin
 strips 2 inches long
1 bell pepper, seeded and cut into
 thin strips
2 tablespoons chopped onion
1 tablespoon chopped fresh cilantro
$\frac{1}{4}$ teaspoon hot sauce

1 teaspoon garlic powder
$\frac{1}{2}$ teaspoon cumin
1 teaspoon chili powder
Salt and freshly ground black pepper
 to taste

4 8-inch flour tortillas

COMBINE all the mixture ingredients in an oiled or nonstick $8\frac{1}{2} \times 8\frac{1}{2} \times 2$-inch square baking (cake) pan.

BROIL for 20 minutes, turning every 5 minutes, or until the pepper and onion are tender and the meat is beginning to brown. Remove from the oven and place equal portions of the mixture in the center of each tortilla. Roll the tortilla around the mixture and lay, seam side down, in a shallow baking pan.

BAKE at 350° F. for 20 minutes, or until the tortillas are lightly browned.

Prep: 12 minutes
Total time: 52 minutes
Serves 4

Turkey Burgers

What the supermarket labels "lean ground turkey" (or chicken) is often high in fat, as much as 15 to 20 percent, because the skin is often ground with the meat. Instead, buy ground turkey breast (or ground chicken breast), which usually has a 3 percent fat content. Homemade Bread Crumbs (recipe follows) enhance these burgers. They are easy to make and have less fat and sodium than most commercial stuffing and bread crumb mixtures. If you prefer purchasing commercial bread crumbs, check out the fat/sodium content before you toss the box in your shopping cart.

1 pound lean ground turkey breast
2 tablespoons bread crumbs
2 tablespoons barbecue sauce
$\frac{1}{2}$ teaspoon garlic powder

$\frac{1}{2}$ teaspoon chili powder
Salt and freshly ground black pepper
  to taste

COMBINE all ingredients in a bowl, mixing well. Divide into 4 portions and shape
  into patties.

BROIL on a rack with a pan underneath for 20 minutes, or until the meat is browned
  and the juice runs clear when pierced with a fork.

Prep: 10 minutes
Total time: 34 minutes
Serves 4

Homemade Bread Crumbs

*I use bread crumbs for coating fish or chicken filets, topping a casserole or quiche, or for
a quick and easy piecrust. I like making my own bread crumbs for these reasons: (1) They
taste better than store-bought, (2) They don't have a lot of undesirable seasonings, fat, or
sodium, (3) I can choose seasonings I like (as in the recipe below) or just make plain
bread crumbs and add the seasonings later, (4) They're easy to make and store well in a
plastic container in the refrigerator. Here's my recipe, the yield of which is about 2 cups.
If you're not convinced that you should take the time to make your own bread crumbs,
check out the sodium and fat content of commercial bread crumbs before you grab the
box and toss it into the shopping cart. Many bread crumb mixes and crumb coatings that
are low in fat are very high in sodium.*

6 slices multigrain or whole wheat
  bread, well toasted and broken
  into pieces
1 teaspoon garlic powder
1 teaspoon curry powder

1 teaspoon cumin
$\frac{1}{2}$ teaspoon salt
$\frac{1}{4}$ teaspoon butcher's pepper

BLEND all ingredients in a food processor or blender to produce fine-textured
  crumbs. Adjust the seasonings to taste.

Prep: 10 minutes
Total time: 10 minutes
Makes approximately 2 cups

Salmon Burgers

Tasty, easy burgers on the table in less than half an hour, thanks to the toaster oven. These burgers are baked instead of broiled because the onion and zucchini need to be cooked well. For something different from the usual burger bun, serve salmon burgers with thick rounds of crusty Italian bread that have been brushed with olive oil and toasted twice, or until browned. For a rounded meal, add a green salad of chopped spinach and leaf lettuce drizzled with olive oil, balsamic vinegar, and seasoned with salt and pepper.

³/₄ cup Homemade Bread Crumbs
  (page 41)
1 15-ounce can salmon, drained
1 small zucchini, finely chopped
2 tablespoons finely chopped onions
1 egg

1 teaspoon dried rosemary
1 teaspoon lemon juice
1 teaspoon garlic powder
Salt and freshly ground black pepper
  to taste
1 teaspoon vegetable oil

PREHEAT the toaster oven to 400° F.

BLEND all ingredients except the oil and form patties 1¹/₂ inches thick. Place on an oiled or nonstick 8¹/₂ × 8¹/₂ × 2-inch square baking (cake) pan.

BAKE for 25 minutes, or until the patties are lightly browned.

Prep: 10 minutes
Total time: 35 minutes
Serves 4

Portobello Burgers

These are delicious vegetarian "burgers." They taste best well done when the liquid within the mushroom has been reduced by broiling and the flavors are concentrated.

4 multigrain hamburger buns
Dijon mustard
4 large portobello mushroom caps,
  stemmed and brushed clean
2 tablespoons olive oil

Garlic powder
Salt and butcher's pepper
4 thin onion slices
4 tomato slices

TOAST the split hamburger buns and spread each slice with mustard. Set aside.

BRUSH both sides of the mushroom caps with olive oil and sprinkle with garlic powder and salt and pepper to taste.

BROIL the caps on a broiling rack with a pan underneath, ribbed side up, for 6 minutes. Turn the mushrooms carefully with tongs and broil again for 6 minutes, or until lightly browned. Place the mushroom caps on the bottom buns and layer each with an onion and tomato slice. Top with the remaining bun halves and serve.

Prep: 8 minutes
Total time: 20 minutes
Serves 4

Nacho Chips

Homemade nachos are easy to make in a toaster oven.

3 jalapeño peppers
4 6-inch flour tortillas

1 cup shredded low-fat Cheddar
   cheese

SEED and cut the jalapeño peppers into thin rings. Arrange one-fourth of the rings on the tortilla. It's a good idea to wear gloves, since the peppers can sometimes cause skin irritation.

PLACE the tortilla in an oiled or nonstick $8^1/_2 \times 8^1/_2 \times 2$-inch square baking (cake) pan. Sprinkle evenly with $1/_4$ cup cheese.

BROIL for 5 minutes, or until the cheese is melted. Repeat the process for the remaining tortillas. Cut each into 6 wedges with a sharp knife or scissors.

Prep: 8 minutes
Total time: 28 minutes (4 tortillas)
Makes 24 chips

Smoked Turkey, Walnut, and Pimiento Sandwich

Thick slices of Country Bread (page 183) make this sandwich a cut above the rest. If you don't have time to make the bread, rye bread works well also. It is the toasting that brings the medley of many flavors together to harmonize beautifully. This sandwich is definitely a meal in itself.

Mixture:
Stone-ground mustard
2 tablespoons canned diced pimientos
2 tablespoons finely chopped scallions
2 tablespoons finely chopped walnuts
2 tablespoons chopped raisins

$^1/_2$ teaspoon dill
2 tablespoons reduced-fat mayonnaise
Salt and butcher's pepper to taste

4 slices rye bread
1 2.5-ounce package smoked turkey breast slices

COMBINE the mixture ingredients and spread in equal portions on all bread slices. Layer 2 bread slices with equal portions of smoked turkey breast. Top with the other bread slices to make sandwiches.

TOAST twice on a broiling rack with a pan underneath.

Prep: 8 minutes
Total time: 12 minutes
Serves 2

Oven-Baked Reuben

A delicious substitution for very high-sodium sauerkraut is $^1/_2$ cup finely shredded cabbage that has been tossed with 1 tablespoon wine vinegar and seasoned with a pinch of salt and pepper. Most thin-sliced sandwich corned beef has a relatively low fat content (4 or 5 percent) and some brands are even lower. If you like your Reuben with Russian dressing but can't seem to locate a low-fat brand, try making your own.

4 slices rye bread
2 tablespoons Dijon mustard
6 slices reduced-fat Swiss cheese

1 6-ounce package sliced corned beef
$^1/_2$ cup sauerkraut, drained
Russian Dressing (recipe follows)

SPREAD each slice of bread with mustard. Layer 2 slices with 3 slices each of Swiss cheese and equal portions of corned beef and sauerkraut. Top with the remaining bread slices and place on a broiling rack with the pan underneath.

TOAST twice, or until the cheese is melted. Serve with Russian Dressing.

Prep: 5 minutes
Total time: 8 minutes
Serves 2

Russian Dressing

¾ cup low-fat or fat-free sour cream
1 tablespoon ketchup
1 tablespoon chopped dill pickles

1 tablespoon fat-free half-and-half
Salt and freshly ground black pepper
  to taste

COMBINE all the ingredients in a small bowl.

Total time: 6 minutes
Makes 1 cup

Tuna Tarragon Picnic Loaf

This loaf can be made ahead of time and is beautifully portable. After filling and broiling, just reassemble the bread back into a loaf and wrap well to transport to a picnic. At the picnic, simply slice and serve!

1 French baguette, sliced in half
  lengthwise, then quartered

Filling:
1 6-ounce can tuna in water, well
  drained
2 tablespoons chopped onion
2 tablespoons chopped Spanish

olives with pimientos, drained
2 tablespoons chopped fresh parsley
2 tablespoons chopped bell pepper
1 teaspoon dried tarragon
Salt and butcher's pepper to taste

½ cup shredded low-fat mozzarella
  cheese

REMOVE enough bread from each quarter to make a small cavity for the sandwich filling.

Continued

COMBINE all the filling ingredients and spoon the mixture in equal portions into each of the bread quarter cavities. Sprinkle each quarter with equal portions of mozzarella cheese.

BROIL on a broiling rack with a pan underneath for 10 minutes, or until the bread is lightly browned and the cheese is melted. If your toaster oven cannot accommodate 4 French bread quarters, broil them in two batches. Slice and serve.

Prep: 12 minutes
Total time: 22 minutes
Serves 4

Chapter 3

Soups

Toaster ovens make beautiful soups! Through baking, the ingredients meld with the broth or water to produce a flavorful, nutritious stock and fully cooked vegetables, meat, grains, or pasta. No nutrients are lost in the process because the liquid reduces and concentrates through the slow simmer of baking. The ease and advantage of making a soup in a toaster oven is in assembling all of the ingredients in one dish and baking it to completion. No need to stand at the stove sautéing, browning, or stirring. In the average time of an hour, the soup is ready for the table. All of the ingredients—grains, vegetables, meat, or pasta—are cooked to perfection by a constant heat. In this chapter, you'll find wonderful soup recipes for the toaster oven, including French Onion, Narragansett Clam Chowder, Lentil and Carrot, Tomato Bisque, Chicken Noodle, and more.

Narragansett Clam Chowder

This is based on a recipe a friend scribbled on a napkin for me years ago, but I have replaced the heavy cream base with fat-free half-and-half thickened with unbleached flour. The flavor is rich, the texture smooth and silky. Like most soup, a day or two in the refrigerator will enhance the flavor of the stock. Serve with warm slices of Yogurt Bread (page 182).

1 cup fat-free half-and-half
2 tablespoons unbleached flour
$\frac{1}{2}$ cup chopped onion
1 cup peeled and diced potato
1 tablespoon vegetable oil
1 tablespoon chopped fresh parsley

1 6-ounce can clams, drained and chopped
1 15-ounce can fat-free low-sodium chicken broth
Salt and freshly ground black pepper
Continued

WHISK together the half-and-half and flour in a small bowl. Set aside.

COMBINE the onion, potato, and oil in an $8^1/_2 \times 8^1/_2 \times 2$-inch square baking (cake) pan.

BROIL 15 minutes, turning every 5 minutes with tongs, or until the potato is tender and the onion is cooked. Transfer to a 1-quart baking dish. Add the parsley, clams, broth, and half-and-half/flour mixture. Stir well and season to taste with salt and pepper.

BAKE, uncovered, at 375° F. for 20 minutes, stirring after 10 minutes, or until the stock is reduced and thickened. Ladle into bowls and serve with Yogurt Bread (page 182).

Prep: 15 minutes
Total time: 50 minutes
Serves 4

French Onion Soup

Onion soup does admirably in a toaster oven. Often a bouillon stock reduced by boiling becomes too salty and the seasonings diluted or unbalanced. The slow, steady simmering heat of the toaster oven brings out the flavor of the onions and integrates it with all of the ingredients, gently harmonizing them. Sesame oil adds a subtle, toasted flavor to the stock; white wine introduces a mild edge of tartness, which contrasts well with the mellow richness of the bread and Parmesan cheese.

1 cup finely chopped onions	Freshly ground black pepper to taste
1 teaspoon toasted sesame oil	4 French bread rounds, sliced 1 inch
1 tablespoon vegetable oil	thick
$^1/_2$ cup dry white wine	4 tablespoons grated Parmesan
2 teaspoons soy sauce	cheese
$^1/_2$ teaspoon garlic powder	1 tablespoon chopped fresh parsley

PLACE the onions, sesame oil, and vegetable oil in an $8^1/_2 \times 8^1/_2 \times 2$-inch square baking (cake) pan.

BROIL for 10 minutes, stirring every 3 minutes until the onions are tender. Remove from the oven and transfer to a 1-quart $8^1/_2 \times 8^1/_2 \times 4$-inch ovenproof baking dish. Add 2 cups water, the wine, and the soy sauce. Add the garlic powder and pepper and adjust the seasonings.

BAKE, covered, at 400° F. for 30 minutes. Remove from the oven, uncover, and add the 4 bread rounds, letting them float on top of the soup. Sprinkle each with 1 tablespoon Parmesan cheese.

BROIL, uncovered, for 6 minutes, or until the cheese is lightly browned. With tongs, transfer the bread rounds to 4 individual soup bowls. Ladle the soup on top of the bread rounds. Garnish with the parsley and serve immediately.

Prep: 10 minutes
Total time: 56 minutes
Serves 4

Roasted Vegetable Gazpacho

Vegetables are baked to tenderness, then roasted under the broiler. It's the flavor of the roasted vegetables that gives the chilled tomato-based stock depth and character. One or two days in the refrigerator will enhance the flavor of the stock even further.

Vegetables and seasonings:
1 bell pepper, thinly sliced
$1/2$ cup chopped celery
$1/2$ cup frozen or canned corn
1 medium onion, thinly sliced
1 small yellow squash, cut into
 1-inch slices
1 small zucchini, cut into 1-inch
 slices

3 garlic cloves, chopped
$1/2$ teaspoon ground cumin
2 tablespoons olive oil
Salt and freshly ground black pepper
 to taste

1 quart tomato juice
1 tablespoon lemon juice
3 tablespoons chopped fresh cilantro

PREHEAT the toaster oven to 400° F.

COMBINE the vegetables and seasonings in an oiled or nonstick $8^{1}/_{2} \times 8^{1}/_{2} \times 2$-inch square baking (cake) pan, mixing well.

BAKE, covered, for 25 minutes, or until the onions and celery are tender. Remove from the oven, uncover, and turn the vegetable pieces with tongs.

BROIL for 10 minutes, or until the vegetables are lightly browned. Remove from the oven and cool. Transfer to a large nonaluminum container and add the tomato juice, lemon juice, and cilantro. Adjust the seasonings.

CHILL, covered, for several hours, preferably a day or two to enrich the flavor of the stock.

Prep: 20 minutes
Total time: 55 minutes
Serves 4

Pea Soup

Peas that are not completely pulverized by processing in a blender give the soup texture. The powder becomes, through baking, a smooth, creamy base and additions of carrots, onions, and bacon give this soup a delicious homemade flavor. This is good old-fashioned nourishment!

Shortcut: Grating the carrot, celery, and onion in a food processor shortens prep time by 8 minutes.

1 cup dried split peas, ground in a blender to a powderlike consistency

3 strips lean turkey bacon, uncooked and chopped

$\frac{1}{4}$ cup grated carrots

$\frac{1}{4}$ cup grated celery

2 tablespoons grated onion

$\frac{1}{2}$ teaspoon garlic powder

Salt and freshly ground black pepper to taste

Garnish:

2 tablespoons chopped fresh chives

PREHEAT the toaster oven to 400° F.

COMBINE all the ingredients in a 1-quart $8\frac{1}{2} \times 8\frac{1}{2} \times 4$-inch ovenproof baking dish, mixing well. Adjust the seasonings.

BAKE, covered, for 35 minutes. Remove from the oven and stir.

BAKE, covered, for another 20 minutes, or until the soup is thickened. Ladle the soup into individual soup bowls and garnish each with chopped fresh chives.

Prep: 17 minutes

Total time: 1 hour and 12 minutes

Serves 6

Connecticut Garden Chowder

Inspired by my garden's produce, this chowder base is made with fat-free half-and-half and reduced-fat cream cheese thickened with unbleached flour. Letting the soup sit for an hour after cooking strengthens the flavors. Refrigeration for a day or two will further enhance the flavors by allowing the stock and vegetables to "get intimate."

Shortcut: Shredding the carrot, celery, potato, and zucchini in a food processor reduces prep time to 9 minutes.

Soup:
$^1/_2$ cup peeled and shredded potato
$^1/_2$ cup shredded carrot
$^1/_2$ cup shredded celery
2 plum tomatoes, chopped
1 small zucchini, shredded
2 bay leaves
$^1/_4$ teaspoon sage
1 teaspoon garlic powder
Salt and butcher's pepper to taste

Chowder base:
2 tablespoons reduced-fat cream
  cheese, at room temperature
$^1/_2$ cup fat-free half-and-half
2 tablespoons unbleached flour
2 tablespoons chopped fresh parsley

PREHEAT the toaster oven to 375°F.

COMBINE the soup ingredients in a 1-quart $8^1/_2 \times 8^1/_2 \times 4$-inch ovenproof baking
  dish, mixing well. Adjust the seasonings to taste.

BAKE, covered, for 40 minutes, or until the vegetables are tender.

WHISK the chowder mixture ingredients together until smooth. Add the mixture to
  the cooked soup ingredients and stir well to blend.

BAKE, uncovered for 20 minutes, or until the stock is thickened. Ladle the soup into
  individual soup bowls and garnish with the parsley.

Prep: 20 minutes
Total time: 1 hour and 20 minutes
Serves 4

Crab Chowder

*For maximum flavor, allow the soup to cool after cooking, then chill for 3 hours. Reheat
and serve with thick slabs of Country Bread (page 183).*

1 6-ounce can lump crabmeat,
  drained and chopped, or $^1/_2$ pound
  fresh crabmeat, cleaned and
  chopped
1 cup skim milk or low-fat soy milk
1 cup fat-free half-and-half
2 tablespoons unbleached flour
$^1/_4$ cup chopped onion
$^1/_2$ cup peeled and diced potato

1 carrot, peeled and chopped
1 celery stalk, chopped
2 garlic cloves, minced
2 tablespoons chopped fresh parsley
$^1/_2$ teaspoon ground cumin
1 teaspoon paprika
Salt and butcher's pepper to taste

Continued

PREHEAT the toaster oven to 400° F.

WHISK together the milk, half-and-half, and flour in a bowl. Transfer the mixture to a 1-quart $8\frac{1}{2} \times 8\frac{1}{2} \times 4$-inch ovenproof baking dish. Add all the other ingredients, mixing well. Adjust the seasonings to taste.

BAKE, covered, for 40 minutes, or until the vegetables are tender.

Prep: 10 minutes
Total time: 50 minutes
Serves 4

Green Bean Soup

This recipe was passed down to me by my grandmother. Little is changed here, except margarine is substituted for butter, the roux for the stock is browned in the broiler, and the soup is baked in a toaster oven rather than simmered on a stovetop. Indescribably delicious! It is difficult to have just one bowl of this soup.

Roux mixture:
2 tablespoons unbleached flour
1 tablespoon margarine

3 cups water or low-sodium vegetable stock

1 cup ($\frac{1}{2}$ pound) fresh string beans, trimmed and cut into 1-inch pieces
$\frac{1}{2}$ teaspoon dried oregano
$\frac{1}{2}$ teaspoon ground cumin
Salt and freshly ground black pepper to taste

COMBINE the roux mixture in an $8\frac{1}{2} \times 8\frac{1}{2} \times 2$-inch baking (cake) pan.

BROIL for 5 minutes, or until the margarine is melted. Remove from the oven and stir, then broil again for 2 minutes, or until the mixture is brown but not burned. Remove from the oven and stir to mix well. Set aside.

COMBINE the water or broth, string beans, and seasonings in a 1-quart $8\frac{1}{2} \times 8\frac{1}{2} \times 4$-inch ovenproof baking dish. Stir in the roux mixture, blending well. Adjust the seasonings to taste.

BAKE, covered, at 375° F. for 40 minutes, or until the string beans are tender.

Prep: 10 minutes
Total time: 57 minutes
Serves 4

Lentil and Carrot Soup

A good and hearty soup, Lentil and Carrot is my fall favorite. A bowl enables one to face a long cold winter cheerfully. When the soup is done and slightly cooled, puree one half in the blender or food processor for a smoother texture and thickened stock. Serve with Garlic Basil Bread (page 187).

$\frac{1}{2}$ cup lentils
$\frac{1}{2}$ cup dry white wine
1 small onion, chopped
3 carrots, peeled and finely chopped
$\frac{1}{2}$ cup fresh mushrooms, cleaned
 and sliced, or 1 5-ounce can
 mushroom pieces, well drained

3 garlic cloves, minced
1 tablespoon chopped fresh parsley
1 tablespoon Worcestershire sauce
Salt and freshly ground black pepper
 to taste

PREHEAT the toaster oven to 375°F.

COMBINE all the ingredients with 2 cups water in a 1-quart $8\frac{1}{2} \times 8\frac{1}{2} \times 4$-inch ovenproof baking dish. Adjust the seasonings.

BAKE for 40 minutes, or until the lentils, carrots, and onions are tender. Ladle into individual soup bowls and serve.

Prep: 13 minutes
Total time: 53 minutes
Serves 4

Chicken Noodle Soup

Noodles, chicken, and vegetables all cook together, blended exquisitely by baking in the toaster oven. This quintessential soup has a full, rich flavor without adding a commercial broth or stock. The slow baking process integrates the soup ingredients and the liquid to produce a wonderful taste and aroma. One bowl of this soup raises the bedridden to a chair in front of the TV. Caution: Two bowls gets them out of the house and back to work!

 Shortcut: *Chopping the carrot, celery, tomato, onion, and parsley in a food processor reduces the prep time to 10 minutes.*

Continued

1 cup egg noodles, uncooked
1 skinless, boneless chicken breast
  filet, cut into 1-inch pieces
1 carrot, peeled and chopped
1 celery stalk, chopped
1 plum tomato, chopped

1 small onion, peeled and chopped
1 tablespoon chopped fresh parsley
1 teaspoon dried basil
Salt and freshly ground black pepper
  to taste

PREHEAT the toaster oven to 400° F.

COMBINE all the ingredients with 3 cups water in a 1-quart $8^{1}/_{2} \times 8^{1}/_{2} \times 4$-inch oven-proof baking dish.

BAKE, covered, for 45 minutes, or until the vegetables and chicken are tender.

Prep: 20 minutes
Total time: 1 hour and 5 minutes
Serves 4

Creamy Roasted Pepper Basil Soup

Serve this smooth, rose-colored soup hot or cold. To serve hot, sprinkle with Parmesan cheese. To serve cold, garnish with chopped fresh basil leaves.

1 5-ounce jar roasted peppers,
  drained
$^{1}/_{2}$ cup fresh basil leaves
1 cup fat-free half-and-half
1 cup skim milk
2 tablespoons reduced-fat cream
  cheese
1 teaspoon garlic powder

1 teaspoon paprika
Salt and freshly ground black pepper
  to taste
2 tablespoons chopped fresh basil
  leaves (garnish for cold soup)
2 tablespoons grated Parmesan
  cheese (topping for hot soup)

PREHEAT the toaster oven to 400° F.

PROCESS all the ingredients in a blender or food processor until smooth. Transfer the mixture to a 1-quart $8^{1}/_{2} \times 8^{1}/_{2} \times 4$-inch ovenproof baking dish.

BAKE, covered, for 35 minutes. Ladle into individual soup bowls and serve.

Prep: 8 minutes
Total time: 43 minutes
Serves 4

Tomato Bisque

This is a light soup, full of flavor—smooth and rich tasting. The color is a beautiful light orange and a garnish of fresh basil leaves makes this soup an elegant beginning or a lovely light lunch. Good served hot or cold.

1 8-ounce can tomato sauce
1 7-ounce jar diced pimientos, drained
1 tablespoon finely chopped onion
2 cups low-fat buttermilk
1 cup fat-free half-and-half
1 tablespoon low-fat cream cheese

1 teaspoon garlic powder
$1/2$ teaspoon paprika
$1/2$ teaspoon ground bay leaf
1 teaspoon hot sauce (optional)
Salt and white pepper to taste
2 tablespoons minced fresh basil leaves

PREHEAT the toaster oven to 350° F.

PROCESS all the ingredients except the basil in a blender or food processor until smooth. Pour into a 1-quart $8^{1}/_{2} \times 8^{1}/_{2} \times 4$-inch ovenproof baking dish. Adjust the seasonings to taste.

BAKE, covered, for 25 minutes. Ladle into small soup bowls and garnish each with fresh basil leaves before serving.

Prep: 15 minutes
Total time: 40 minutes
Serves 4

Chapter 4

Pizza

When you think of pizza, perhaps you think of buying a frozen pizza and putting it in the oven to bake. With a toaster oven it's easy to do that, but it's almost as easy to make your own pizza, which is just as delicious but with less fat, calories, additives, and sodium than a commercial pizza. By its very nature, pizza is not a dietetic food, but by making the crust and topping yourself, you can be in control of the ingredients. Included in this chapter are recipes for making your own crust (Yeast Dough for Two Pizzas) and sauce (Homemade Pizza Sauce), as well as recipes for a variety of provocative toppings for ready-made crusts. The Sun-Dried Tomato Pizza, My Favorite Pizza, Fresh Herb Veggie Pizza, and Inspirational Personal Pizza recipes will inspire you to create the pizza of your dreams. Or, if you desire pizza out of the ordinary, there's Spanakopizza and Pesto Pizza to whet your appetite for the deliciously different.

My Favorite Pizza

Making this pizza is like painting a picture. A swirl of red tomato sauce, a sparkle of olive oil, white sprinklings of mozzarella cheese and chicken breast meat, and green dots of bell pepper are interspersed with multicolored spatters of garlic and seasonings. From palette to palate—a thoroughly delectable artistic journey!

1 9-inch ready-made pizza crust
1 8-ounce can tomato sauce
1 tablespoon olive oil

1 cup skinless, boneless chicken
   breast, cooked and cubed
3 plum tomatoes, chopped

1 bell pepper, quartered, seeded,
  and chopped
2 garlic cloves, minced
1/2 teaspoon dried oregano

1/2 teaspoon dried basil
1/2 teaspoon red pepper flakes
1 cup shredded part-skim, low-
  moisture mozzarella cheese

PREHEAT the toaster oven to 400° F.

SPREAD the pizza crust with the tomato sauce. Drizzle with the olive oil and sprinkle with the chicken, tomatoes, pepper, garlic, seasonings, and cheese. Place the pizza on the toaster oven rack.

BAKE for 25 minutes, or until the topping is cooked and the crust is lightly browned.

Prep: 15 minutes
Total time: 45 minutes
Serves 4

Italian Bread Pizza

A quick and easy pizza can be made using a loaf of Italian or French bread. The filling of tomato, olives, onion, and zucchini makes this bread great with pasta. Or as an appetizer, cut the baked bread into 1-inch slices.

Shortcut: *Grating the zucchini, onion, and pepper in a food processor will shorten prep time to 10 minutes.*

1 loaf Italian or French bread,
  unsliced

Filling:
1/2 cup tomato sauce
2 tablespoons tomato paste
2 tablespoons olive oil
1/2 cup grated zucchini
1/2 cup grated onion
2 tablespoons grated bell pepper

1 teaspoon garlic powder
2 tablespoons chopped pitted black
  olives
1 teaspoon dried oregano or 1
  tablespoon chopped fresh oregano
Salt to taste
1/4 cup mozzarella cheese

PREHEAT the toaster oven to 375° F.

CUT the loaf of bread in half lengthwise, then in quarters crosswise. Remove some of the bread from the center to make a cavity for the pizza topping.

Continued

COMBINE all the topping ingredients and spoon equal portions into the cavities in the bread. Sprinkle with mozzarella cheese. Place the bread quarters on the toaster oven rack.

BAKE for 30 minutes, or until the cheese is melted and the crust is lightly browned.

Prep: 15 minutes
Total time: 45 minutes
Serves 4

Yeast Dough for Two Pizzas

It's fun making a pizza crust! Kneading the dough bonds you to the ancient tradition of pizza making, the aroma of the dough baking is exquisite, and the prospect of assembling and layering a medley of your favorite toppings on the crust is a wonderful and rewarding experience. Make two pizza crusts, or make one and wrap up the other dough ball in plastic to store in the refrigerator for up to two weeks.

1/4 cup tepid water
1 cup tepid skim milk
1/2 teaspoon sugar

1 1 1/4-ounce envelope dry yeast
2 cups unbleached flour
1 tablespoon olive oil

PREHEAT the toaster oven to 400° F.

COMBINE the water, milk, and sugar in a bowl. Add the yeast and set aside for 3 to 5 minutes, or until the yeast is dissolved.

STIR in the flour gradually, adding just enough to form a ball of the dough.

KNEAD on a floured surface until the dough is satiny, and then put the dough in a bowl in a warm place with a damp towel over the top. In 1 hour or when the dough has doubled in bulk, punch it down and divide it in half. Flatten the dough and spread it out to the desired thickness on an oiled or nonstick 9 3/4-inch-diameter pie pan. Spread with Homemade Pizza Sauce (recipe follows) and add any desired toppings.

BAKE for 20 minutes, or until the topping ingredients are cooked and the cheese is melted.

Prep: 15 minutes
Total time: 35 minutes (Dough rising: 1 hour)
Makes 2 9-inch pizza crusts

Homemade Pizza Sauce

1 9-inch ready-made pizza crust or
  1 homemade pizza crust (page 58)
2 plum tomatoes, chopped
1 tablespoon olive oil
3 garlic cloves, peeled and chopped
$1/4$ cup chopped onion
2 tablespoons tomato paste
2 tablespoons dry red wine

1 tablespoon chopped fresh basil
  or 1 teaspoon dried basil
1 tablespoon chopped fresh oregano
  or 1 teaspoon dried oregano
1 bay leaf
Salt and freshly ground black pepper
  to taste

COMBINE all ingredients in an $8^{1}/_{2} \times 8^{1}/_{2} \times 2$-inch square baking (cake) pan. Adjust the seasonings to taste.

BROIL for 20 minutes, or until the onions and tomatoes are tender. Remove the bay leaf and cool before spreading on the pizza crust. Bake the pizza according to instructions on the ready-made crust package or in the homemade pizza crust recipe.

Prep: 15 minutes
Total time: 35 minutes
Makes 1 cup

Sun-Dried Tomato Pizza

Sun-dried tomatoes amplify the flavors, tomato paste gives the sauce substance, and the cheese, black olives, and mushrooms make this a perfect vegetarian delight.

Tomato mixture:
1 cup chopped sun-dried tomatoes
2 tablespoons tomato paste
2 tablespoons olive oil
2 tablespoons chopped onion
2 garlic cloves, minced
1 teaspoon dried oregano
1 teaspoon dried basil
Salt and red pepper flakes to taste

1 9-inch ready-made pizza crust
1 5-ounce can mushrooms
$1/4$ cup pitted and sliced black olives
$1/2$ cup shredded low-fat mozzarella
  cheese

Continued

COMBINE the tomato mixture ingredients with $1/2$ cup water in an $8^1/_2 \times 8^1/_2 \times 2$-inch square baking (cake) pan.

BROIL for 8 minutes, or until the tomatoes are softened. Remove from the oven and cool for 5 minutes.

PROCESS the mixture in a blender or food processor until well blended. Spread on the pizza crust and layer with the mushrooms, olives, and cheese.

BAKE at 400°F. for 25 minutes, or until the cheese is melted.

Prep: 15 minutes
Total time: 40 minutes
Serves 4

Inspirational Personal Pizza

Just sprinkle on whatever you desire. Anchovies? Why not? Pepperoni? Black olives? How about mushrooms or maybe tuna? Or perhaps you would prefer broccoli florets, chopped spinach, or tons of onions. Here's a chance to make your own pizza, exactly the way you like it. Look in the cupboard and refrigerator and get inspired! This recipe is my preference.

1 9-inch ready-made pizza crust
1 teaspoon olive oil
2 tablespoons tomato paste
4 ounces ($1/2$ cup) ground lean turkey breast
2 tablespoons sliced marinated artichokes
2 tablespoons pitted and chopped kalamata olives

2 tablespoons crumbled feta cheese
1 tablespoon chopped fresh basil leaves
1 tablespoon chopped fresh oregano leaves
2 tablespoons grated Parmesan cheese
$1/4$ teaspoon red pepper flakes

PREHEAT the toaster oven to 375°F.

BRUSH the pizza crust with the olive oil and spread on the tomato paste. Add all the other ingredients. Place the pizza on the toaster oven rack.

BAKE for 30 minutes, or until the topping is cooked and the crust is lightly browned.

Prep: 15 minutes
Total time: 45 minutes
Serves 1

Very Quick Pizza

Why not have pizza as a quick snack? Here's a fast, low-fat solution that truly satisfies a pizza craving!

2 tablespoons salsa
1 6-inch whole wheat pita bread

2 tablespoons shredded part-skim, low-moisture mozzarella cheese

SPREAD the salsa on the pita bread and sprinkle with the cheese.
TOAST once, or until the cheese is melted.

Prep: 3 minutes
Total time: 3 minutes
Serves 1

Fresh Herb Veggie Pizza

Add chopped fresh broccoli, cauliflower, grated carrots, or chopped spinach to this herb pizza for a medley of flavors and textures.

1 9-inch ready-made pizza crust
1 tablespoon olive oil
1 4-ounce can tomato paste
2 tablespoons shredded part-skim mozzarella
2 tablespoons grated Parmesan cheese
2 tablespoons crumbled feta cheese

$1/2$ bell pepper, chopped
1 tablespoon chopped fresh parsley
1 tablespoon chopped fresh oregano
1 tablespoon chopped fresh basil
$1/2$ teaspoon red pepper flakes
Salt and freshly ground black pepper to taste

Pizza mixture:
2 garlic cloves, minced
1 plum tomato, chopped

PREHEAT the toaster oven to 400° F.
BRUSH the pizza crust with olive oil and spread the tomato paste evenly to cover.
COMBINE the ingredients for the pizza mixture and spread evenly on top of the

Continued

tomato paste layer. Sprinkle the cheeses over all and season to taste. Place the pizza on the toaster oven rack.

BAKE for 25 minutes, or until the vegetables are cooked and the cheese is melted.

Prep: 13 minutes
Total time: 38 minutes
Serves 4

Pesto Pizza

And now for something entirely different. If you like pesto, you will love pesto pizza! Fresh basil is essential here, as well as a good-quality Parmesan cheese and olive oil.

Topping:
1/2 cup chopped fresh basil
1 tablespoon pine nuts (pignoli)
1 tablespoon olive oil
2 tablespoons shredded Parmesan
  cheese
1 garlic clove, minced
1/2 teaspoon dried oregano or 1
  tablespoon chopped fresh oregano

1 plum tomato, chopped
Salt and pepper to taste

1 9-inch ready-made pizza crust
2 tablespoons shredded low-fat
  mozzarella

PREHEAT the toaster oven to 375°F.

COMBINE the topping ingredients in a small bowl.

PROCESS the mixture in a blender or food processor until smooth. Spread the mixture on the pizza crust, then sprinkle with the mozzarella cheese. Place the pizza crust on the toaster oven rack.

BAKE for 20 minutes, or until the cheese is melted and the crust is brown.

Prep: 10 minutes
Total time: 30 minutes
Serves 1

Spanakopizza

Press the thawed spinach into a sieve with your hands to drain excess water (you'll be surprised how much water comes out!). This is delicious as a meal for two or cut into small wedges for appetizers. Phyllo sheets can be folded to fit just about any baking pan you are using.

8 sheets phyllo dough, thawed and folded in half
4 tablespoons olive oil
4 tablespoons grated Parmesan cheese

Topping mixture:
1 10-ounce package frozen chopped spinach, thawed and well drained
1 plum tomato, finely chopped

¼ cup finely chopped onion
¼ cup shredded low-fat mozzarella cheese
3 tablespoons crumbled feta cheese or part-skim ricotta cheese
2 garlic cloves, minced
Salt and freshly ground black pepper to taste

PREHEAT the toaster oven to 375°F.

LAYER the sheets of phyllo dough in an oiled or nonstick 9¾-inch-diameter baking pan, lightly brushing the top of each sheet with olive oil and folding in the corner edges to fit the pan.

COMBINE the topping mixture ingredients in a bowl and adjust the seasonings to taste. Spread the mixture on top of the phyllo pastry layers and sprinkle with the Parmesan cheese.

BAKE for 30 minutes, or until the cheese is melted and the topping is lightly browned. Remove carefully from the pan with a metal spatula.

Prep: 12 minutes
Total time: 42 minutes
Serves 2

Chapter 5

Vegetables

If there is any appliance capable of bringing out the beauty of vegetables, it is the toaster oven. Baking and broiling elevates carrots, potatoes, broccoli, and squashes to new levels of texture and flavor. The recipes in this chapter were designed to prove that vegetables need not be relegated to the sidelines of an entrée, steamed into submission, diluted by boiling, or microwaved to mush. Broccoli and cauliflower are tasty and toothsome, zucchini seductive, and carrots can glow like sunsets in a lemon haze. The recipes in this chapter will show you how to roast skewered vegetables to perfection (Roasted Veggie Kabobs), paint an autumn table with the harvest colors of baked yellow squash with bell peppers (Yellow Squash with Bell Peppers), serve up broiled eggplant and tomato slices that are delectable and nearly fat free (Eggplant and Tomato Slices), and stir-fry broccoli, mushrooms, and water chestnuts under the broiler (Broccoli with Chinese Mushrooms and Water Chestnuts). No need for rich sauces to hide them, butter to slather them, or a puree to disguise them. Baked and broiled vegetables can stand on their own—full of nourishment, amplified in flavor, and sophisticated in style and texture.

Roasted Vegetables

A wide variety of frozen packaged vegetable mixtures are available in the supermarket these days. Because the pieces are basically all the same small size, they roast quickly and evenly. Broiling in a toaster oven makes these medleys tastier and more nutritious than the prescribed microwave or stovetop cooking methods. I hope that in the near future toaster oven preparation instructions will be added as a viable cooking option for packaged frozen vegetables.

1 1-pound package frozen vegetable
  mixture
1 tablespoon olive oil
1 tablespoon bread crumbs
1 teaspoon dried oregano
1 teaspoon ground cumin

Salt and freshly ground black pepper
  to taste
1 tablespoon grated Parmesan
  cheese
1 tablespoon chopped walnuts

BLEND all the ingredients in an oiled or nonstick $8\frac{1}{2} \times 8\frac{1}{2} \times 2$-inch square baking (cake) pan, tossing to coat the vegetable pieces with the oil, bread crumbs, and seasonings. Adjust the seasonings.

BROIL for 10 minutes. Remove the pan from the oven and turn the pieces with tongs. Add the cheese and walnuts. Broil for another 10 minutes, or until the vegetables are lightly browned. Adjust the seasonings and serve.

Prep: 3 minutes
Total time: 23 minutes
Serves 4

Rolled Chinese (Napa) Cabbage with Chickpea Filling

Crafting this dish is fun and very rewarding. You can make these rolls ahead of time, store them in the refrigerator in a covered dish for several days, then reheat them at 400° F., covered, for 15 minutes before serving. I created a filling that harmonizes well with this cabbage's mild flavor. Lightly browning by broiling produces a pleasing veinlike pattern on the cabbage rolls and toasted almonds further enhance their flavor.

6 Chinese cabbage leaves, approximately 7 inches long

Filling:
2 tablespoons low-fat ricotta cheese
  or Yogurt Cheese Spread (page 32)

1 cup canned chickpeas (garbanzos),
  drained and mashed
1 teaspoon lemon juice
Salt and butcher's pepper to taste

2 tablespoons olive oil for brushing
2 tablespoons chopped almonds

LAYER an $8\frac{1}{2} \times 8\frac{1}{2} \times 2$-inch square baking (cake) pan with the cabbage leaves and add enough water to barely cover them.

Continued

BROIL 5 minutes, turn the leaves with tongs, and broil another 5 minutes, or until the leaves are partially cooked and just pliable. Spread the leaves on paper towels to drain and cool.

MIX the filling ingredients together in a medium bowl and adjust the seasonings to taste. Place equal portions of filling 2 inches from the stem end (base of the leaf) and roll up the leaf, enclosing the filling. Place each roll with the leaf edge down in an oiled or $8\frac{1}{2} \times 8\frac{1}{2} \times 2$-inch square baking (cake) pan. Sprinkle with the almonds. Cover the pan with aluminum foil.

BAKE at 400° F. for 30 minutes, or until the rolls are tender. Remove the cover.

BROIL 6 minutes, or until the almonds and cabbage leaves are lightly browned.

Prep: 10 minutes
Total time: 56 minutes
Serves 4

Roasted Veggie Kebabs

Skewered vegetables are baked to tenderness, then broiled to produce a roasted flavor. I love to make these kebabs, using whatever I have available: Brussels sprouts, small wedges of cabbage, parsnips, turnip chunks, potato pieces, and the like. Cut harder or firmer veggies (carrots, potatoes, parsnips, turnips, and the like) smaller and softer veggies (zucchini, cabbage, Brussels sprouts, and the like) a little larger. While baking, test them periodically by piercing them with a fork until they are done to your liking. Serve one skewer per dinner guest, accompanied by a small pitcher of Italian dressing or 1 part olive oil/1 part lemon juice to drizzle. Note: *If your toaster oven cannot accommodate a 9-inch metal skewer, purchase a package of the wooden (bamboo) skewers and break off the nonpointed end to fit your oven.*

Shortcut: *Microwave the vegetable pieces for 5 minutes at Medium, or until almost tender. Cool and skewer the pieces, brush with the mixture, and broil as directed.*

Brushing mixture:
3 tablespoons olive oil
1 tablespoon soy sauce
1 teaspoon garlic powder
1 teaspoon ground cumin
2 tablespoons balsamic vinegar
Salt and freshly ground black pepper
  to taste

Cauliflower, zucchini, onion, broccoli, bell pepper, mushrooms, celery, cabbage, beets, and the like, cut into approximately 2×2-inch pieces

PREHEAT the toaster oven to 400°F.

COMBINE the brushing mixture ingredients in a small bowl, mixing well. Set aside.

SKEWER the vegetable pieces on 4 9-inch metal skewers and place the skewers lengthwise on a broiling rack with a pan underneath.

BAKE for 40 minutes, or until the vegetables are tender, brushing with the mixture every 10 minutes.

BROIL for 5 minutes, or until lightly browned.

Prep: 15 minutes
Total time: 1 hour
Serves 4

Pecan Parmesan Cauliflower

Cauliflower is not one of my favorite vegetables, but I took up the challenge and decided to make a recipe that would turn cauliflower into an exciting complement for steaks, chicken, or fish. A combination of baking and broiling plus the addition of ground pecans, pepper, and Parmesan create a nutlike, toasted flavor that emphasizes the mild and flavorful personality of cauliflower.

2$\frac{1}{2}$ cups (frozen thawed or fresh) thinly sliced cauliflower florets
Salt and freshly ground black pepper

3 tablespoons freshly grated Parmesan cheese
$\frac{1}{2}$ cup ground pecans

PREHEAT the toaster oven to 400°F.

COMBINE the florets and oil in a 1-quart 8$\frac{1}{2}$ × 8$\frac{1}{2}$ × 4-inch ovenproof baking dish, tossing to coat well. Season to taste with salt and pepper. Cover the dish with aluminum foil.

BAKE for 25 minutes, or until tender. Uncover and sprinkle with the cheese and pecans.

BROIL for 10 minutes, or until lightly browned.

Prep: 10 minutes
Total time: 45 minutes
Serves 4

Empty-the-Refrigerator Roasted Vegetables

I created this recipe to use up whatever fresh vegetables I had on hand, such as cauliflower, broccoli, zucchini, peppers, potatoes, string beans, and so on. Many times, the combinations are quite colorful and, regardless of what combination of vegetables I have used, it always comes out tasty with a grilled look and flavor thanks to the toaster oven broiler. Here's a chance for seasonings and herbs to work their magic.

Shortcut: Microwave the vegetables for 5 minutes at Medium, or until almost tender. Transfer to the toaster oven and broil as directed. Total time is reduced to 25 minutes.

3 cups assorted fresh vegetables, cut into 1 × 1-inch pieces
2 garlic cloves, minced
2 tablespoons olive oil
3 tablespoons dry white wine

Salt and freshly ground black pepper to taste
1 tablespoon chopped fresh basil
1 tablespoon chopped fresh oregano
1 tablespoon chopped fresh parsley

PREHEAT the toaster oven to 400° F.

COMBINE all the ingredients with 2 tablespoons water in a 1-quart $8\frac{1}{2} \times 8\frac{1}{2} \times 4$-inch ovenproof baking dish, mixing well. Cover the dish with aluminum foil.

BAKE, covered, for 25 minutes, until the vegetables are tender. Remove from the oven and stir to blend the vegetables and sauce.

BROIL, uncovered, for 10 minutes, or until lightly browned.

Prep: 15 minutes
Total time: 50 minutes
Serves 4

Asparagus Ronald

This recipe comes from Ronald, my aerobics instructor of many years ago, who attributed his energy and agility to eating asparagus three times a week.

20 asparagus spears, rinsed and hard stem ends cut off
1 tablespoon soy sauce
3 tablespoons lemon juice

3 tablespoons olive oil
Salt and freshly ground black pepper
3 tablespoons crumbled feta cheese

PREHEAT the toaster oven to 400° F.

PLACE the asparagus spears in a 1-quart 8½ × 8½ × 4-inch ovenproof baking dish.

DRIZZLE the soy sauce, lemon juice, and olive oil over the asparagus spears. Season to taste with salt and pepper. Cover the dish with aluminum foil.

BAKE for 25 minutes, or until tender. Sprinkle with the feta cheese before serving.

Prep: 10 minutes
Total time: 35 minutes
Serves 4

Yogurt Zucchini with Onion

Yogurt gives the zucchini a mellow, creamy consistency and pine nuts add an unexpect-edly rich taste that enhances the zucchini's mild flavor. Simple ingredients come together to make a unique and delectable dish. Serve with chicken, fish, meat, or pasta.

½ cup plain fat-free yogurt
1 tablespoon unbleached flour
4 small zucchini, scrubbed and
  sliced into ½-inch strips
3 tablespoons minced fresh onion

1 tablespoon olive oil
3 tablespoons pine nuts, ground in a
  blender
Salt and freshly ground black pepper

PREHEAT the toaster oven to 400° F.

WHISK together the yogurt and flour in a small bowl until smooth. Transfer to a 1-quart 8½ × 8½ × 4-inch ovenproof baking dish. Add all the remaining ingredients, mixing well. Adjust the seasonings to taste. Cover the dish with aluminum foil.

BAKE, covered, for 25 minutes, or until the zucchini is tender. Uncover and toss gently to blend.

BROIL for 5 minutes, or until the top is lightly browned.

Prep: 12 minutes
Total time: 42 minutes
Serves 4

Yellow Squash with Bell Peppers

Yellow summer squash, green bell pepper, and red pimientos create a colorful and autumnal combination, while artichoke, basil, oregano, cheese, and bread crumbs introduce an aromatic, mellow, and slightly tart flavor. This squash is excellent served with baked or broiled fish (see Light Trout Amandine, page 127). Cilantro, used as a garnish, adds one more flavor to the spectrum.

Squash mixture:
2 cups yellow (summer) squash, thinly sliced
$1/3$ cup dry white wine
1 bell pepper, seeded and sliced into thin strips
1 $6^{1}/_{2}$-ounce jar marinated artichoke hearts, drained and sliced
1 tablespoon minced fresh garlic
1 5-ounce can diced pimientos, drained
Salt and freshly ground black pepper to taste

$1/4$ cup shredded part-skim mozzarella cheese
3 tablespoons Homemade Bread Crumbs (page 41)
2 tablespoons chopped fresh cilantro

PREHEAT the toaster oven to 400° F.

COMBINE the squash mixture ingredients in a 1-quart $8^{1}/_{2} \times 8^{1}/_{2} \times 4$-inch ovenproof baking dish, mixing well. Adjust the seasonings.

BAKE, covered, for 40 minutes, or until the vegetables are tender. Uncover and sprinkle with the cheese and bread crumbs.

BROIL 10 minutes, or until the top is lightly browned. Garnish with the chopped cilantro before serving.

Prep: 10 minutes
Total time: 1 hour
Serves 4

Oregano Zucchini

Fresh oregano is best to use with this recipe. Broiling reduces the moisture from the zucchini and concentrates the flavors. Basting the zucchini midbroiling enhances the flavor further. This dish is great with pasta.

Mixture:
3 tablespoons olive oil
1 tablespoon Roasted Garlic
  (page 75)
2 tablespoons tomato paste
2 tablespoons dry white wine
1 tablespoon chopped fresh oregano
Salt and freshly ground pepper to
  taste

4 small zucchini squash, rinsed well,
  halved, then quartered
3 tablespoons grated Parmesan
  cheese

WHISK together the mixture ingredients in a small bowl, adjusting the seasonings to taste. Add the zucchini and toss gently to coat well. Transfer to an oiled or nonstick 8½ × 8½ × 2-inch square baking (cake) pan.

BROIL, uncovered, for 20 minutes. Remove the pan from the oven, turn the pieces with tongs, and spoon the sauce over the zucchini. Broil again for 10 minutes, or until tender. Before serving, sprinkle with the grated Parmesan cheese.

Prep: 10 minutes
Total time: 40 minutes
Serves 4

Eggplant and Tomato Slices

It's a challenge to find a recipe using eggplant that does not require a lot of fat or oil, which eggplant readily absorbs. Brushing the eggplant slices with a mixture of olive oil and garlic, topping each with a large slice of tomato, and finishing the broiling with mozzarella cheese makes a great-tasting accompaniment for pasta or chicken. This simple recipe is eggplant at its best: flavored with oil and garlic, melded with tomato and cheese, and with a minimum of oil. Fresh herbs complete the flavor spectrum. A good substitute for the cheese is a topping of bread crumbs, using the same amount.

Continued

2 tablespoons olive oil

1/4 teaspoon garlic powder

4 1/2-inch-thick slices eggplant

4 1/4-inch-thick slices fresh tomato

2 tablespoons tomato sauce or salsa

1/2 cup shredded Parmesan cheese

Salt and freshly ground black pepper
  to taste

2 tablespoons chopped fresh basil,
  cilantro, parsley, or oregano

WHISK together the oil and garlic powder in a small bowl. Brush each eggplant slice
  with the mixture and place in an oiled or nonstick 8 1/2 × 8 1/2 × 2-inch square baking (cake) pan.

BROIL for 20 minutes. Remove the pan from the oven and turn the pieces with
  tongs. Top each with a slice of tomato and broil another 10 minutes, or until tender. Remove the pan from the oven, brush each slice with tomato sauce or salsa,
  and sprinkle generously with Parmesan cheese. Season to taste with salt and pepper. Broil again for 6 minutes, until the tops are browned.

GARNISH with the fresh herb and serve.

Prep: 6 minutes

Total time: 42 minutes

Serves 4

Quick Broccoli Quiche

*Phyllo (filo) pastry is a delicious alternative to piecrust and can be found in the freezer
section in the supermarket. Variations on this quiche include fresh or frozen spinach
instead of broccoli, feta cheese instead of ricotta, and sunflower seeds instead of shredded mozzarella on top.*

12 sheets phyllo dough

Olive oil for brushing phyllo sheets

Filling:

1/2 cup chopped fresh broccoli
  or 1/2 cup frozen chopped broccoli,
  thawed and well drained

4 eggs, well beaten

2 tablespoons fat-free half-and-half

3 tablespoons nonfat plain yogurt

1/2 cup low-fat ricotta cheese

3 tablespoons finely chopped onion

Salt and freshly ground pepper

1/4 cup shredded part-skim mozzarella cheese

PREHEAT the toaster oven to 300° F.

LAYER the phyllo sheets in an oiled or nonstick 9³⁄₄-inch-diameter pie pan, brushing each sheet with olive oil and folding it to fit the pan. Bake for 5 minutes, or until lightly browned. Remove from the oven and set aside.

MIX together all the filling ingredients in a medium bowl and season to taste with salt and pepper. Pour the mixture into the phyllo dough crust and sprinkle with the mozzarella cheese.

BAKE at 400° F. for 30 minutes, or until the surface is springy to touch and browned.

Prep: 15 minutes
Total time: 50 minutes
Serves 6

Lemon-Glazed Baby Carrots

Peeled, bite-size baby carrots are now available in most supermarkets. The glaze is made in the broiler in a baking dish and the carrots are added and baked to completion. Very simple and very good! Buy several lemons if they are on sale, squeeze them, and store the juice in a jar in the refrigerator or in an ice cube tray in the freezer. Fresh lemon juice gives a fuller flavor to the glaze than reconstituted lemon juice.

Shortcut: Microwave the carrots with glaze ingredients in an oven-safe glass or ceramic dish at Medium for 8 minutes, or until the carrots are almost tender. Stir to blend well and transfer to the toaster oven. Broil for 5 minutes, or until tender. Total time is reduced to 23 minutes.

Glaze:
1 tablespoon margarine
2 tablespoons lemon juice
1 tablespoon honey
1 teaspoon garlic powder
Salt and freshly ground black pepper
  to taste

2 cups peeled baby carrots (approximately 1 pound)
1 tablespoon chopped fresh parsley
  or cilantro

PLACE the glaze ingredients in a 1-quart 8¹⁄₂ × 8¹⁄₂ × 4-inch ovenproof baking dish and broil for 4 minutes, or until the margarine is melted. Remove from the oven and mix well. Add the carrots and toss to coat. Cover the dish with aluminum foil.

Continued

BAKE, covered, at 350°F. for 30 minutes, or until the carrots are tender. Garnish with chopped parsley or cilantro and serve immediately.

Prep: 10 minutes
Total time: 43 minutes
Serves 4

Almond-Crusted Spinach Soufflé

My affection for spinach soufflé goes back to cooking class in high school. Making this dish was the ultimate test, but I remember it never tasted all that good, possibly because we never drained the spinach well. Frozen spinach has a high water content; when it's thawed, it must be pressed into a sieve with paper towels to remove as much of the excess water as possible. Especially in a soufflé, if there is too much liquid, subtle flavors are lost, as is the light, fluffy consistency. For this reason, chopped fresh spinach is preferable for the best flavor and texture of this dish.

2 tablespoons reduced-fat sour
  cream
1 tablespoon unbleached flour
2 cups fresh spinach, rinsed well,
  drained, and finely chopped, or 1
  10-oz. package frozen spinach,
  thawed, drained, and blotted dry

1 egg, separated
1 teaspoon olive oil
Salt and freshly ground black pepper
Grated nutmeg
$\frac{1}{4}$ cup finely chopped almonds

PREHEAT the toaster oven to 350°F.

STIR together the sour cream and flour in a medium bowl until smooth. Add the spinach, egg yolk, and oil, mixing well and seasoning to taste with the salt, pepper, and nutmeg.

BEAT the egg white until stiff and fold into the spinach mixture. Pour into a 1-quart $8\frac{1}{2} \times 8\frac{1}{2} \times 4$-inch ovenproof baking dish. Sprinkle with the almonds.

BAKE, uncovered, for 25 minutes, or until firm and the topping is lightly browned.

Prep: 12 minutes
Total time: 37 minutes
Serves 4

Roasted Garlic

Roasted garlic is easy to make in a toaster oven and you don't have to heat up the kitchen or use a lot of energy to do it! As an appetizer, seasoned roasted garlic with olive oil on crusty Italian bread is far less fattening than cheese or dips with crackers. Use roasted garlic wherever fresh garlic or garlic powder is called for in a recipe. Roasted garlic can be stored in the refrigerator in an airtight container.

3 whole garlic buds
3 tablespoons olive oil

Salt and freshly ground black pepper

PREHEAT the toaster oven to 450° F.

PLACE the garlic buds in an oiled or nonstick $8\frac{1}{2} \times 8\frac{1}{2} \times 2$-inch square baking (cake) pan.

BAKE, uncovered, for 20 minutes, or until the buds are tender when pierced with a skewer or sharp knife. When cool enough to handle, peel and mash the baked cloves with a fork into the olive oil. Season with salt and pepper to taste.

Prep: 2 minutes
Total time: 22 minutes
Makes $\frac{3}{4}$ cup

Broiled Tomatoes

Quick to prepare, a broiled tomato on a bed of mixed lettuce greens or spinach makes an excellent, healthy lunch. Broiled tomatoes are great cut up and tossed with Roasted Garlic (above) and olive oil on pasta, a nice alternative to the usual tomato sauce.

2 medium tomatoes

Filling:
2 tablespoons grated Parmesan
  cheese
2 tablespoons bread crumbs
2 tablespoons olive oil

1 teaspoon dried oregano or 1 tablespoon chopped fresh oregano
1 teaspoon garlic powder or 2 garlic
  cloves, minced
Salt and freshly ground black pepper
  to taste

Continued

SLICE the tomatoes in half through the stem scar (top) and carefully scoop out the seeds and flesh with a teaspoon. (Remove and discard about 1 tablespoon each.)

MIX together the filling ingredients in a small bowl and adjust the seasonings. Fill each tomato half cavity with equal portions of the mixture. Place the tomato halves in an oiled or nonstick $8^{1}/_{2} \times 8^{1}/_{2} \times 2$-inch square baking (cake) pan.

BROIL for 10 minutes, or until the tomatoes are cooked and the tops are browned.

Prep: 10 minutes
Total time: 20 minutes
Serves 4

Broccoli with Chinese Mushrooms and Water Chestnuts

Stir-fry with the broiler of your toaster oven without stirring or frying! Chinese dried mushrooms have a unique, meaty flavor and aroma, and can be found in the ethnic food section of most supermarkets, Asian food stores, or gourmet food stores. You can use a 6-ounce can of mushrooms instead, but the flavor will not be the same. To cook Chinese dried mushrooms, simmer them in 2 cups of water for 10 minutes, then rinse them in fresh water and slice the caps (the stems remain tough and need to be cut off).

2 cups broccoli florets, cut in half
$^{1}/_{2}$ cup Chinese dried mushrooms, cooked, drained, stemmed, and sliced
$^{1}/_{4}$ cup dry white wine

1 5-ounce can sliced water chestnuts, well drained
1 tablespoon vegetable oil
1 teaspoon toasted sesame oil
1 teaspoon oyster sauce

COMBINE all the ingredients with $^{1}/_{4}$ cup water in an oiled or nonstick $8^{1}/_{2} \times 8^{1}/_{2} \times 2$-inch square baking (cake) pan. Adjust the seasonings to taste.

BROIL 20 minutes, turning with tongs every 5 minutes, or until the vegetables are tender.

Prep: 10 minutes
Total time: 30 minutes
Serves 4

Baked Stuffed Acorn Squash

I created this recipe, making a filling that compliments the flavor of the squash without exceeding or overwhelming it. Corn, onion, bread crumbs, and capers introduce a medley of flavors that harmonize with the squash, which becomes a small casserole for the filling.

Stuffing:
1/4 cup multigrain bread crumbs
1 tablespoon olive oil
1/4 cup canned or frozen thawed
  corn
2 tablespoons chopped onion

1 teaspoon capers
1 teaspoon garlic powder
Salt and freshly ground black pepper

1 medium acorn squash, halved and
  seeds scooped out

PREHEAT the toaster oven to 400°F.

COMBINE the stuffing ingredients and season to taste. Fill the squash cavities with the mixture and place in an oiled or nonstick 8½ × 8½ × 2-inch square baking (cake) pan.

BAKE for 25 minutes, or until the squash is tender and the stuffing is lightly browned.

Prep: 10 minutes
Total time: 35 minutes
Serves 2

Chapter 6

Potatoes

T his chapter is solely devoted to potatoes and the toaster oven. There is a wide variety of recipes including microwave/toaster oven quick baked potato, crisp hash browns and potato wedges in the broiler, low-fat topping options, stuffed potato fillings, "French fries" without the frying and without the fat, and even a slimming Potatoes au Gratin. Also included are several sweet potato recipes that far exceed the usual candied versions.

Classic Baked Potatoes

Here is a classic baked potato recipe and a list of toppings I have tried and really like. What inspires you? Any experimentation will, more than likely, taste great!

Shortcut: Microwave the potatoes at High for 6 minutes, or until almost cooked. Transfer to the toaster oven rack and bake for 20 minutes, until tender and the skin is browned to your preference. Total time is reduced to 29 minutes.

   4 medium baking potatoes,
     scrubbed and pierced with a fork

PREHEAT the toaster oven to 450° F.
BAKE the potatoes on the oven rack for 50 minutes, or until tender when pierced with a fork.

   Prep: 4 minutes
   Total time: 54 minutes
   Serves 4

Favorite Toppings

- 1 tablespoon low-fat sour cream and 1 teaspoon finely chopped scallion or chives
- 1 tablespoon crumbled lean cooked turkey bacon and 1 tablespoon Italian dressing
- 2 tablespoons mashed avocado, 1 teaspoon lemon juice, and 1 teaspoon olive oil
- 1 teaspoon finely chopped onion, 1 teaspoon finely chopped sun-dried tomato, and 1 teaspoon Worcestershire sauce
- 1 tablespoon finely crumbled Roquefort or Saga blue cheese
- 1 tablespoon sesame oil, 1 teaspoon soy sauce, and 1 teaspoon sesame seeds

Classic Stuffed Baked Potatoes

Baked stuffed potatoes are a variation of baked potatoes. After baking, all you need to do is open the slit enough to scoop out the insides of the potatoes with a teaspoon. Once extracted and placed in a bowl, the potato pulp can be mixed with any number of exciting ingredients. Here is a classic baked stuffed potato recipe everyone likes and that can be served to your most conservative guests. But keep in mind that these fillings are amenable to all kinds of creative inspiration. What can you create? I dare you to try barbecue sauce, Worcestershire sauce, artichoke hearts, marinated artichokes, or anchovies (maybe not all at once). I'm including a list of my favorite mixtures for baked stuffed potatoes.

Shortcut: Microwave the potatoes at High for 6 minutes, or until almost cooked. Transfer to the toaster oven rack and bake for 20 minutes until tender and the skin is browned to your preference.

2 large baking potatoes, slit on top
with a knife

Stuffing:
1 teaspoon margarine
1 egg, lightly beaten
$\frac{1}{2}$ cup nonfat sour cream

$\frac{1}{8}$ teaspoon paprika
Salt and freshly ground black pepper
to taste

4 tablespoons fresh or frozen and
thawed chives

PREHEAT the toaster oven to 400° F.

BAKE the potatoes on the oven rack for 50 minutes, or until tender. Open the slits with a knife and scoop out the pulp with a teaspoon. Set the potato shells aside.

COMBINE the stuffing ingredients and add the pulp, mixing well, until light and fluffy. Refill the potato shells.

Continued

BROIL 8 minutes, or until the top is lightly browned. Sprinkle with the chives before serving.

> *Prep:* 10 minutes
> *Total time:* 1 hour and 8 minutes
> Serves 4

Baked Stuffed Potatoes with Vegetables

This recipe is good for using up leftover vegetables—the baking time may be shortened to 15 minutes if the vegetables are already cooked. If you prefer, substitute sesame, poppy, or sunflower seeds for the caraway seeds.

Shortcut: *Shredding the carrot, bell pepper, broccoli, and cauliflower in a food processor shortens the prep time to 8 minutes.*

2 large baking potatoes, baked, cooked, and pulp scooped out to make shells

Stuffing:
1 carrot, shredded
$\frac{1}{2}$ bell pepper, seeded and shredded
2 tablespoons broccoli, shredded
2 tablespoons cauliflower, shredded
3 tablespoons fat-free half-and-half
1 teaspoon paprika
$\frac{1}{2}$ teaspoon garlic powder
$\frac{1}{2}$ teaspoon caraway seeds
Salt and butcher's pepper to taste

PREHEAT the toaster oven to 400° F.

COMBINE the stuffing mixture ingredients, mixing well. Fill the potato shells with the mixture and place the shells in an oiled $8\frac{1}{2} \times 8\frac{1}{2} \times 2$-inch square baking (cake) pan.

BAKE for 25 minutes or until vegetables are cooked.

BROIL for 5 minutes, or until the tops are lightly browned.

> *Prep:* 15 minutes
> *Total time:* 45 minutes
> Serves 2

Pimiento-and-Olive Stuffed Potatoes

Here are fillings for stuffed potatoes that are imaginative departures from the usual sour cream that is so adept at expanding waistlines. These can be used without reservation because they are low-fat alternatives and have less calories than most fillings. So, bring on the potatoes!

2 large baking potatoes, baked

Stuffing:
3 tablespoons minced pimientos
3 tablespoons pitted and chopped
   black olives

3 tablespoons nonfat sour cream
1 teaspoon paprika
Salt and butcher's pepper to taste

SCOOP out the pulp of the baked potatoes and place in a bowl.
ADD the stuffing ingredients, blending well, and fill the potato shells. Place the potatoes on a broiling rack with a pan underneath.
BROIL for 8 minutes, or until the top is lightly browned.

Prep: 10 minutes
Total time: 18 minutes (Baking potatoes: 40 minutes)
Serves 2

Inspirational stuffed potato fillings:

Here's my mix-and-match list of fillings. What's yours? Be bold!
- 1 tablespoon in any combination: Chopped scallions; grated carrots; shredded cheese; crumbled lean bacon; chopped black or green olives; capers; chopped walnuts, pecans, or almonds; finely chopped watercress; radishes; or cucumbers
- 1 teaspoon in any combination to add to the above: Finely chopped jalapeños, hard-boiled eggs, smoked paprika, bourbon, hot pepper sauce, horseradish, pickle relish, spicy brown mustard

Potato Skins

Broiling this delectable appetizer assures it will be crunchy and tasty. I have added my list of toppings for potato skins and hope you will be inspired to create your own.

PLACE 4 potato shells in an oiled or nonstick $8\frac{1}{2} \times 8\frac{1}{2} \times 2$-inch square baking (cake) pan.

BRUSH, SPRINKLE, AND FILL with a variety of seasonings or ingredients (see mix-and-match options below).

BROIL 20 minutes, or until browned and crisped to your preference.

Prep: 15 minutes
Total time: 35 minutes
Serves 4

Inspirational Potato Skin Toppings:

Brush on:
1 tablespoon sesame oil
1 tablespoon tomato sauce
1 tablespoon hot sauce
1 tablespoon olive oil
1 tablespoon barbecue sauce
1 teaspoon soy sauce

Sprinkle:
1 tablespoon chopped fresh basil, parsley, oregano, or cilantro
1 tablespoon chopped fresh parsley
1 tablespoon crumbled cooked lean turkey bacon
1 tablespoon grated Parmesan cheese
2 tablespoons shredded low-fat mozzarella cheese
1 teaspoon garlic powder

2 tablespoons crumbled feta cheese
$\frac{1}{2}$ teaspoon curry powder
$\frac{1}{2}$ teaspoon ground cumin
1 tablespoon chopped onion

Fill with:
2 tablespoons nonfat sour cream
2 tablespoons yogurt cheese
2 tablespoons low-fat ricotta cheese
2 tablespoons chopped avocado
2 tablespoons chopped plum tomato
2 tablespoons frozen vegetables
2 tablespoons chopped fresh vegetables
2 tablespoons cooked ground turkey
3 slices low-fat cheese, shredded
3 slices smoked turkey, chopped
3 slices honey ham, chopped

Tasty Golden Potatoes

Use any kind of potatoes. The carrots will make them golden and lend a pleasant sweetness that contrasts with the onion and seasonings.

Shortcut: *Shredding the carrots, onion, and potatoes in a food processor reduces prep time to 8 minutes.*

2 cups peeled and shredded potatoes
$\frac{1}{2}$ cup peeled and shredded carrots
$\frac{1}{4}$ cup shredded onion
1 teaspoon salt
1 teaspoon dried rosemary

1 teaspoon dried cumin
3 tablespoons vegetable oil
Salt and freshly ground black pepper
  to taste

PREHEAT the toaster oven to 400° F.
MIX all the ingredients together in a 1-quart $8\frac{1}{2} \times 8\frac{1}{2} \times 2$-inch ovenproof baking dish. Adjust the seasonings to taste. Cover the dish with aluminum foil.
BAKE, covered, for 30 minutes, or until tender. Remove the cover.
BROIL for 8 minutes, or until the top is browned.

Prep: 10 minutes
Total time: 48 minutes
Serves 4

Potato Shells with Cheese and Bacon

These potato shells look sumptuous and they taste terrific. Okay, they have half the fat and calories of traditional potato shells. If you don't say anything when you serve these as appetizers, no one will ever know.

4 tablespoons shredded reduced-fat
  cheddar cheese
4 slices lean turkey bacon, cooked
  and crumbled
4 potato shells

4 tablespoons nonfat sour cream
4 teaspoons chopped fresh or frozen
  chives
Salt and freshly ground black pepper

Continued

SPRINKLE 1 tablespoon Cheddar cheese and 1 tablespoon crumbled bacon into each potato shell. Place the shells on a broiling rack with a pan underneath.

BROIL for 8 minutes, or until the cheese is melted and the shells lightly browned. Spoon 1 tablespoon sour cream into each shell and sprinkle with 1 teaspoon chives. Add salt and pepper to taste.

Prep: 10 minutes
Total time: 18 minutes
Serves 4

Ranch Potatoes

These are always my favorite to make on an open grill at a campsite after a day of hiking, but I discovered that a toaster oven can roast potatoes as well as a grill! Potatoes are sealed in aluminum packets and baked until done, then the packet is opened and the potatoes browned to your preference under the broiler.

2 medium russet potatoes, scrubbed and cut lengthwise into ¼-inch strips
1 medium onion, chopped

2 tablespoons vegetable oil
2 tablespoons barbecue sauce
¼ teaspoon hot sauce
Salt and freshly ground black pepper

PREHEAT the toaster oven to 400° F.

COMBINE all the ingredients in a medium bowl, mixing well and adjusting the seasonings to taste.

PLACE equal portions of the potatoes on two 12 × 12-inch squares of heavy-duty aluminum foil. Fold up the edges of the foil to form a sealed packet and place on the oven rack.

BAKE for 40 minutes, or until the potatoes are tender. Carefully open the packet and fold back the foil.

BROIL 10 minutes, or until the potatoes are browned.

Prep: 8 minutes
Total time: 58 minutes
Serves 2

Marjoram New Potatoes

Fresh marjoram has a strong rosemarylike fragrance, but broiling mellows its essence. As a dried seasoning, it is less potent, but either lends a unique and aromatic flavor to the mild taste of new potatoes without overpowering them.

6 small new red potatoes, scrubbed
 and halved
1 tablespoon olive oil
1 tablespoon balsamic vinegar

1 tablespoon fresh marjoram leaves,
 chopped, or 1 teaspoon dried
 marjoram
Salt and freshly ground black pepper
 to taste

PREHEAT the toaster oven to 400° F.

COMBINE all the ingredients in a medium bowl and mix well to coat the potatoes. Place in an oiled or nonstick $8^1/_2 \times 8^1/_2 \times 2$-inch square baking (cake) pan.

BAKE, covered, for 30 minutes, or until the potatoes are tender.

BROIL 10 minutes to brown to your preference. Serve with balsamic vinegar in a small pitcher to drizzle over.

Prep: 8 minutes
Total time: 48 minutes
Serves 2

Hasty Home Fries

I love to make home fries on Saturday morning, accompanied by fried eggs that I also make in the toaster oven (see chapter 1). To complete the meal, I broil six strips of lean turkey bacon for 5 minutes in a shallow baking pan, blotting the excess fat from the cooked strips with paper towels before serving.

Shortcut: Shredding onion and potatoes in a food processor reduces prep time to 6 minutes.

2 medium baking potatoes,
 scrubbed and finely chopped
$^1/_4$ cup onions, finely chopped

1 teaspoon hot sauce
Salt and freshly ground black pepper

Continued

COMBINE all the ingredients in a bowl. Transfer the mixture to an oiled or nonstick $8^{1}/_{2} \times 8^{1}/_{2} \times 2$-inch square baking (cake) pan, adjusting the seasonings to taste.

BROIL for 10 minutes, then turn with tongs and broil again for 10 minutes, or until browned and crisped to your preference.

Prep: 15 minutes
Total time: 35 minutes
Serves 4

Potatoes au Gratin

These potatoes are rich tasting but low in fat. I have adapted a traditional recipe for the toaster oven to meet the contemporary standards of less fat and more flavor.

Mixture:
$^{1}/_{2}$ cup fat-free half-and-half
$^{1}/_{4}$ cup nonfat plain yogurt
2 tablespoons margarine
2 tablespoons unbleached flour
1 teaspoon garlic powder
$^{1}/_{4}$ cup shredded low-fat mozzarella cheese

2 tablespoons grated Parmesan cheese
Salt and butcher's pepper to taste

2 cups peeled and diced potatoes
$^{1}/_{2}$ cup chopped onion
1 tablespoon fresh or frozen chives
$^{1}/_{4}$ teaspoon paprika

PREHEAT the toaster oven to 400° F.

PROCESS the mixture ingredients in a food processor or blender until smooth. Pour into a 1-quart $8^{1}/_{2} \times 8^{1}/_{2} \times 4$-inch ovenproof baking dish.

ADD the potatoes, onion, chives, and paprika and stir to mix well. Cover the dish with aluminum foil.

BAKE, covered, for 40 minutes, or until the potatoes and onion are tender.

Prep: 10 minutes
Total time: 50 minutes
Serves 4

Roasted Garlic Potatoes

See page 75 for the recipe for Roasted Garlic. Garlic potatoes are simply delicious and great served with Bourbon Broiled Steak (page 112).

2 medium potatoes, peeled and
  chopped
6 garlic cloves, roasted

1 tablespoon olive oil
Salt and freshly ground black pepper
1 tablespoon chopped fresh parsley

PREHEAT the toaster oven to 400° F.

PLACE the potatoes in an oiled or nonstick $8^{1}/_{2} \times 8^{1}/_{2} \times 2$-inch square baking (cake) pan. Add the garlic, oil, and salt and pepper to taste. Toss to coat well. Cover the pan with aluminum foil.

BAKE, covered, for 40 minutes, or until the potatoes are tender. Remove the cover.

BROIL 10 minutes, or until lightly browned. Garnish with fresh parsley before serving.

Prep: 8 minutes
Total time: 48 minutes
Serves 2

Crisp Cajun Potato Wedges

"French fried" potatoes without frying! Crisping is done by broiling and all with only one tablespoon of vegetable oil. If you cover the baking pan with aluminum foil, remove it slowly and allow the steam to escape. Always wear oven mitts when placing a pan in the toaster oven or removing it.

2 medium baking potatoes,
  scrubbed, halved, and cut lengthwise into $^{1}/_{2}$-inch-wide wedges
1 tablespoon vegetable oil

Cajun seasonings:
$^{1}/_{4}$ teaspoon chili powder
$^{1}/_{8}$ teaspoon cayenne

$^{1}/_{8}$ teaspoon dry mustard
$^{1}/_{8}$ teaspoon salt
$^{1}/_{8}$ teaspoon cumin
$^{1}/_{4}$ teaspoon onion powder
$^{1}/_{4}$ teaspoon paprika

Continued

PREHEAT the toaster oven to 450° F.

SOAK the potato wedges in cold water for 10 minutes to crisp. Drain on paper towels. Brush with the oil.

COMBINE the Cajun seasonings in a small bowl, add the wedges, and toss to coat well. Transfer to an oiled or nonstick $8\frac{1}{2} \times 8\frac{1}{2} \times 2$-inch square baking (cake) pan.

BAKE, covered, for 40 minutes, or until the potatoes are tender. Carefully remove the cover.

BROIL for 20 minutes to crisp, turning with a tongs every 5 minutes until the desired crispness is achieved.

Prep: 12 minutes
Total time: 1 hour and 22 minutes (Soaking: 10 minutes)
Serves 2

Spicy Sweet Potatoes

This recipe expands the personality of sweet potatoes and gives them a new role on the dinner plate. Serve with Cilantro-Crusted Flank Steak (page 114).

2 sweet potatoes, peeled and sliced
   into 1-inch rounds
1 tablespoon vegetable oil

Salt and freshly ground black pepper
   to taste

Seasonings:
$\frac{1}{2}$ teaspoon each: grated nutmeg,
   ground cinnamon, cardamom, and
   ginger

PREHEAT the toaster oven to 400° F.

BRUSH the potato slices with oil and set aside.

COMBINE the seasonings in a 1-quart $8\frac{1}{2} \times 8\frac{1}{2} \times 4$-inch ovenproof baking dish and add the potato slices. Toss to coat well and adjust the seasonings to taste. Cover the dish with aluminum foil.

BAKE for 25 minutes, or until the potatoes are tender.

Prep: 10 minutes
Total time: 35 minutes
Serves 4

Simply Sweet Potatoes

The lemon juice contrasts and tempers the sweetness of the potatoes and thyme adds depth to the subtle flavor. A dot of margarine adds richness, or, as a variation, serve these sweet potatoes with Gorgonzola Dip (recipe follows).

2 medium sweet potatoes, scrubbed and slit on top

$^1\!/_4$ teaspoon ground thyme per potato

1 tablespoon lemon juice per potato

$^1\!/_2$ teaspoon margarine per potato

Salt and freshly ground black pepper

PREHEAT the toaster oven to 425°F.

BAKE the potatoes on the oven rack for 35 minutes, or until tender.

OPEN the slit and fluff the sweet potato pulp with a fork. Sprinkle the pulp with equal portions of thyme, lemon juice, and margarine. Fluff again. Season with salt and pepper to taste.

Prep: 5 minutes
Total time: 40 minutes
Serves 2

Gorgonzola Dip

3 tablespoons crumbled Gorgonzola cheese

1 cup nonfat sour cream

1 tablespoon chopped fresh or frozen chives

1 teaspoon raspberry vinaigrette

Salt and freshly ground black pepper to taste

COMBINE all the ingredients in a small bowl, mixing well.

Total time: 5 minutes
Makes 1$^1\!/_2$ cups

Balsamic Sweet Potatoes

I created this sweet potato recipe in self-defense to prove that sweet potatoes can be tasty without marshmallows. I prefer leaving the skins on for texture; however, they're just as good peeled. Balsamic vinegar, molasses, and garlic powder combine to flavor the potatoes with a sweet/sour tartness. A garnish of lemon zest completes the flavor spectrum.

    Shortcut: *Microwave the sweet potatoes for 5 minutes on High, or until almost baked. Transfer to the toaster oven, add the remaining ingredients, and broil as directed.*

2 medium sweet potatoes, scrubbed (or peeled) and sliced into 1-inch rounds	2 teaspoons molasses
	$\frac{1}{2}$ teaspoon garlic powder
	Salt and freshly ground black pepper to taste
3 tablespoons olive oil	
2 tablespoons balsamic vinegar	1 tablespoon grated lemon zest

PREHEAT the toaster oven to 400° F.

MIX the potatoes, oil, balsamic vinegar, molasses, and garlic powder together in an oiled or nonstick $8\frac{1}{2} \times 8\frac{1}{2} \times 2$-inch square baking (cake) pan. Cover the pan with aluminum foil.

BAKE, covered, for 30 minutes, or until tender. Remove the cover.

BROIL for 10 minutes, or until the potatoes are lightly browned. Season to taste with salt and pepper and garnish with the lemon zest.

Prep: 7 minutes
Total time: 47 minutes
Serves 4

Poultry

Crisp-coated chicken, spice-rubbed game hens, tasty meat loaf, rosemary chicken breasts baked in aluminum foil packets—here are easy-to-create delectable dishes—and your toaster oven does practically all of the work! All you do is assemble the ingredients and while your toaster oven is baking or broiling your meal, you are free to weed the garden, read a magazine, make those phone calls, or help the kids with their homework. Your kitchen is not heating up because your toaster oven radiates less than half the heat your full-size stove oven does. Whether it is crisped, browned, crusted, or baked with a sauce, flavors are heightened and fat content reduced through baking and broiling chicken, turkey, and game hen in your toaster oven. See pages 10–11 for poultry baking and broiling times.

Poultry Notes

Most of the fat content is in the skin and the bones cannot be consumed, so purchasing skinless and boneless chicken and turkey will save you money. For dark meat, use skinless, boneless thighs and for white meat, use skinless, boneless breasts. If skinless is not available, remove the skin by pulling it away from the meat. Snip or cut out the fat deposits in the meat with a scissors or sharp knife. Storing the discarded skin in a resealable plastic bag in the refrigerator until garbage pickup day will eliminate any odors due to its decomposition.

On the other hand, the skin is an automatic baster during broiling. Meat retains its juices better when baked or broiled with the skin on, and afterward, you still have the option of removing the skin, which pulls off quite easily. Better alternatives to skin, however, are crusts, coatings, basting, or marinating, which instill flavor in the meat and create a barrier on the meat surface so moisture within the meat is retained during baking or broiling. The Pesto-Crusted Chicken and Oven-Crisped Chicken recipes, for example, employ coatings and crusts for this purpose. Marinades, as in the Marinated Green Pepper and Pineapple Chicken and Lemon Chicken recipes, impart flavor as well as tenderize the meat through absorption of the marinade. Basting and brushing (as in Orange-Glazed Roast Chicken) give flavor and moisture to the meat as it bakes or broils. A word of caution about marinating: If you want to baste with the marinating liquid, reserve a portion of it for that purpose before marinating poultry. If you use the liquid the meat has marinated in, you may introduce harmful bacteria into the meat during cooking.

Liquid remaining in the broiling or baking pan makes an excellent stock. Add a cup of water to the pan and, after an hour, scrape to loosen any baked-on pieces, then pour the liquid into a plastic storage container. I usually add a little more water to increase the volume of the stock, but not so much as to compromise the flavor. Refrigerate the liquid for several hours or until the fat rises to the top and solidifies. Remove all of the fat and discard it. This liquid rivals any high-quality canned commercial broth or stock you can buy. It is nearly fat free and has a low sodium content as well as a wonderful depth of flavor. It can be strained or pureed in a blender and it will store well (for several months) in a plastic container or heavy-duty resealable plastic bag in the freezer.

Marinated Green Pepper and Pineapple Chicken

Unsweetened grated coconut is available in most food specialty or gourmet stores. If desired, reserve 2 tablespoons of the marinade mixture (before putting the chicken strips into the marinade) for spooning over the chicken, pepper, and onion for the last broiling procedure.

Marinade:
1 teaspoon finely chopped fresh ginger
2 garlic cloves, finely chopped
1 teaspoon toasted sesame oil
1 tablespoon brown sugar
2 tablespoons soy sauce
¾ cup dry white wine

2 skinless, boneless chicken breasts, cut into 1 × 3-inch strips
2 tablespoons chopped onion
1 bell pepper, chopped
1 5-ounce can pineapple chunks, drained
2 tablespoons grated unsweetened coconut

COMBINE the marinade ingredients in a medium bowl and blend well. Add the chicken strips and spoon the mixture over them. Marinate in the refrigerator for at least 1 hour. Remove the strips from the marinade and place in an oiled or non-stick $8^{1}/_{2} \times 8^{1}/_{2} \times 2$-inch square (cake) pan. Add the onion and pepper and mix well.

BROIL for 8 minutes. Then remove from the oven and, using tongs, turn the chicken, pepper, and onion pieces. (Spoon the reserved marinade over the pieces, if desired.)

BROIL again for 8 minutes, or until the chicken, pepper, and onion are cooked through and tender. Add the pineapple chunks and coconut and toss to mix well.

BROIL for another 4 minutes, or until the coconut is lightly browned.

Prep: 15 minutes
Total time: 35 minutes
Serves 4

Sesame Chicken Breasts

Skinless, boneless chicken breasts can be bland and boring. Sesame oil, balsamic vinegar, and soy sauce imbue them with a nutty, toasted flavor and sesame seeds give them a great texture. I serve these breasts with Oven-Baked Rice (page 175) and a salad of baby spinach greens, fresh basil, and oregano leaves tossed with olive oil, balsamic vinegar, and freshly ground pepper.

Mixture:
2 tablespoons sesame oil
2 teaspoons soy sauce
2 teaspoons balsamic vinegar

2 skinless, boneless chicken breast
  filets
3 tablespoons sesame seeds

COMBINE the mixture ingredients in a small bowl and brush the filets liberally. Reserve the mixture. Place the filets on a broiling rack with a pan underneath.

BROIL 15 minutes, or until the meat is tender and the juices, when the meat is pierced, run clear. Remove from the oven and brush the filets with the remaining mixture. Place the sesame seeds on a plate and press the chicken breast halves into the seeds, coating well.

BROIL for 5 minutes, or until the sesame seeds are browned.

Prep: 6 minutes
Total time: 26 minutes
Serves 2

Chicken in Mango Sauce

Mangoes are very sweet, so I have created a sauce to temper their sweetness and add moisture and spicy flavors to the chicken breasts. Use fresh ginger and ripe mangoes (they should be soft and fragrant). Serve this with Moroccan Couscous (page 171) and Rolled Chinese (Napa) Cabbage with Chickpea Filling (page 65).

2 skinless and boneless chicken breast halves	$\frac{1}{2}$ teaspoon garlic powder
1 tablespoon capers	1 teaspoon fresh ginger, peeled and minced
1 tablespoon raisins	$\frac{1}{2}$ teaspoon soy sauce
	$\frac{1}{2}$ teaspoon curry powder
Mango mixture:	1 tablespoon pimientos, minced
1 cup mango pieces	Salt and pepper to taste
1 teaspoon balsamic vinegar	

PREHEAT the toaster oven to 375°F.

PROCESS the mango mixture ingredients in a food processor or blender until smooth. Transfer to an oiled or nonstick $8\frac{1}{2} \times 8\frac{1}{2} \times 2$-inch square (cake) pan and add the capers, raisins, and pimientos, stirring well to blend. Add the chicken breasts and spoon the mixture over the breasts to coat well.

BAKE for 40 minutes. Serve the breasts with the sauce.

Prep: 15 minutes
Total time: 55 minutes
Serves 2

Tasty Meat Loaf

Using Homemade Bread Crumbs (page 41) adds a deeper, richer flavor to this meat loaf. Because this is a one-step recipe and the uncooked meat is combined with all the other ingredients, it is important to use very lean ground turkey breast or chicken breast meat. If ground breast meat is unavailable, buy any ground chicken or turkey meat, crumble it into a baking pan, and brown it under the broiler (usually 8 minutes, turning it with tongs every 2 minutes). Transfer the ground meat to several layers of paper towels and press the fat and moisture out of the meat with several more layers of paper towels on top. Then add to the meat loaf ingredients and bake as directed.

1 to 1½ pounds ground turkey or
  chicken breast
1 egg
1 tablespoon chopped fresh parsley
2 tablespoons chopped bell pepper
3 tablespoons chopped canned
  mushrooms

2 tablespoons chopped onion
2 garlic cloves, minced
½ cup multigrain bread crumbs
1 tablespoon Worcestershire sauce
1 tablespoon ketchup
Freshly ground black pepper to taste

PREHEAT the toaster oven to 400°F.

COMBINE all the ingredients in a large bowl and press into a regular-size 4½ × 8½
  × 2¼-inch loaf pan.

BAKE for 35 minutes, or until browned on top.

Prep: 10 minutes
Total time: 45 minutes
Serves 4

Roasted Game Hens with Vegetable Stuffing

*Game hens, for the most part, are leaner than chickens. Sometimes there is fat on the
flaps of skin beneath the tail. This fat can be snipped off easily with a sharp scissors.
Here is a stuffing that is fat free, low in sodium, and full of flavor.*

Shortcut: *Shredding the onion, carrot, celery, and parsley in a food processor shortens prep time to 10 minutes.*

Stuffing:
1 cup multigrain bread crumbs
2 tablespoons chopped onion
1 carrot, shredded
1 celery stalk, shredded
1 garlic clove, minced
2 tablespoons chopped fresh parsley
Salt and freshly ground black pepper
  to taste

2 whole game hens (thawed or
  fresh), giblets removed, rinsed,
  and patted dry with paper towels

PREHEAT the toaster oven to 350°F.

COMBINE the stuffing ingredients in a medium bowl. Stuff the cavities of the game
  hens and place them in a baking dish.

Continued

BAKE, covered, for 45 minutes, or until the meat is tender and the juices run clear when the breast is pierced with a fork.

BROIL, uncovered, for 8 minutes, or until lightly browned.

Prep: 20 minutes
Total time: 1 hour and 10 minutes
Serves 2

Ginger Chicken

"Stir-fry" the chicken, pea pods, water chestnuts, and bok choy using the BROIL *function of your toaster oven. The result is a great stir-fried taste with no fat and less sodium, and you don't have to put in all the wok time! Bok choy, or Chinese cabbage, is available in the fresh produce sections of most supermarkets. Oyster sauce is available in most Asain, food specialty, or gourmet stores. Five-spice powder is available in the ethnic food section of the supermarket. Fresh ginger is essential.*

2 skinless, boneless chicken breast halves cut into 1-inch cubes
1 tablespoon Chinese oyster sauce or 1 teaspoon five-spice powder
1 teaspoon soy sauce
1 teaspoon toasted sesame oil
2 tablespoons vegetable oil
2 tablespoons lemon juice
2 tablespoons peeled and finely chopped fresh ginger

2 tablespoons fresh garlic, finely chopped
1 tablespoon brown sugar
1 cup fresh snow pea pods, ends snipped
1 6-ounce can water chestnuts, drained
1 cup bok choy, cut into $1/4 \times 1$-inch pieces

COMBINE all the ingredients in a large bowl and mix thoroughly. Transfer to an oiled or nonstick $8^{1}/_{2} \times 8^{1}/_{2} \times 2$-inch square (cake) pan.

BROIL for 20 minutes, remove from the oven, and turn the pieces with tongs.

BROIL for another 20 minutes, or until the chicken and vegetables are well cooked.

Prep: 8 minutes
Total time: 48 minutes
Serves 4

Spice-Rubbed Split Game Hen

Cornish game hens have a wonderful flavor, reminiscent of the way chicken used to taste when I was a kid. Fresh or frozen, they are readily available in your grocery store. Allow at least 5 or 6 hours to thaw a frozen game hen in the refrigerator or use your microwave (see shortcut below). Once thawed, remove the giblets, if any, rinse thoroughly, and pat with a paper towel. I boil the giblets in 2 cups water to make a stock, which I refrigerate, then skim off the fat. It is fairly easy to split a game hen; the bones are small and the flesh tender. Place the game hen on its back on a cutting board. Use a large, sharp knife and draw the blade lengthwise from the sternum (chest) downward. Repeat until you have cut entirely through the game hen.

Shortcut: Microwave the game hen halves at High for 6 to 10 minutes to partially cook. Transfer the halves to a baking dish and bake, skin side up, for 20 minutes, or until tender. Broil for 5 minutes, or until brown.

Spice rub mixture:
1 teaspoon ground cumin
1 teaspoon garlic powder
1 teaspoon onion powder
1 teaspoon paprika

1 teaspoon ground coriander
1 teaspoon salt (optional)

1 Cornish game hen, split

PREHEAT the toaster oven to 400° F.

MIX all the spices together in a small bowl and rub each half of the game hen well and on both sides to coat evenly. Place the pieces skin side down in a baking dish. Cover the dish with aluminum foil.

BAKE for 20 minutes. Turn the pieces over and bake, covered, for another 20 minutes, or until the meat is tender. Remove from the oven and uncover.

BROIL 8 minutes, or until browned to your preference.

Prep: 10 minutes
Total time: 58 minutes
Serves 2

Pesto-Crusted Chicken

Many herbs can be used for a pesto. I have used combinations of fresh basil, oregano, marjoram, cilantro, and mint, as well as the leaves of Swiss chard, spinach, and arugula. The variations are mainly in the taste. Marjoram is more aromatic, spinach and Swiss chard produce a very mild flavor, and blends of cilantro, oregano, and basil, multiple shadings of their own tastes. Here, cilantro, parsley, and basil combine for a pesto crust for chicken. The chicken remains moist because of the coating and is wonderfully herb-flavored. If you have some fresh herbs available, this is the recipe to try!

Pesto:
1 cup fresh cilantro, parsley, and
   basil leaves
3 tablespoons nonfat plain yogurt
¼ cup pine nuts, walnut, or pecans
3 tablespoons grated Parmesan
   cheese
2 peeled garlic cloves

1 tablespoon lemon juice
3 tablespoons olive oil
Salt and freshly ground black pepper
   to taste

2 skinless, boneless chicken breast
   halves

PREHEAT the toaster oven to 450° F.

BLEND the pesto ingredients in a blender or food processor until smooth. Set aside.

PLACE the chicken breast halves in an oiled or nonstick 8½ × 8½ × 2-inch square (cake) pan. With a butter knife or spatula, spread the mixture liberally on both sides of each chicken breast. Cover the dish with aluminum foil.

BAKE, covered, for 25 minutes, or until the chicken is tender. Remove from the oven and uncover.

BROIL for 6 minutes, or until the pesto coating is lightly browned.

Prep: 10 minutes
Total time: 41 minutes
Serves 2

Chicken Ranch Roll-Ups

If necessary, heat the tortillas for 1 or 2 minutes under the broiler to make them pliable. Serve each roll-up with a tablespoon of low-fat sour cream sprinkled with chili powder.

4 6-inch flour tortillas
Low-fat sour cream
Chili powder

Filling mixture:
1 cup cooked chopped chicken
  breast
4 tablespoons canned black beans
2 tablespoons shredded low-fat
  cheddar cheese

2 tablespoons finely chopped green
  bell pepper
2 tablespoons finely chopped onion
1 finely chopped plum tomato
2 tablespoons tomato salsa
1 seeded and chopped chili pepper
Hot sauce or Salt and pepper

PREHEAT the toaster oven to 350°F.
BLEND filling ingredients together well in a bowl and season to taste.
FILL tortillas with equal portions of mixture, roll into cylinders and lay, seam side
  down, in an oiled or nonstick $8\frac{1}{2}'' \times 8\frac{1}{2}'' \times 2''$ square (cake) pan.
BAKE for 20 minutes or until browned and cheese is melted.

Prep: 15 minutes
Total time: 25 minutes
Serves 4

Hot Thighs

These chicken thighs make an excellent appetizer served with a low-fat Blue Cheese Dip (recipe follows) or an entrée with Crisp Cajun Potato Wedges (page 87).

6 skinless, boneless chicken thighs
$\frac{1}{4}$ cup fresh lemon juice

Seasonings:
1 teaspoon garlic powder
$\frac{1}{4}$ teaspoon cayenne

$\frac{1}{2}$ teaspoon chili powder
1 teaspoon onion powder
Salt and freshly ground black pepper
  to taste

Continued

PREHEAT the toaster oven to 450° F.

BRUSH the chicken thighs liberally with the lemon juice. Set aside.

COMBINE the seasonings in a small bowl and transfer to a paper or plastic bag. Add the thighs and shake well to coat. Remove from the bag and place in an oiled or nonstick $8^1/_2 \times 8^1/_2 \times 2$-inch square (cake) pan. Cover the pan with aluminum foil.

BAKE, covered, for 20 minutes. Turn the pieces with tongs and bake again for another 20 minutes, or until the meat is tender and lightly browned.

Prep: 10 minutes
Total time: 50 minutes
Serves 4

Blue Cheese Dip

$^1/_4$ cup crumbled blue cheese
1 cup nonfat sour cream
3 tablespoons low-fat buttermilk

Salt and freshly ground black pepper
to taste

COMBINE all the ingredients in a small bowl, adjusting the seasonings to taste. If the consistency is too thick, add a little buttermilk. If it's too thin, add a little blue cheese.

Prep: 5 minutes
Total time: 5 minutes
Makes 1 cup

I Forgot to Thaw—Garlic Capered Chicken Thighs

It would be nice to have chicken for supper, you decide, but the chicken is in the freezer and you do not have a microwave to thaw it. You can use your toaster oven to thaw, then bake, your chicken. Here's how.

Run hot water over the frozen package of chicken until you are able to separate the chicken from the package. Place the frozen chicken in a 1-quart $8^1/_2 \times 8^1/_2 \times 4$-inch ovenproof baking dish and bake uncovered at 400° F. for 30 minutes, or until you can separate the pieces of chicken. Add the garlic mixture ingredients and bake, covered. The baking time will be longer than normal, but the results will be the same.

6 frozen skinless, boneless chicken
   thighs

Garlic mixture:
3 garlic cloves, minced
¾ cup dry white wine

2 tablespoons capers
½ teaspoon paprika
¼ teaspoon ground cumin
Salt and freshly ground black pepper
   to taste

PREHEAT the toaster oven to 400° F.

THAW the chicken as directed (see page 100). Separate the pieces and add the garlic mixture, which has been combined in a small bowl, stirring well to coat. Cover the dish with aluminum foil.

BAKE for 30 minutes, or until the chicken is tender. Remove the cover and turn the chicken pieces, spooning the sauce over them.

BROIL for 8 minutes, or until the chicken is lightly browned.

Prep: 5 minutes
Total time: 55 minutes
Serves 4

Oven-Crisped Chicken

The longer the baking time, the browner and crisper the coating will be. By extending the baking time, you can brown and crisp the chicken to your preference. Because of the coating, the chicken pieces will remain moist, even if you prefer very crisp-coated chicken and bake them a little longer than the time specified by the recipe. A minimal amount of oil is used, just enough to coat the chicken pieces. Because the chicken is on a broiling rack and not sitting in the oil and absorbing it, as in frying, even less oil is present in the coating. Is oven-crisped chicken as tasty as fried? Dare to compare! Serve this crisp chicken with my Ginger Peachy Salsa (recipe follows).

Coating mixture:
1 cup cornmeal
¼ cup wheat germ
1 teaspoon paprika
1 teaspoon garlic powder
Salt and butcher's pepper to taste

3 tablespoons olive oil
1 tablespoon spicy brown mustard
6 skinless, boneless chicken thighs

Continued

PREHEAT the toaster oven to 375°F.

COMBINE the coating mixture ingredients in a small bowl and transfer to a plate, spreading the mixture evenly over the plate's surface. Set aside.

WHISK together the oil and mustard in a bowl. Add the chicken pieces and toss to coat thoroughly. Press both sides of each piece into the coating mixture to coat well. Chill in the refrigerator for 10 minutes. Transfer the chicken pieces to a broiling rack with a pan underneath.

BAKE, uncovered, for 35 minutes, or until the meat is tender and the coating is crisp and golden brown or browned to your preference.

Prep: 10 minutes
Total time: 45 minutes
Serves 4

Ginger Peachy Salsa

Some like it hotter! I made this salsa hot enough for me. You may want to add more chilies. If possible, give the salsa a day or two in the refrigerator so that the flavors have time to meld.

1 cup peeled, pitted, and finely chopped fresh peaches or 1 cup finely chopped canned peaches, drained well

2 tablespoons finely chopped bell pepper

2 tablespoons canned diced pimientos, drained

2 tablespoons chopped onion

1 small chili pepper, seeded and chopped

1 tablespoon peeled and grated fresh ginger

3 tablespoons tomato paste

1 tablespoon capers

Salt and freshly ground black pepper to taste

COMBINE all the ingredients in a large bowl, mixing well. Transfer to a glass or ceramic storage container. Chill for at least 3 hours before serving.

Total time: 15 minutes
Makes 2 cups

Chicken Potpie

I wanted to create a chicken potpie recipe that did not require any stovetop browning or sautéing. Treating the ingredients like a casserole reduced the steps to mainly two: (1) assembling the pie filling ingredients and (2) topping with the phyllo pastry to finish the baking. Phyllo pastry crust is thinner and lighter than pastry dough and tends to brown quickly.

Pie filling:
1 tablespoon unbleached flour
$\frac{1}{2}$ cup evaporated skim milk
4 skinless, boneless chicken thighs,
   cut into 1-inch cubes
1 cup potatoes, peeled and cut into
   $\frac{1}{2}$-inch pieces
$\frac{1}{2}$ cup frozen green peas
$\frac{1}{2}$ cup thinly sliced carrot

2 tablespoons chopped onion
$\frac{1}{2}$ cup chopped celery
1 teaspoon garlic powder
Salt and freshly ground black pepper
   to taste

8 sheets phyllo pastry, thawed
Olive oil

PREHEAT the toaster oven to 400°F.

WHISK the flour into the milk until smooth in a 1-quart $8\frac{1}{2} \times 8\frac{1}{2} \times 4$-inch oven-proof baking dish. Add the remaining filling ingredients and mix well. Adjust the seasonings to taste. Cover the dish with aluminum foil.

BAKE for 40 minutes, or until the carrot, potatoes, and celery are tender. Remove from the oven and uncover.

PLACE one sheet of phyllo pastry on top of the baked pie-filling mixture, bending the edges to fit the shape of the baking dish. Brush the sheet with olive oil. Add another sheet on top of it and brush with oil. Continue adding the remaining sheets, brushing each one, until the crust is completed. Brush the top with oil.

BAKE for 6 minutes, or until the phyllo pastry is browned.

Prep: 10 minutes
Total time: 58 minutes
Serves 4

Orange-Glazed Roast Chicken

If you have a medium- to large-size toaster oven that can hold four to six slices of toast, roasting a chicken will be amazingly easy. Cover the chicken with aluminum foil, making sure that it does not touch the upper elements or sides of the oven. An easy stuffing that adds a wonderful flavor and moisture to the roast chicken is made from apple wedges and mandarin oranges (recipe follows). It makes a good warm condiment that compliments the chicken and goes well with Oven-Baked Rice (page 175).

1 3-pound whole chicken, rinsed and patted dry with paper towels

Brushing mixture:
2 tablespoons orange juice concentrate
1 tablespoon soy sauce

1 tablespoon toasted sesame oil
1 teaspoon ground ginger
Salt and freshly ground black pepper to taste

PREHEAT the toaster oven to 400° F.

PLACE the chicken, breast side up, in an oiled or nonstick $8\frac{1}{2} \times 8\frac{1}{2} \times 2$-inch square (cake) pan and brush with the mixture, which has been combined in a small bowl, reserving the remaining mixture. Cover with aluminum foil.

BAKE for 1 hour and 20 minutes. Uncover and brush the chicken with remaining mixture.

BAKE, uncovered, for 20 minutes, or until the breast is tender when pierced with a fork and golden brown.

Prep: 10 minutes
Total time: 1 hour and 50 minutes
Serves 6

Apple and Orange Stuffing

1 cup apples, peeled, cored, and sliced into thin pieces
1 11-ounce can mandarin oranges, drained well
1 teaspoon grated lemon zest

2 tablespoons raisins
2 tablespoons capers, drained well
$\frac{1}{2}$ cup Homemade Bread Crumbs (page 41)
Salt and white pepper

COMBINE all the ingredients in a medium bowl, mixing well. Adjust the seasonings to taste. Stuff the chicken with the mixture and bake.

Total time: 10 minutes
Makes 2 cups

Foiled Rosemary Chicken Breasts

To double this recipe, wrap four individual foil packets instead of two breasts per packet. They will bake faster than two breasts per packet. A final broiling enhances the flavors and concentrates the juices. Do not overbake the breasts or they will dry out with the broiling. Make a small slit with a knife in one of the breasts to test for doneness. The juice should be clear and the meat white, but better to have it a little pink than very white and too well done. Fresh rosemary is absolutely necessary for this recipe.

2 skinless, boneless chicken breast
   halves

Sauce:
3 tablespoons dry white wine
1 tablespoon Dijon mustard

2 tablespoons nonfat plain yogurt
Salt and freshly ground black pepper
   to taste
2 rosemary sprigs

PREHEAT the toaster oven to 400° F.

PLACE each breast on a 12 × 12-inch square of heavy-duty aluminum foil (or regular foil doubled) and turn up the edges of the foil.

MIX together the sauce ingredients and spoon over the chicken breasts. Lay a rosemary sprig on each breast. Bring up the edges of the foil and fold to form a sealed packet.

BAKE for 25 minutes or until juices run clear when the meat is pierced with a fork. Remove the rosemary sprigs.

BROIL for 5 minutes, or until lightly browned. Replace the sprigs and serve.

Prep: 10 minutes
Total time: 40 minutes
Serves 2

Lemon Chicken

Reserve three tablespoons of the marinade mixture before putting the chicken thighs in to marinate, then just before broiling, spoon it on the baked chicken to give a lift to the flavor. I serve this chicken with Moroccan Couscous (page 171).

Marinade:
Juice of 1 lemon, plus pulp (no seeds)
$\frac{1}{4}$ cup dry white wine
2 tablespoons olive oil
1 tablespoon minced garlic
2 bay leaves
1 teaspoon dried thyme

1 teaspoon freshly ground black pepper
Salt to taste

8 skinless, boneless chicken thighs
Juice of 1 lemon
2 tablespoons olive oil

PREHEAT the toaster oven to 400° F.

BLEND the marinade ingredients in a bowl (reserving 3 tablespoons for basting), add the chicken thighs, cover, and chill for at least 1 hour. Transfer the chicken thighs to a 1-quart $8\frac{1}{2} \times 8\frac{1}{2} \times 4$-inch ovenproof baking dish. Adjust the seasonings. Cover the dish with aluminum foil.

BAKE for 30 minutes, or until the chicken is tender. Uncover and spoon the reserved marinade over the chicken.

BROIL for 8 minutes, or until lightly browned. Remove the bay leaves before serving.

Prep: 6 minutes
Total time: 42 minutes
Serves 4

Light and Lovely Loaf

I created this recipe as a welcome alternative to traditional weighty and fatty meat loaf recipes. The texture is aerated, grainy, and hearty, and using ground turkey breast or chicken breast meat makes the fat content much lower than that in meat loaf made with ground beef.

***Shortcut:** Grating the carrot, celery, and onion in a food processor shortens the prep time by 8 minutes.*

2 cups ground chicken or turkey
  breast

1 egg

$\frac{1}{2}$ cup grated carrot

$\frac{1}{2}$ cup grated celery

1 tablespoon finely chopped onion

$\frac{1}{2}$ teaspoon garlic powder

Salt and freshly ground black pepper
  to taste

PREHEAT the toaster oven to 400° F.

BLEND all ingredients in a bowl, mixing well, and transfer to an oiled or nonstick regular-size $4\frac{1}{2} \times 8\frac{1}{2} \times 2\frac{1}{4}$-inch loaf pan.

BAKE, uncovered, for 30 minutes, until lightly browned.

Prep: 15 minutes

Total time: 45 minutes

Serves 4

East Indian Chicken

The combination of wine, broth, and spices produces a flavorful sauce that is a richly colored vehicle for the onion, pepper, and tomato. This is an excellent dish to make a day ahead and marinate in the refrigerator. The chicken and vegetables will deepen in flavor bathed in the wine/broth liquid.

Sauce mixture:

$\frac{1}{4}$ cup white wine

$\frac{1}{4}$ cup red wine

$\frac{1}{2}$ cup low-sodium vegetable broth

$\frac{1}{2}$ cup finely chopped onion

$\frac{1}{2}$ cup finely chopped bell pepper

$\frac{1}{2}$ cup finely chopped fresh tomato

3 garlic cloves, minced

1 tablespoon peeled and minced
  fresh ginger

2 teaspoons curry powder

$\frac{1}{4}$ teaspoon ground cinnamon

$\frac{1}{4}$ teaspoon ground cumin

4 small dried chilies

Salt and freshly ground black pepper
  to taste

6 skinless, boneless chicken thighs

PREHEAT the toaster oven to 400° F.

COMBINE the sauce mixture ingredients in a 1-quart $8\frac{1}{2} \times 8\frac{1}{2} \times 4$-inch ovenproof baking dish and mix well. Add the chicken and toss together to coat well. Cover the dish with aluminum foil.

Continued

BAKE for 45 minutes, or until the chicken is tender. Uncover and spoon the sauce over the chicken. Remove the chilies before serving.

> *Prep:* 13 minutes
> *Total time:* 58 minutes
> Serves 4

Guiltless Bacon

One of my favorite Saturday breakfasts is scrambled eggs, bacon, and toast. I feel no twinges of guilt using turkey bacon, which is actually a kind of pressed dark and light turkey meat that has a rather nice smoky flavor and only a fraction of the fat of regular pork bacon. Any excess fat can be pressed out of the cooked bacon with layers of paper towels. Monitor the broiling time and take note of when the bacon is done to your preference so that next time you can gauge your preparation time accordingly.

> 6 slices lean turkey bacon, placed on
>   a broiling pan

BROIL 5 minutes, turn the pieces, and broil again for 5 more minutes, or until done to your preference. Press the slices between paper towels and serve immediately.

> *Prep:* 2 minutes
> *Total time:* 12 minutes
> Serves 4

Chapter 8

Meat

T oaster ovens are superb for baking and broiling chops, steaks, and ground beef. Broiling meat on a rack reduces the fat content by draining it away from the meat as it broils, while baking and broiling enhance flavors by reducing the exterior moisture content and concentrating seasonings and natural juices within the meat. You can even "stir-fry" meat and vegetables under the broiler, producing the same results with less fat. It is important to purchase lean cuts only or trim all fat away. Ground beef claiming to be lean often has a comparatively high fat content of 10, 12, or even 15 percent. Buy ground sirloin or try pressing cooked ground beef between paper towels to reduce the fat content.

The recipes in this chapter include broiled steaks, pork and lamb chops, curries, kebabs, meatballs, meat loaf, beef birds, and yes, stir-fry. All take less than an hour to prepare, are simple and simply delicious, and all can be done to perfection in the toaster oven! See page 11 for steak broiling times. Toaster ovens vary, but generally a ¾-inch steak will take approximately 8 minutes for rare, 12 minutes for medium, and 14 minutes for well done.

In Praise of Marinades

A marinade of only fifteen minutes will enhance the flavor of most meat, and a longer marinating time, of course, produces more depth of flavor. Large portions require more marinating time than smaller portions and marinating the meat for one day or overnight produces the best flavor results. Basting the meat with the marinade while cooking further enhances the flavor to the meat.

Seasoned Boneless Pork Sirloin Chops

With the new emphasis on lean pork as an alternative to higher-fat-content beef, new cuts are appearing in the meat section at the supermarket. Pork sirloin chops require no trimming and are very lean. Broiling to medium (the timing in this recipe reflects this) produced excellent, tender, and juicy chops. Broiling to well done, however, produced a rather tough and dry piece of meat. Pork requires less cooking time because it's lower in fat and has low water content. This recipe also highlights Pickapeppa sauce, which is sweeter, thicker, and hotter than Worcestershire sauce. If you like Worcestershire, try Pickapeppa, which is available in most supermarkets.

Seasoning mixture:
1/2 teaspoon ground cumin
1/4 teaspoon turmeric
Pinch of ground cardamom
Pinch of grated nutmeg
1 teaspoon vegetable oil
1 teaspoon Pickapeppa sauce

2 1/2- to 3/4-pound boneless lean pork
   sirloin chops

COMBINE the seasoning mixture ingredients in a small bowl and brush on both sides of the chops. Place the chops on the broiling rack with a pan underneath.
BROIL 8 minutes, remove the chops, turn, and brush with the mixture. Broil again for 8 minutes, or until the chops are done to your preference.

Prep: 8 minutes
Total time: 24 minutes
Serves 2

Spicy Little Beef Birds

Thinly sliced lean beef has many names in the supermarket meat section—pepper, skillet, or sandwich steaks, to name a few. Take round steak or any lean boneless beef cut and pound it with a meat mallet, flat side of a large knife, or a rolling pin until it is 1/4 inch thick. These little birds are excellent appetizers to serve with a Roquefort dip of 1 1/2 cups low-fat sour cream blended with 2 tablespoons Roquefort cheese. Yogurt Zucchini with Onion (page 69) and Classic Baked Potatoes (page 78) make excellent accompaniments. Appetizer or entrée, beef birds are a delicious low-fat meal—simple and fun to make!

Spicy mixture:
1 tablespoon olive oil
1 tablespoon brown mustard
1 teaspoon chili powder
1 teaspoon garlic powder
1 teaspoon hot sauce

1 tablespoon barbecue sauce or salsa
Salt and freshly ground black pepper
to taste

$^1\!/_2$ to $^3\!/_4$ pound pepper steaks, cut
into 3 × 4-inch strips

BLEND the spicy mixture ingredients in a small bowl and brush both sides of the beef strips.

ROLL up the strips lengthwise and fasten with toothpicks near each end. Place the beef rolls in an oiled or nonstick $8^1\!/_2$ × $8^1\!/_2$ × 2-inch square baking (cake) pan.

BROIL for 6 minutes, remove from the oven, and turn with tongs. Brush with the spicy mixture and broil again for 6 minutes, or until done to your preference.

Prep: 10 minutes
Total time: 22 minutes
Serves 2

Minted Lamb Chops

The combination of lamb and mint is undisputedly delicious. However, for me, mint jelly is annoyingly sweet. I created this recipe as an alternative to the usual lamb/jelly combo. I wanted the balsamic vinegar to give one side of the lamb chops a mild tang and a mint coating on the other side to provide an aromatic mint flavor that harmonized beautifully with the lamb. I think I got it!

Mint mixture:
4 tablespoons finely chopped fresh
mint
2 tablespoons nonfat yogurt
1 tablespoon olive oil
Salt and freshly ground black pepper
to taste

4 lean lamb chops, fat trimmed,
approximately $^3\!/_4$ inch thick
1 tablespoon balsamic vinegar

COMBINE the mint mixture ingredients in a small bowl, stirring well to blend. Set aside. Place the lamp chops on a broiling rack with a pan underneath.

BROIL the lamb chops for 10 minutes, or until they are slightly pink. Remove

Continued

from the oven and brush one side liberally with balsamic vinegar. Turn the chops over with tongs and spread with the mint mixture, using all of the mixture.

BROIL again for 5 minutes, or until lightly browned.

Prep: 6 minutes
Total time: 21 minutes
Serves 4

Bourbon Broiled Steak

The brushing mixture makes an excellent sauce or gravy. When the steak is done, quickly broil the mixture for 3 minutes, or until it begins to bubble. The alcohol, which is considerable, will be dispersed by the cooking, leaving a flavorful sauce that is good as a drizzle for the potatoes or vegetables. Bourbon Broiled Steak is excellent with Classic Stuffed Baked Potatoes (page 79) and Lemon-Glazed Baby Carrots (page 73).

Brushing mixture:
1/4 cup bourbon
1 teaspoon garlic powder
1 tablespoon olive oil
1 teaspoon soy sauce

2 6- to 8-ounce sirloin steaks, 3/4 inch thick

COMBINE the brushing mixture ingredients in a small bowl. Brush the steaks on both sides with the mixture and place on the broiling rack with a pan underneath.

BROIL 4 minutes, remove from the oven, turn with tongs, brush the top and sides, and broil again for 4 minutes, or until done to your preference. To use the brushing mixture as a sauce or gravy, pour the mixture into a baking pan.

BROIL the mixture for 6 minutes, or until it begins to bubble.

Prep: 5 minutes
Total time: 19 minutes
Serves 2

Curry Powder

Ideally, a curry's flavor should be balanced and no single spice should dominate. Households in India create their own garam masala (hot spice mixture), a blend of spices used in cooking, usually a mixture of cloves, cinnamon, and cardamom seeds together in equal amounts. To prepare this, roast equal portions (about $1/4$ cup each) cinnamon sticks, cardamom pods, and cloves in a baking pan at 200° F. for about 30 minutes, turning frequently to toast evenly. Shell the cardamom pods and grind the seeds, cinnamon sticks, and cloves in a blender until they form a fine powder. Stored in a sealed jar, these spices will keep fresh for months. Commercial curry powders are quite satisfactory, but if you make your own, you will find it to be more flavorful and with a depth of taste that a store-bought curry powder may not have. Here's a recipe for creating your own curry powder. Adjust the ingredients to your own preference for flavor and hotness.

$1/2$ cup coriander seeds
2 tablespoons ground cumin
2 tablespoons black peppercorns
1 tablespoon sesame seeds
1 tablespoon cardamom seeds,
  extracted from the pods

2 small dried chili peppers
3 tablespoons turmeric
2 tablespoons ground ginger

COMBINE the coriander seeds, cumin, peppercorns, sesame seeds, cardamom seeds, and chili peppers in an oiled or nonstick $8^1/2 \times 8^1/2 \times 2$-inch square baking (cake) pan.

TOAST once, then turn with tongs and toast again, or continue toasting and turning until evenly toasted. Cool and grind the spices in a blender until the mixture becomes a powder. Add the turmeric and ground ginger and mix well. Store in a covered container in the refrigerator.

Prep: 15 minutes
Total time: 20 minutes
Makes approximately 1 cup

Lamb Curry

If you prefer using a commercial curry powder, I recommend purchasing an Indian curry powder at a gourmet, food specialty, or Indian food store, or a Jamaican or Mexican curry powder in the ethnic foods section of the supermarket.

1 pound lean lamb for stewing, trimmed and cut into 1 × 1-inch pieces
1 small onion, chopped
3 garlic cloves, minced

2 plum tomatoes, chopped
$^1/_2$ cup dry white wine
2 tablespoons curry powder
Salt and cayenne to taste

PREHEAT the toaster oven to 400° F.
COMBINE all the ingredients in an 8$^1/_2$ × 8$^1/_2$ × 4-inch ovenproof baking dish. Adjust the seasonings.
BAKE, covered, for 40 minutes, or until the meat is tender and the onion is cooked.

Prep: 8 minutes
Total time: 48 minutes
Serves 4

Cilantro-Crusted Flank Steak

Flank steak is a cut of meat that is almost error free: tender, moist when broiled to well done, and amenable to crusts like the cilantro crust I created here. I like the long, stringy grain of the meat, and flank steak has more flavor than many other cuts of meat. If fresh cilantro is not available, parsley works well. Serve with Eggplant and Tomato Slices (page 71) or Broiled Tomatoes (page 75).

Coating:
2 tablespoons chopped onion
1 tablespoon olive oil
2 tablespoons plain nonfat yogurt
1 plum tomato
$^1/_2$ cup fresh cilantro leaves
2 tablespoons cooking sherry

$^1/_4$ teaspoon hot sauce
1 teaspoon garlic powder
$^1/_2$ teaspoon chili powder
Salt and freshly ground black pepper

2 8-ounce flank steaks

PROCESS the coating ingredients in a blender or food processor until smooth. Spread half of the coating mixture on top of the flank steaks. Place the steaks on a broiling rack with a pan underneath.

BROIL for 8 minutes. Turn with tongs, spread the remaining mixture on the steaks, and broil again for 8 minutes, or until done to your preference.

Prep: 10 minutes
Total time: 26 minutes
Serves 2

Lime and Cumin Lamb Kebabs

If you have a small toaster oven, you can still do kebabs even if the metal skewers are too large. Purchase a package of the thin wooden skewers, available in most cooking utensil sections in supermarket, kitchen, or gourmet stores, and shorten them by breaking off the nonpointed end to fit your oven. If you are using large pieces of meat or vegetables, use two or three of these skewers instead of one. Serve with Oven-Baked Rice (page 175) or Moroccan Couscous (page 171).

1 pound boneless lean lamb, trimmed and cut into 1 × 1-inch pieces
2 plum tomatoes, cut into 2 × 2-inch pieces
1 bell pepper, cut into 2 × 2-inch pieces
1 small onion, cut into 2 × 2-inch pieces

Brushing mixture:
¼ cup lime juice
½ teaspoon soy sauce
1 tablespoon honey
½ teaspoon ground cumin

SKEWER alternating pieces of lamb, tomato, pepper, and onion on four 9-inch skewers.
COMBINE the brushing mixture ingredients in a small bowl and brush on the kebabs. Place the skewers on a broiling rack with a pan underneath.
BROIL for 8 minutes. Turn the skewers, brush the kebabs with the mixture, and broil for 8 minutes, or until the meat and vegetables are cooked and browned.

Prep: 12 minutes
Total time: 28 minutes
Serves 4

Barbecued Broiled Pork Chops

You don't have to fire up the grill. Barbecue pork chops in your toaster oven! Whether you marinate or brush on the barbecue sauce, the taste is smoky and piquant. As in grilling, the more you brush, the better it gets. Liquid smoke is available in the condiments or barbecue sauce section of the supermarket.

Barbecue sauce mixture:
1 tablespoon ketchup
1/4 cup dry red wine
1 tablespoon vegetable oil
1/8 teaspoon smoked flavoring (liquid smoke)
1 teaspoon chili powder

1 teaspoon ground cumin
1 teaspoon brown sugar
1/4 teaspoon butcher's pepper

2 large (6- to 8-ounce) lean pork chops, approximately 3/4 to 1 inch thick

COMBINE the barbecue sauce mixture ingredients in a small bowl. Brush the chops with the sauce and place on a broiling rack with a pan underneath.

BROIL 8 minutes, turn with tongs, and broil for another 8 minutes, or until the meat is cooked to your preference.

Prep: 8 minutes
Total time: 24 minutes
Serves 2

Steak Pinwheels with Pepper Slaw and Minneapolis Potato Salad

Add Pepper Slaw and Minneapolis Potato Salad (recipes follow) and you have a perfect picnic!

Brushing mixture:
1/2 cup cold strong brewed coffee
2 tablespoons molasses
1 tablespoon tomato paste
2 garlic cloves, minced
1 tablespoon olive oil
Garlic powder
1 teaspoon butcher's pepper

1 pound lean, boneless beefsteak, flattened to 1/8-inch thickness with a meat mallet or rolling pin (place steak between 2 sheets of heavy-duty plastic wrap)

COMBINE the brushing mixture ingredients in a small bowl and set aside.

CUT the steak into 2 × 3-inch strips, brush with the mixture, and roll up, securing the edges with toothpicks. Brush again with the mixture and place in an oiled or nonstick $8\frac{1}{2}$ × $8\frac{1}{2}$ × 2-inch square baking (cake) pan.

BROIL for 8 minutes, then turn with tongs, brush with the mixture again, and broil for another 8 minutes, or until browned.

Prep: 20 minutes
Total time: 36 minutes
Serves 4

Pepper Slaw

Shortcut: Grating the carrots, pepper, and cabbage in a food processor reduces the prep time to 8 minutes.

2 carrots, grated
1 bell pepper, seeded and grated
1 cup grated cabbage
2 scallions, chopped
3 tablespoons nonfat plain yogurt

1 tablespoon balsamic vinegar
1 tablespoon honey
$\frac{1}{4}$ teaspoon celery seed
$\frac{1}{4}$ teaspoon butcher's pepper
Salt to taste

COMBINE the slaw ingredients in a medium bowl and chill for 1 hour.

Prep: 15 minutes
Serves 4

Minneapolis Potato Salad

2 cups potatoes, peeled, cooked, and cut into 1 × 1-inch pieces
3 hard-boiled eggs, peeled and finely chopped
$\frac{1}{4}$ cup low-fat mayonnaise

$\frac{1}{4}$ cup nonfat sour cream
2 tablespoons finely chopped onion
2 tablespoons white vinegar
Salt and butcher's pepper to taste

COMBINE all the ingredients in a large bowl. Adjust the seasonings to taste. Chill before serving.

Total time: 25 minutes
Makes approximately 3 cups

Beef, Onion, and Pepper Shish Kebab

If you don't have time to marinate the beef, brush the kebabs with the marinade ingredients before broiling, then every 5 minutes while broiling. If your toaster oven cannot accommodate an 8-inch skewer, use wooden (bamboo) skewers, which come in packages of several dozen. You can shorten these to fit your oven by simply breaking off the non-pointed end. Wear oven mitts when placing a pan with the skewers in the oven or removing it.

Marinade:
2 tablespoons olive oil
1/2 cup dry red wine
1 tablespoon soy sauce
1 teaspoon chili powder
1 teaspoon Worcestershire sauce
1 teaspoon garlic powder
1 teaspoon spicy brown mustard
1 teaspoon brown sugar

8 onion quarters, approximately 2 ×
    2-inch pieces
8 bell pepper quarters, 2 × 2-inch
    pieces
1 pound lean boneless beef (sirloin,
    round steak, London broil), cut
    into 8 2-inch cubes
4 8-inch metal or wooden (bamboo)
    skewers

COMBINE the marinade ingredients in a large bowl. Add the onion, peppers, and beef. Refrigerate, covered, for at least 1 hour or

SKEWER alternating beef, pepper, and onion pieces. Brush with the marinade mixture and place the skewers on a broiling rack with the pan underneath.

BROIL for 5 minutes, remove the pan with the skewers from the oven, turn the skewers, brush again, then broil for another 5 minutes. Repeat turning and brushing every 5 minutes, until the peppers and onions are well cooked and browned to your preference.

Prep: 15 minutes
Total time: 35 minutes
Serves 4

Italian Meatballs

The meatballs are browned under the toaster oven broiler. In using the broiler, remember that you are dealing with a small, very hot space and always wear oven mitts! Remove the pan completely from the oven and then turn the meatballs with tongs. When you transfer the meatballs to a baking dish, add the sauce ingredients and return the baking dish to the toaster oven. For this dish, the usual partner is spaghetti, but I like to serve it with ziti on the side and liberal applications of grated Parmesan cheese.

Olive oil

Meatball mixture:
1 pound lean ground sirloin
2 tablespoons multigrain bread crumbs
1 egg
2 tablespoons grated Parmesan cheese
Salt and freshly ground black pepper

Tomato sauce:
1 15-ounce can tomato sauce
2 garlic cloves, minced
$\frac{1}{4}$ teaspoon dried oregano or 1 tablespoon chopped fresh oregano leaves
$\frac{1}{2}$ teaspoon dried basil or 1 tablespoon chopped fresh basil leaves

COMBINE the meatball mixture ingredients in a medium bowl and adjust the seasonings to taste. Form into 2-inch balls and place in an oiled or nonstick $8\frac{1}{2} \times 8\frac{1}{2} \times 2$-inch square baking (cake) pan.

BROIL 10 minutes, remove from the oven, and turn with tongs. Broil another 10 minutes, or until the meatballs are cooked through and lightly browned. Drain the meatballs on paper towels for several minutes, then transfer to an oiled or nonstick $8\frac{1}{2} \times 8\frac{1}{2} \times 4$-inch ovenproof baking dish.

COMBINE the tomato sauce ingredients in a medium bowl and pour over the meatballs to cover thoroughly. Cover with aluminum foil.

BAKE, covered, at 350° F. for 25 minutes.

Prep: 15 minutes
Total time: 1 hour
Serves 4

Beer-Baked Pork Tenderloin

Beer imparts a delectable aromatic flavor to pork. When the weather gets chilly, this pot roast–type recipe is extremely satisfying—great with Marjoram New Potatoes (page 85), Asparagus Ronald (page 68), or Pecan Parmesan Cauliflower (page 67). Perfect for supper after a day of raking leaves, the liquid is delicious drizzled over a baked potato (page 78). Spiced apple slices can be found in the canned vegetable or fruit section of the supermarket.

1 pound lean pork tenderloin, fat trimmed off
3 garlic cloves, minced
1 cup good-quality dark ale or beer

2 bay leaves
Salt and freshly cracked black pepper
Spiced apple slices

PREHEAT the toaster oven to 400° F.

PLACE the tenderloin in an $8\frac{1}{2} \times 8\frac{1}{2} \times 4$-inch ovenproof baking dish. Sprinkle the minced garlic over the pork, pour over the beer, add the bay leaves, and season to taste with the salt and pepper. Cover with aluminum foil.

BAKE, covered, for 40 minutes, or until the meat is tender. Discard the bay leaves and serve sliced with the liquid. Garnish with the spiced apple slices.

Prep: 8 minutes
Total time: 48 minutes
Serves 4

Chinese Pork and Vegetable Non-Stir-Fry

Yes, you can use your toaster oven broiler to stir-fry! There's no fattening, sodium-loaded sauce, no stirring, and no frying. Just turn the pork and vegetables with tongs every 8 minutes. Five-spice powder and sesame oil can be purchased in the ethnic food section of the supermarket. Serve with Oven-Baked Rice (page 175).

Seasoning sauce:
1 tablespoon soy sauce
$\frac{1}{4}$ cup dry white wine
1 tablespoon sesame oil

1 tablespoon vegetable oil
1 teaspoon Chinese five-spice powder

2 6-ounce lean boneless pork chops
  cut into $1/4 \times 2$-inch strips
1 1-pound package frozen vegetable
  mix or 2 cups sliced assorted fresh
  vegetables: broccoli, carrots, cauliflower, bell pepper, and the like

1 4-ounce can mushroom pieces,
  drained, or $1/2$ cup cleaned and
  sliced fresh mushrooms
2 tablespoons sesame seeds
2 tablespoons minced fresh garlic

WHISK together the seasoning sauce ingredients in a small bowl. Set aside.

COMBINE the pork, vegetables, mushrooms, sesame seeds, and garlic in an oiled or
nonstick $8\frac{1}{2} \times 8\frac{1}{2} \times 2$-inch square baking (cake) pan. Add the seasoning sauce
ingredients and toss to coat the pork, vegetables, and mushrooms well.

BROIL for 30 minutes, turning with tongs every 8 minutes, until the vegetables and
meat are well cooked and lightly browned.

Prep: 8 minutes
Total time: 38 minutes
Serves 4

Chapter 9

Fish

Did you ever want to buy a swordfish steak or a salmon fillet to broil but didn't because the thought of heating up the oven broiler and cleaning the big rack and pan later wasn't appealing? Did you think of frying the fish in a skillet, but didn't want all the grease? Did the thought of microwaving a fish fillet turn you off because you thought it might be rubbery after it was cooked? If you have experienced any of these apprehensions and therefore deprived yourself of a delicious fish dinner, then it's time you discovered that baking and broiling fish is easy and fast using a toaster oven. The average broiling time for two $\frac{1}{2}$-inch fillets is 12 minutes, with 15 minutes for 1-inch-thick steaks. The average baking times for $\frac{1}{2}$-inch fillets is 20 minutes and 30 minutes for 1-inch steaks. Downsized, nonstick broiling racks and baking pans make cleanup a snap. Broiling recipes for fish include Oven-Crisped Fish Fillets with Salsa, Catfish Kebabs, Snapper with Capers and Olives, and Light Trout Amandine. There is a great offering of baked fish recipes as well, including Mediterranean Baked Fish, Best-Dressed Trout, Rolled Asparagus Flounder, and Baked Tomato Pesto Bluefish. The toaster oven can produce not only delicious crisp-coated fish fillets with a slimming minimum of fat, but also poached fish, kebabs, appetizers, and much more.

Broiled Dill and Lemon Salmon

This recipe produces the best broiled salmon I've ever tasted. I found that if I did not have time to marinate the salmon, I could adjust the marinade ingredients, increasing the dill, lemon juice, and soy sauce and brushing the steaks with this mixture, and let them sit at room temperature for 10 minutes. By brushing the steaks again midbroiling, a depth of flavor is achieved without marinating.

Brushing mixture:
2 tablespoons lemon juice
2 tablespoons olive oil
1 tablespoon soy sauce
1 teaspoon dried dill or dill weed

$\frac{1}{2}$ teaspoon garlic powder
1 teaspoon soy sauce

2 6-ounce salmon steaks

COMBINE the brushing mixture ingredients in a small bowl and brush the salmon steak tops, skin side down, liberally, reserving the remaining mixture. Let the steaks sit at room temperature for 10 minutes, then place on a broiling rack with a pan underneath.

BROIL 15 minutes, remove from the oven, and brush the steaks with the remaining mixture. Broil again for 5 minutes, or until the meat flakes easily with a fork.

Prep: 5 minutes
Total time: 30 minutes
Serves 2

Roasted Pepper Tilapia

Tilapia or any mild-flavored, thin fish fillet (such as flounder or scrod) will work for this delectable appetizer recipe. Serve drizzled with dip or cut into 1-inch slices, insert a toothpick into each slice, and serve with the dip in a bowl.

6 5-ounce tilapia fillets
2 tablespoons olive oil

Filling:
1 cucumber, peeled, seeds scooped
  out and discarded, and chopped
$\frac{1}{2}$ cup chopped roasted peppers,
  drained
2 tablespoons lemon juice
2 tablespoons chopped fresh parsley
  or cilantro

1 teaspoon garlic powder
1 teaspoon paprika
Salt and freshly ground black pepper
  to taste

Dip mixture:
1 cup nonfat sour cream
2 tablespoons low-fat mayonnaise
3 tablespoons Dijon mustard
1 teaspoon Worcestershire sauce
1 teaspoon dried dill

COMBINE the filling ingredients in a bowl, adjusting the seasonings to taste.
SPOON equal portions of filling in the centers of the tilapia filets. Roll up the fillets, starting at the smallest end. Secure each roll with toothpicks and place the rolls

Continued

in an oiled or nonstick baking pan. Carefully brush the fillets with oil and place them in an oiled or nonstick $8\frac{1}{2} \times 8\frac{1}{2} \times 2$-inch square baking (cake) pan.

BROIL for 20 minutes, or until the fillets are lightly browned. Combine the dip mixture ingredients in a small bowl and serve with the fish.

Prep: 16 minutes
Total time: 36 minutes
Makes 6 tilapia rolls

Oven-Poached Salmon

Poached salmon may be served hot or cold. To serve hot, remove the fish from the poaching liquid, drain briefly on paper towels, and serve garnished with chopped watercress and lemon wedges. To serve cold, leave the fish in the poaching liquid for 15 to 20 minutes to allow the flavors from the liquid to be absorbed by the fish. Then drain briefly on paper towels and serve chilled with the garnishes or Cucumber Sauce.

Poaching liquid:
1 cup dry white wine
2 bay leaves
1 tablespoon mustard seed
Salt and freshly ground black pepper
   to taste

2 6-ounce salmon steaks
2 tablespoons fresh watercress,
   rinsed, drained, and chopped (for
   serving hot)
1 lemon, cut into small wedges (for
   serving hot)
Cucumber Sauce (recipe follows)

PREHEAT the toaster oven to 350°F.

COMBINE the poaching liquid ingredients with 1 cup water in a small bowl and set aside.

PLACE the salmon steaks in an oiled or nonstick $8\frac{1}{2} \times 8\frac{1}{2} \times 2$-inch square baking (cake) pan and pour enough poaching liquid over the steaks to barely cover them. Adjust the seasonings to taste.

BAKE, uncovered, for 20 minutes, or until the fish feels springy to the touch. Remove the bay leaves and serve the fish hot with watercress and lemon or cold with Cucumber Sauce.

Prep: 10 minutes
Total time: 30 minutes
Serves 2

Cucumber Sauce

1 cucumber, peeled, halved, seeds
  scooped out with a teaspoon and
  discarded, and finely chopped
$\frac{1}{2}$ teaspoon white vinegar
$\frac{1}{2}$ teaspoon honey
$\frac{1}{4}$ teaspoon salt

$\frac{1}{2}$ cup plain fat-free yogurt
$\frac{1}{2}$ cup fat-free or reduced-fat sour
  cream
1 tablespoon finely chopped fresh
  dill or 1 teaspoon dried dill weed

COMBINE the cucumber, vinegar, honey, and salt in a small bowl and set aside.
BLEND the yogurt, sour cream, and dill in a small bowl, add the cucumber mixture,
  and chill before serving.

Prep: 10 minutes
Makes 2 cups

Marinated Catfish

*This recipe so enhances the flavor of catfish, taking it to another level because of the
marinade. Spoon a generous amount of the marinade sauce over each portion of fillet.*

Marinade:
1 tablespoon olive oil
1 tablespoon lemon juice
$\frac{1}{4}$ dry white wine

1 tablespoon garlic powder
1 tablespoon soy sauce

4 6-ounce catfish fillets

COMBINE the marinade ingredients in an $8\frac{1}{2} \times 8\frac{1}{2} \times 4$-inch ovenproof baking dish.
  Add the fillets and let stand for 10 minutes, spooning the marinade over the fil-
  lets every 2 minutes.
BROIL the fillets for 15 minutes, or until the fish flakes easily with a fork.

Prep: 10 minutes
Total time: 20 minutes (marinade: 10 minutes)
Serves 4

Tasty Fillets with Poblano Sauce

This recipe works well with the thinner fillets like scrod, catfish, flounder, and the like. Poblano sauce gives the fish a bold, spicy flavor.

4 5-ounce thin fish fillets—perch, scrod, catfish, or flounder
1 tablespoon olive oil

Poblano sauce:
1 poblano chili, seeded and chopped
1 bell pepper, seeded and chopped

2 tablespoons chopped onion
5 garlic cloves, peeled
1 tablespoon flour
1 cup fat-free half-and-half
Salt to taste

PREHEAT the toaster oven to 350°F.
BRUSH the fillets with olive oil and transfer to an oiled or nonstick $8\frac{1}{2} \times 8\frac{1}{2} \times 2$-inch square baking (cake) pan. Set aside.
COMBINE the poblano sauce ingredients and process in a blender or food processor until smooth. Spoon the poblano sauce over the fillets, covering them well.
BAKE, uncovered, for 20 minutes, or until the fish flakes easily with a fork.

Prep: 15 minutes
Total time: 35 minutes
Makes $1\frac{1}{2}$ cups sauce

Mediterranean Baked Fish

Serve this quick and easy baked fish with Oven-Baked Rice (page 175) or Oven-Baked Barley (page 172).

Baking mixture:
1 tablespoon olive oil
2 tablespoons tomato paste
3 plum tomatoes, chopped
2 garlic cloves, minced
2 tablespoons capers
2 tablespoons pitted and chopped black olives

2 tablespoons chopped fresh basil leaves
2 tablespoons chopped fresh parsley

4 6-ounce fish fillets (red snapper, cod, whiting, sole, or mackerel)

PREHEAT the toaster oven to 350°F.

COMBINE the baking mixture ingredients in a small bowl. Set aside.

LAYER the fillets in an oiled or nonstick 8½ × 8½ × 2-inch square baking (cake) pan, overlapping them if necessary, and spoon the baking mixture over the fish.

BAKE, covered, for 25 minutes, or until the fish flakes easily with a fork.

Prep: 10 minutes
Total time: 35 minutes
Serves 4

Light Trout Amandine

In adapting the traditional recipe for a lower fat content, I heightened the flavors with Worcestershire sauce and lemon juice and deepened them by adding almonds, which toast while the trout browns in the broiler.

1 tablespoon margarine
½ cup sliced almonds
1 tablespoon lemon juice
1 teaspoon Worcestershire sauce

Salt and freshly ground black pepper
4 6-ounce trout fillets
2 tablespoons chopped fresh parsley

COMBINE the margarine and almonds in an oiled or nonstick 8½ × 8½ × 2-inch square baking (cake) pan.

BROIL for 5 minutes, or until the margarine is melted. Remove the pan from the oven and add the lemon juice and Worcestershire sauce. Season to taste with salt and pepper, and stir again to blend well. Add the trout fillets and spoon the mixture over them to coat well.

BROIL for 10 minutes, or until the almonds and fillets are lightly browned. Garnish with the chopped parsley before serving.

Prep: 5 minutes
Total time: 20 minutes
Serves 4

Oven-Crisped Fish Fillets with Salsa

If you like crisply fried fish but don't like the calories and fat, try this oven-crisped fish! Preheating the pan helps make the fish coating crisp. Use thinner filets, such as trout, catfish, tilapia, scrod, or flounder. Serve with Black Bean Tomato Salsa (recipe follows) and add a green salad to complete the meal. If you prefer a very crisp coating, broil until crisped to your preference.

Coating ingredients:
1 cup cornmeal
1 teaspoon garlic powder
1 teaspoon ground cumin
1 teaspoon paprika
Salt to taste

4 6-ounce fish fillets, approximately
   ¼ to ½ inch thick
2 tablespoons vegetable oil

COMBINE the coating ingredients in a small bowl, blending well. Transfer to a large plate, spreading evenly over the surface. Brush the fillets with vegetable oil and press both sides of each fillet into the coating.

BROIL an oiled or nonstick 8½ × 8½ × 2-inch square baking (cake) pan for 1 or 2 minutes to preheat. Remove the pan and place the fillets in the hot pan, laying them flat.

BROIL for 7 minutes, then remove the pan from the oven and carefully turn the fillets with a spatula. Broil for another 7 minutes, or until the fish flakes easily with a fork and the coating is crisped to your preference. Serve immediately.

Prep: 15 minutes
Total time: 29 minutes
Serves 4

Black Bean Tomato Salsa

This is a great accompaniment for broiled chicken or steaks, or as a dip for nachos. Make this salsa ahead of time and keep it chilled in the refrigerator for a day or two to improve the flavor. Make your own low-fat, less-sodium nachos by cutting flour tortillas into triangles and baking them in a shallow baking pan at 400° F. for 8 minutes, or until crisp.

1 garlic bud, roasted, peeled, and mashed (page 75)

1 cup or 1 15-ounce can black beans, drained and rinsed

$\frac{1}{2}$ cup finely chopped onion

1 cup finely chopped fresh tomato

2 tablespoons tomato paste

$\frac{1}{2}$ cup finely chopped green or red bell pepper

1 tablespoon finely chopped fresh cilantro

1 teaspoon chili powder

3 tablespoons lemon juice

Salt and freshly ground black pepper to taste

COMBINE all the ingredients in a medium bowl, stirring well to blend, and adjust the seasonings to taste. Chill before serving.

Total time: 10 minutes
Serves 4

Rolled Asparagus Flounder

To cut off the tough part of the asparagus stem, start at the end of the asparagus stalk where it is the toughest and most fibrous and continue making slices every $\frac{1}{8}$ inch or so until the stalk is tender. Any thin-fillet fish (trout, scrod, catfish, or tilapia) works well in this recipe.

1 dozen asparagus stalks, tough stem part cut off

4 6-ounce flounder fillets

4 tablespoons chopped scallions

4 tablespoons shredded carrots

4 tablespoons finely chopped almonds

1 teaspoon dried dill weed

Salt and freshly ground black pepper

1 lemon, cut into wedges

PREHEAT the toaster oven to 400° F.

PLACE 3 asparagus stalks lengthwise on a flounder fillet. Add 1 tablespoon scallions, 1 tablespoon carrots, 1 tablespoon almonds, and a sprinkling of dill. Season to taste with salt and pepper and roll the fillet together so that the long edges overlap. Secure the edges with toothpicks or tie with cotton string. Carefully place the rolled fillet in an oiled or nonstick $8\frac{1}{2} \times 8\frac{1}{2} \times 2$-inch square baking (cake) pan. Repeat the process for the remaining ingredients. Cover the pan with aluminum foil.

BAKE, covered, for 20 minutes, or until the asparagus is tender. Remove the cover.

Continued

BROIL, uncovered, for 10 minutes, or until the fish is lightly browned. Remove and discard the toothpicks or string. Serve the rolled filets with lemon wedges.

Prep: 10 minutes
Total time: 40 minutes
Serves 4

Fish with Sun-Dried Tomato Pesto

A mildly tart tomato coating adds a wonderful flavor to the fish fillets. Only 1 table-spoon of reduced-fat mayonnaise goes a long way in producing a rich flavor.

Tomato sauce:
$1/4$ cup chopped sun-dried tomatoes
2 tablespoons chopped fresh basil
$2/3$ cup dry white wine
2 tablespoons grated Parmesan cheese
2 tablespoons olive oil
1 tablespoon pine nuts
2 garlic cloves
Salt and freshly ground black pepper
  to taste

4 6-ounce fish fillets (trout, catfish, flounder, or tilapia)
1 tablespoon reduced-fat mayon-naise
2 tablespoons chopped fresh cilantro
Olive oil

PREHEAT the toaster oven to 400° F.
PROCESS the tomato sauce ingredients in a blender or food processor until smooth.
LAYER the fish fillets in an oiled or nonstick $8^1/2 \times 8^1/2 \times 2$-inch square baking (cake) pan. Spoon the sauce over the fish, spreading evenly.
BAKE, uncovered, for 25 minutes, or until the fish flakes easily with a fork. Remove from the oven, spread the mayonnaise on top of the fish, and garnish with the cilantro.
BROIL for 6 minutes, or until lightly browned.

Prep: 15 minutes
Total time: 46 minutes
Serves 4

Catfish Kebabs

Use any thin fillet that can be rolled, including flounder, trout, cod, and tilapia. Plum tomatoes work best because they are firmer and keep together on the skewer. The onions will become pleasantly sweet in broiling, a nice contrast to the tomatoes and fish. Cut firm or crisp items like onions, peppers, broccoli, and the like a little smaller than softer, moister items like meat, fish, poultry, tomatoes, and squash. Gauging the size this way will help cook everything to completion at the same time. For a fuller, richer flavor, prepare the marinade the evening before and let the fish marinate all day in the refrigerator.

Marinade:
3 tablespoons lemon juice
3 tablespoons tomato juice
2 garlic cloves, minced
2 tablespoons olive oil
1 teaspoon soy sauce

4 5-ounce catfish fillets
4 9-inch metal skewers
2 plum tomatoes, quartered
1 onion, cut into 1 × 1-inch pieces

COMBINE the marinade ingredients in a small bowl. Set aside.

CUT the fillets into 2 by 3-inch strips and place in a shallow glass or ceramic dish. Add the marinade and refrigerate, covered, for at least 20 minutes. Remove the strips from the marinade, roll, and skewer, alternating the rolled strips with the tomatoes and onion.

BRUSH the kebabs with marinade, reserving the remaining marinade for brushing again later. Place the skewers on a broiling rack with a pan underneath.

BROIL for 10 minutes, then remove the pan from the oven and carefully turn the skewers. Brush the kebabs with the marinade and broil again for 10 minutes, or until browned.

Prep: 15 minutes
Total time: 35 minutes (marinade: 20 minutes)
Serves 4

Best-Dressed Trout

One autumn evening many years ago, I had the best-dressed trout I'd ever tasted at a restaurant in Bar Harbor, Maine. Alas, the restaurant is long gone, but I set about trying to duplicate the flavor and I think I've come pretty close with this recipe. "Dressed" means the fish is whole, the innards have been removed, and often the fins, head, and tail are left on. This makes the fish ideal for stuffing. There is really no stuffing here, simply two slices of lemon. My own preference is to remove the head (with a sharp knife, cutting directly behind the gills), tail, and fins (with a good pair of scissors). The extra preparation is well worth it for anyone who appreciates the exquisite flavor of trout. Smoked paprika (pimenton ahumado), which is available in the ethnic (Latin) food section in the grocery store, adds a rich color and flavor to the trout.

2 dressed trout
1 egg, beaten
2 tablespoons finely ground almonds
2 tablespoons unbleached flour
1 teaspoon paprika or smoked
  paprika

Pinch of salt (optional)
4 lemon slices, approximately $\frac{1}{4}$
  inch thick
1 teaspoon lemon juice

PREHEAT the toaster oven to 400° F.

BRUSH the trout (both sides) with the beaten egg. Blend the almonds, flour, paprika, and salt in a bowl and sprinkle both sides of the trout. Insert 2 lemon slices in each trout cavity and place the trout in an oiled or nonstick $8\frac{1}{2} \times 8\frac{1}{2} \times 2$-inch square baking (cake) pan.

BAKE for 20 minutes, or until the meat is white and firm. Remove from the oven and turn the trout carefully with a spatula.

BROIL for 5 minutes, or until the trout is lightly browned.

Prep: 10 minutes
Total time: 35 minutes
Serves 2

Snapper with Capers and Olives

Olives, capers, and a shading of oregano enhance the flavor of snapper. Garnish with fresh tomato wedges.

2 tablespoons capers
$\frac{1}{4}$ cup pitted and sliced black olives
2 tablespoons olive oil
$\frac{1}{2}$ teaspoon dried oregano

Salt and freshly ground black pepper
  to taste
2 6-ounce red snapper fillets
1 tomato, cut into wedges

COMBINE the capers, olives, olive oil, and seasonings in a bowl.

PLACE the fillets in an oiled or nonstick $8\frac{1}{2} \times 8\frac{1}{2} \times 2$-inch square baking (cake) pan and spoon the caper mixture over them.

BROIL for 10 minutes, or until the fish flakes easily with a fork. Serve with the tomato wedges.

Prep: 5 minutes
Total time: 15 minutes
Serves 2

Crispy Pecan Fish

Even those of us who are not particularly fond of fish like Crispy Pecan Fish. The toasted nutty coating makes the fish almost irresistible, especially with a good old standby like tartar sauce (a low-fat version follows).

3 tablespoons multigrain bread
  crumbs
3 tablespoons ground pecans
4 6-ounce fish fillets, approximately
  $\frac{1}{4}$ inch thick

1 egg white, whisked until frothy
1 tablespoon olive oil
Salt and freshly ground black pepper
  to taste

COMBINE the bread crumbs and pecans in a small bowl and transfer to a platter or plate.

BRUSH both sides of the fillets with egg white and dredge in the bread crumb/pecan mixture. Transfer the fillets to an oiled or nonstick $8\frac{1}{2} \times 8\frac{1}{2} \times 2$-inch square baking (cake) pan.

Continued

BROIL for 10 minutes. Remove from the oven and carefully turn the fillets with a spatula. Broil again for 10 minutes, or until the fillets are lightly browned. Season to taste with the salt and pepper.

Prep: 10 minutes
Total time: 30 minutes
Serves 4

Low-Fat Tartar Sauce

2 tablespoons sweet pickle relish, drained well
1 cup (8-ounce carton) nonfat sour cream

2 tablespoons low-fat mayonnaise
$\frac{1}{4}$ teaspoon garlic powder
Salt to taste

Total time: 8 minutes
Makes approximately 1 cup

Spiced Sea Bass

Brushing with a lemon/garlic/parsley mixture and spicy seasonings combine to flavor sea bass fillets. I like to serve this highly seasoned fish with mellow Yellow Squash with Bell Peppers (page 70) or Yogurt Zucchini with Onion (page 69).

Brushing mixture:
2 tablespoons lemon juice
1 tablespoon chopped fresh parsley
2 garlic cloves, minced

2 6-ounce sea bass fillets, approximately 1 inch thick

Spice mixture:
2 teaspoons paprika
2 teaspoons ground cumin
1 teaspoon allspice
2 teaspoons garlic powder
Pinch of cayenne
Salt to taste

COMBINE the brushing mixture ingredients in a small bowl, mixing well. Place the fillets on a plate or platter.
BRUSH the fillets on both sides with the brushing mixture. Let stand at room temperature for 10 minutes.
COMBINE the spice mixture ingredients in a small bowl, mixing well. Transfer to a

plate and press the fillets into the spice mixture to coat well. Transfer the fillets to an oiled or nonstick $8\frac{1}{2} \times 8\frac{1}{2} \times 2$-inch square baking (cake) pan.

BROIL for 15 minutes, or until the fish flakes easily with a fork.

> *Prep:* 10 minutes
> *Total time:* 25 minutes
> Serves 4

Stuffed Baked Red Snapper

A filling of shrimp flavored with anchovy paste heightens snapper in a rich-tasting egg and sherry sauce. Unique flavors mingle into one delicious taste.

Stuffing mixture:
12 medium shrimp, cooked, peeled, and chopped
2 tablespoons multigrain bread crumbs
1 teaspoon anchovy paste
$\frac{1}{4}$ teaspoon paprika
Salt to taste

2 6-ounce red snapper fillets
1 egg
$\frac{1}{2}$ cup fat-free half-and-half
2 tablespoons cooking sherry

PREHEAT the toaster oven to 350°F.

COMBINE all the stuffing mixture ingredients in a medium bowl and place a mound of mixture on one end of each fillet. Fold over the other fillet end, skewering the edge with toothpicks.

PLACE the rolled fillets in an oiled or nonstick $8\frac{1}{2} \times 8\frac{1}{2} \times 2$-inch square baking (cake) pan.

WHISK the egg in a small bowl until light in color, then whisk in the half-and-half and sherry. Pour over the fillets. Cover the pan with aluminum foil.

BAKE for 30 minutes.

> *Prep:* 15 minutes
> *Total time:* 45 minutes
> Serves 2

Baked Tomato Pesto Bluefish

Bluefish is a distinctly flavored fish similar to mackerel or lake trout. Good just broiled with a bit of olive oil and garlic, bluefish is better tempered with tomato and best with a pesto!

Pesto:
2 plum tomatoes
2 tablespoons tomato paste
$\frac{1}{4}$ cup fresh basil leaves
1 tablespoon olive oil
2 garlic cloves

2 tablespoons pine nuts
$\frac{1}{4}$ cup grated Parmesan cheese
1 teaspoon dried oregano
Salt to taste

2 6-ounce bluefish fillets

PREHEAT the toaster oven to 400° F.

PROCESS the pesto ingredients in a blender or food processor until smooth.

PLACE the bluefish fillets in an oiled or nonstick $8\frac{1}{2} \times 8\frac{1}{2} \times 2$-inch square baking (cake) pan.

BAKE, covered, for 15 minutes, or until the fish flakes with a fork. Remove from the oven, uncover, and spread the pesto mixture on both sides of the fillets.

BROIL, uncovered, for 8 minutes, or until the pesto is lightly browned.

Prep: 12 minutes
Total time: 35 minutes
Serves 2

Chapter 10

Seafood

If you love seafood, you'll love your toaster oven! Skewered shrimp, baked mussels, and broiled scallops are all done easily. The toaster oven is on the countertop and very accessible for skewering, basting, and brushing. As an added plus, toaster ovens emit less than half the heat of a large oven so you really won't have to sweat over preparing a beautiful seafood meal. Sauces and dips compliment many of the seafood recipes here and there are a wide variety of entrées and appetizers, including a crab stuffing for peppers, crispy crab cakes, shrimp-filled romaine wraps, coconut-crusted shrimp, and broiled calamari flavored with Japanese miso. Lobster tails are brushed with a flavorful thyme/lemon mixture that replaces high-fat butter sauce and simple but elegant clam appetizers are baked to perfection in their shells. The subtle flavors of seafood, enhanced by baking or broiling, are showcased in these easy preparation recipes. Use the index in the first chapter of this book as a reference for estimated cooking times for seafood.

Baked Parsley Mussels with Zucchini

Domestic mussels are cleaner and safer to consume than wild mussels, which are often harvested from polluted waters. Preparing fresh mussels is one of the few procedures in this cookbook that cannot be done in a toaster oven! Rinse them in cold water, discarding any with broken shells or mussels that are open. Fill a large pot with salted water and bring it to a boil, then add the mussels and boil them for several minutes. Transfer them to a colander or sieve to drain well, then pick through them, discarding any that haven't opened. Gently pull the rest from their shells. Now they are ready to be combined with the other ingredients.

I like to serve this dish with rounds of crusty Italian bread. Slice the bread diago-nally, brush with olive oil, wrap in aluminum foil, and bake at 350° F. for 10 minutes. To brown the bread, open the aluminum foil on top and return to the toaster oven to bake for another 5 minutes.

2 pounds (approximately 40) mus-sels, cooked, shells discarded

4 small zucchini squash, scrubbed, halved, and cut lengthwise into ½-inch-wide strips

½ cup dry white wine

1 tablespoon chopped fresh oregano or 1 teaspoon dried oregano

2 garlic cloves, minced

¼ cup chopped fresh Italian parsley

2 tablespoons olive oil

Freshly ground black pepper to taste

¼ cup grated low-fat Parmesan cheese

PREHEAT the toaster oven to 350° F.

COMBINE all the ingredients except the Parmesan cheese in a 1-quart 8½ × 8½ × 4-inch ovenproof baking dish, mixing well. Adjust the seasonings to taste and cover with aluminum foil.

BAKE for 35 minutes, or until the zucchini is tender. Uncover and sprinkle with Parmesan cheese.

BROIL for 5 minutes, or until the cheese is melted and the top is lightly browned.

Prep: 10 minutes

Total time: 50 minutes

Serves 6

Broiled Lemon Coconut Shrimp

To butterfly shrimp, deepen the cut made by deveining and spread at the slice, pressing the shrimp flat (leave the shrimp tail on). Grated unsweetened coconut, often used in Indian or Indonesian cooking, can be found in most health food, gourmet, or food specialty stores.

Brushing mixture:

2 tablespoons lemon juice

4 tablespoons olive oil

1 tablespoon grated lemon zest

Salt to taste

1 pound fresh shrimp, peeled, deveined, and butterflied

½ cup grated unsweetened coconut

COMBINE the brushing mixture ingredients in a small bowl. Add the shrimp and toss to coat well. Set aside.

PLACE the coconut on a plate, spreading it out evenly.

PRESS each shrimp into the coconut, coating well on all sides. Place the shrimp in an $8\frac{1}{2} \times 8\frac{1}{2} \times 2$-inch oiled or nonstick square (cake) pan.

BROIL the shrimp for 5 minutes, turn with tongs, and broil for 5 more minutes, or until browned lightly.

Prep: 15 minutes
Total time: 25 minutes
Serves 4

Skewered Salsa Verde Shrimp

Salsa verde or tomatillo salsa is available in the ethnic foods section of the supermarket. Combined with cumin, cilantro, and yogurt, salsa verde imparts a rich flavor to the shrimp, while adding a light coating of moisture and color. A squeeze of lemon works to add one more splash to these flavors.

$1\frac{1}{2}$ pounds large fresh shrimp, peeled and deveined

Brushing mixture:
1 7-ounce can salsa verde
1 teaspoon ground cumin

$\frac{1}{2}$ teaspoon chopped fresh cilantro or parsley
1 teaspoon garlic powder
3 tablespoons plain yogurt
1 tablespoon olive oil

Lemon wedges

THREAD the shrimp onto the skewers.

COMBINE the brushing mixture ingredients in a small bowl. Adjust the seasonings and brush the shrimp with the mixture.

BROIL the shrimp for 4 minutes. Turn the skewers, brush the shrimp again, and broil for another 4 minutes, or until the shrimp are firm and cooked. Remove the shrimp from the skewers and serve with lemon wedges.

Prep: 15 minutes
Total time: 23 minutes
Serves 4

Shrimp with Jalapeño Dip

I serve this shrimp and dip with homemade nachos (see Chapter 2, "Sandwiches") and a Sangria wine cooler. Or, for a nonalcoholic beverage, try the juice of 3 limes and $^1/_2$ cup sugar dissolved in 32 ounces water—add crushed ice and mint sprigs.

Seasonings:
1 teaspoon ground cumin
1 tablespoon minced garlic
1 teaspoon paprika
1 teaspoon chili powder

Pinch of cayenne
Salt to taste

$1^1/_2$ pounds large shrimp, peeled and
  deveined

COMBINE the seasonings in a plastic bag, add the shrimp, and shake well to coat. Transfer the shrimp to an oiled or nonstick $8^1/_2 \times 8^1/_2 \times 2$-inch square baking (cake) pan.

BROIL for 5 minutes. Remove the pan from the oven and turn the shrimp with tongs. Broil 5 minutes again, or until the shrimp are cooked (they should be firm but not rubbery.) Serve with Jalapeño Dip (recipe follows).

Prep: 5 minutes
Total time: 15 minutes
Serves 4

Jalapeño Dip

Wear protective latex gloves when seeding and cutting hot peppers, since the capsaicin in them can irritate your skin. Make sure to wash your hands with soap and water after handling.

1 jalapeño pepper, seeded and finely
  chopped
2 tablespoons finely chopped onion
1 tablespoon finely chopped fresh
  cilantro

$^1/_2$ cup nonfat yogurt
$^1/_2$ cup reduced-fat sour cream
1 avocado, pitted, peeled, and sliced
Salt to taste

BLEND all the ingredients in a food processor or blender. Adjust the seasonings.

Prep: 10 minutes
Makes approximately $1^1/_2$ cups

Sangria

1 bottle (approximately 1 quart) dry
  red wine
$\frac{1}{2}$ cup orange liqueur
1 cup orange juice

$\frac{1}{4}$ cup lemon juice

1 bottle (approximately 1 quart)
  ginger ale
Orange slices

COMBINE all the ingredients except the ginger ale and orange slices in a pitcher and
  chill well. Before serving, add the ginger ale and garnish with orange slices.

Total time: 5 minutes
Makes 10 cups

Ginger Miso Calamari

*Miso lends itself so well to calamari, instilling a rich flavor without overwhelming the
delicate flavor. Miso, usually quite salty, is tempered and diluted here by the other ingredients. Japanese miso is available in health food or gourmet food stores. A seafood market
will clean the calamari for you—this involves removing the innards and ink sac. Most
supermarkets sell calamari already cleaned.*

15 ounces calamari, cleaned

Sauce:
2 tablespoons dry white wine
2 tablespoons white miso
1 tablespoon balsamic vinegar

1 teaspoon honey
1 teaspoon toasted sesame oil
1 teaspoon olive oil
1 tablespoon grated fresh ginger
Salt and white pepper to taste

SLICE the calamari bodies into $\frac{1}{2}$-inch rings, leaving the tentacles uncut. Set aside.
WHISK together the sauce ingredients in a bowl. Transfer the mixture to a baking
  pan and add the calamari, mixing well to coat.
BROIL for 20 minutes, turning with tongs every 5 minutes, or until cooked but not
  rubbery. Serve with the sauce.

Prep: 15 minutes
Total time: 25 minutes
Serves 4

Chilled Clam Cake Slices with Dijon Dill Sauce

Clam cake slices are a nice alternative to bread or rolls with a meal. Cut into small squares and with a toothpick inserted, they can be served as an appetizer with the sauce as a dip or an entrée with Roasted Vegetables (page 64).

1 10-ounce can minced clams, drained
1 egg
¾ cup multigrain bread crumbs
1 tablespoon vegetable oil
1 cup skim milk
¼ cup chopped onions

2 tablespoons chopped pimientos, drained
Salt and freshly ground black pepper to taste

Dijon Dill Sauce (recipe follows)

PREHEAT the toaster oven to 400° F.

COMBINE all the ingredients in a medium bowl, mixing well. Transfer to an 8½ × 8½ × 2-inch oiled or nonstick square (cake) pan.

BAKE for 30 minutes, or until the top is browned. Let cool, then chill the loaf in the refrigerator. Cut into thin slices or squares and serve with the sauce.

Prep: 12 minutes
Total time: 42 minutes
Serves 6

Dijon Dill Sauce

3 tablespoons low-fat sour cream
½ cup fat-free half-and-half
¼ teaspoon dill weed

2 tablespoons Dijon mustard
Salt and freshly ground black pepper to taste

COMBINE all the ingredients in a small bowl and mix well.

Prep: 5 minutes
Total time: 5 minutes
Makes approximately ¾ cup

Baked Clam Appetizers

If you don't have a collection of clamshells for this purpose, there are assortments of small inexpensive baking dishes that will be ideal for this appetizer. Serve with little forks and small lemon wedges.

1 6-ounce can minced clams, well drained
1 cup multigrain bread crumbs
1 tablespoon minced onion
1 teaspoon garlic powder

1 teaspoon Worcestershire sauce
1 tablespoon chopped fresh parsley
2 tablespoons olive oil
Salt and freshly ground black pepper
Lemon wedges

PREHEAT the toaster oven to 450° F.

COMBINE all the ingredients in a medium bowl and fill 12 scrubbed clamshells or small baking dishes with equal portions of the mixture. Place in an $8^1/_2 \times 8^1/_2 \times$ 2-inch oiled or nonstick square (cake) pan.

BAKE for 10 minutes, or until lightly browned.

Prep: 13 minutes
Total time: 23 minutes
Makes 12 appetizers

Scallops in Orange Sauce

The combination of the scallops, orange sauce, water chestnuts, and watercress is heavenly! If you can't find watercress, parsley is okay, but a bit ordinary for such a unique dish. Better candidates are chopped scallions or chives. The broiling of the sauce is important, because it blends the flavors well and reduces the liquid. Use a deep baking pan or baking dish for the sauce. Take care in placing the pan in the toaster oven and removing it. Don't forget to wear oven mitts!

Broiling mixture:
1 cup orange juice
1 teaspoon soy sauce
2 garlic cloves, finely minced
1 teaspoon grated orange zest

$1^1/_2$ pounds (3 cups) bay scallops, rinsed and drained
1 7-ounce can sliced water chestnuts, drained well
2 tablespoons chopped watercress

Continued

WHISK together the broiling mixture ingredients in a small bowl and transfer to an $8^{1}/_{2} \times 8^{1}/_{2} \times 2$-inch oiled or nonstick square (cake) pan.

BROIL the sauce for 10 minutes to reduce the liquid and meld the flavors. Remove the pan from the oven and add the scallops, spooning the sauce over them.

BROIL for 3 minutes, or until opaque. Serve the scallops with the sauce and garnish with the sliced water chestnuts and chopped watercress.

Prep: 15 minutes
Total time: 18 minutes
Serves 4

Capered Crab Cakes

Serve crab cakes with a Creamy Cucumber Sauce (recipe follows). The cucumber cools the crisp, spicy crab cakes, so be bold and add more hot sauce to the crab cakes! You can always cool off with cucumber.

1 pound fresh lump crabmeat,
  drained and chopped, or
  3 5-ounce cans good-quality
  lump crabmeat
1 cup bread crumbs
$^{1}/_{2}$ cup plain nonfat yogurt
1 tablespoon olive oil

2 tablespoons capers
1 tablespoon garlic powder
1 teaspoon hot sauce
1 egg, beaten
1 tablespoon Worcestershire sauce
Salt and freshly ground black pepper
  to taste

PREHEAT the toaster oven to 350°F.

COMBINE all the ingredients in a bowl. Shape the mixture into patties approximately $2^{1}/_{2}$ inches wide, adding more bread crumbs if the mixture is too wet and sticky and more yogurt if the mixture is too dry and crumbly. Place the patties in an $8^{1}/_{2} \times 8^{1}/_{2} \times 2$-inch oiled or nonstick square (cake) pan.

BAKE, uncovered, for 25 minutes.

BROIL for 5 minutes, until golden brown.

Prep: 8 minutes
Total time: 38 minutes
Serves 6

Creamy Cucumber Sauce

Remove the seeds of the cucumber by scooping out the center with a teaspoon.

$^1/_2$ cup nonfat plain yogurt
$^1/_2$ cup low-fat sour cream
1 cucumber, peeled, seeded, and chopped
1 teaspoon soy sauce

$^1/_2$ teaspoon garlic powder
$^1/_2$ teaspoon celery seed
Salt and white pepper to taste

Paprika

PROCESS all the ingredients except the paprika in a blender or food processor until smooth. Transfer to a serving bowl and sprinkle the top with paprika before serving with the crab cakes.

Total time: 10 minutes
Makes approximately 2 cups

Crab-Stuffed Peppers

Fresh crabmeat is, of course, the best to use. Superior in flavor and texture, even as stuffing for peppers, the difference is notable. There are, however, several varieties of canned crabmeat, so it's important to get the good-quality lump style. Some canned crabmeat is a fibrous, thready substance with little flavor and a very odd texture and appearance. A drizzle of Pimiento Sauce (recipe follows) over the stuffed peppers just before serving expands the spectrum of flavors and colors—the green and red are lovely!

Filling:
$1^1/_2$ cups fresh crabmeat, chopped, or 2 6-ounce cans lump crabmeat, drained
4 plum tomatoes, chopped
2 4-ounce cans sliced mushrooms, drained well
4 tablespoons pitted and sliced black olives

2 tablespoons olive oil
2 garlic cloves, minced
$^1/_2$ teaspoon ground cumin
Salt and freshly ground black pepper to taste

4 large bell peppers, tops cut off, seeds and membrane removed
$^1/_2$ cup shredded low-fat mozzarella cheese

PREHEAT the toaster oven to 375° F.

Continued

COMBINE the filling ingredients in a bowl and adjust the seasonings. Spoon the mixture to generously fill each pepper. Place the peppers upright in an $8^1/_2 \times 8^1/_2 \times$ 2-inch oiled or nonstick square (cake) pan.

BAKE for 40 minutes, or until the peppers are tender. Remove from the oven and sprinkle the cheese in equal portions on top of the peppers.

BROIL 5 minutes, or until the cheese is melted.

Prep: 10 minutes
Total time: 55 minutes
Serves 4

Pimiento Sauce

1 5-ounce jar pimientos, drained
well
1 5-ounce can tomato sauce
3 strips lean turkey bacon, cooked
and chopped
1 tablespoon olive oil

$^1/_2$ teaspoon garlic powder
1 plum tomato, chopped
1 teaspoon chili powder
Pinch of cayenne
Salt and butcher's pepper to taste

PROCESS all the ingredients in a blender or food processor until smooth. Drizzle over the peppers or transfer to a serving bowl with a small ladle to spoon the sauce over the peppers.

Prep: 10 minutes
Total time: 15 minutes
Makes approximately $1^1/_4$ cups sauce

Oysters Broiled in Wine Sauce

Prepare the sauce and shuck the oysters (or buy them already shucked) an hour or two ahead of time. Store in separate containers in the refrigerator, ready to be broiled for a first course to a sumptuous meal. Served as an entrée with Oven-Baked Rice (page 175), the sauce doubles as a delicious drizzle for the rice—a very tasty, low-fat meal! Fresh shucked oysters straight from the seafood counter are best to use for this recipe. Fresh oysters in plastic containers can be used also if they are drained well first. They are smaller and tend to be blander and softer in texture.

Sauce:

2 tablespoons margarine, at room
   temperature
1 cup dry white wine
3 garlic cloves, minced
Salt and freshly ground black pepper
   to taste

24 fresh oysters, shucked and
   drained

COMBINE the sauce ingredients in a 1-quart $8^{1}/_{2} \times 8^{1}/_{2} \times 4$-inch ovenproof baking dish and adjust the seasonings to taste.

BROIL the sauce for 5 minutes, remove the pan from the oven, and stir. Return to the oven and broil for another 5 minutes, or until the sauce begins to bubble. Remove from the oven and cool for 5 minutes. Add the oysters, spooning the sauce over them to cover thoroughly.

BROIL for 5 minutes, or until the oysters are just cooked.

Prep: 12 minutes
Total time: 32 minutes
Serves 2

Lobster Tails

If you have a small toaster oven, broil the lobster tails in pairs. Serve broiled lobster tails with small forks and lemon wedges. If you'd like to have a dipping sauce on the side, double or triple the brushing mixture amount and reserve a portion to heat in a baking pan for 5 minutes, or until it begins to bubble. Transfer to small dipping dishes and serve with the broiled lobster tails. Note: Wear oven mitts when handling the broiling rack and pan. Serve Lobster Tails with Classic Baked Potatoes (page 78) or Classic Stuffed Baked Potatoes (page 79).

Brushing mixture:

2 tablespoons lemon juice
2 tablespoons olive oil
$^{1}/_{2}$ teaspoon garlic powder
$^{1}/_{4}$ teaspoon ground thyme

4 6-ounce lobster tails

WHISK together the brushing mixture ingredients in a small bowl and set aside.

CUT the top of each lobster shell lengthwise from the top edge to the tail with a

Continued

sharp scissors. Place the lobster tails, cut side down, on a broiling rack with a pan underneath. Brush with the brushing mixture.

BROIL for 5 minutes. Remove from the oven and brush again. Broil for 5 minutes, or until the lobster flesh turns from translucent to opaque.

Prep: 15 minutes
Total time: 25 minutes
Serves 4

Broiled Scallops

Serve these broiled scallops with Oven-Baked Barley (page 172)—a delicious combination of flavors, each showcases the other in texture and taste and the sauce makes a nice drizzle for the barley. Watch the scallops carefully when broiling them. It doesn't take long for them to cook, just a few minutes. A good guideline is when they go from being translucent to opaque, they are done. Sea scallops can be used as well. If they are large, you may want to slice them into ¹/₂-inch pieces or adjust the broiling time to allow them to cook longer.

Broiling sauce:
2 tablespoons chopped fresh parsley
3 shallots, finely chopped
³/₄ cup white wine
3 tablespoons margarine, at room
  temperature
¹/₂ teaspoon dried thyme

3 tablespoons sesame seeds
Salt and freshly ground black pepper

1¹/₂ pounds (3 cups) bay scallops,
  rinsed and drained

WHISK together the ingredients for the broiling sauce in a small bowl and transfer to a 1-quart 8¹/₂ × 8¹/₂ × 4-inch ovenproof baking dish. Adjust the seasoning, add the scallops, and spoon the mixture over them.

BROIL for 3 minutes, or until all the scallops are opaque instead of translucent. Serve with the sauce.

Prep: 10 minutes
Total time: 13 minutes
Serves 6

Romaine Wraps with Shrimp Filling

This recipe was inspired by items that happened to be on my pantry shelf and in my refrigerator one day. I gathered them together on the countertop and began to visualize what I could create. I highly recommend this activity for honing your creative skills or just for some good old therapeutic fun. See what you can come up with! Romaine wraps are a great appetizer, chilled and cut into 1 1/2-inch slices. Or, unsliced, they are an excellent accompaniment with chicken or fish.

Filling:
1 6-ounce can tiny shrimp, drained, or 1 cup fresh shrimp, peeled, cooked, and chopped
3/4 cup canned chickpeas, mashed into 1 tablespoon olive oil
2 tablespoons chopped fresh parsley
2 tablespoons grated carrot
2 tablespoons chopped bell pepper

2 tablespoons minced onion
2 tablespoons lemon juice
1 teaspoon soy sauce
Freshly ground black pepper to taste

4 large romaine lettuce leaves
Olive oil
3 tablespoons lemon juice
1 teaspoon paprika

COMBINE the filling ingredients in a bowl, adjusting the seasonings to taste. Spoon equal portions of the filling into the centers of the romaine leaves. Fold the leaves in half, pressing the filling together, overlap the leaf edges, and skewer with toothpicks to fasten. Carefully place the leaves in an oiled or nonstick 8 1/2 × 8 1/2 × 2-inch square baking (cake) pan. Lightly spray or brush the lettuce rolls with olive oil.

BROIL for 8 minutes, or until the filling is cooked and the leaves are lightly browned. Remove from the oven, remove the toothpicks, and drizzle with the lemon juice and sprinkle with paprika.

Prep: 20 minutes
Total time: 28 minutes
Serves 4

Chapter 11

Casseroles

Casseroles, stews, chili, ragouts, gumbos, lasagne, baked beans, moussaka—all of the recipes in this chapter work with your toaster oven to produce complete meals in less than one hour. The majority involve simply combining the ingredients and then baking to completion. Macaroni for a tuna casserole is cooked in the toaster oven, drained, combined with the tuna casserole ingredients, and then baked. The entire ingredients for lasagne, including the uncooked noodles, are combined in a baking dish and baked in less than one hour. No boiling, cooking, sautéing, or browning beforehand! Everything is assembled, then baked. The convenience here is threefold: (1) short preparation time, (2) just an hour for baking—an hour you can use to assemble the rest of the meal—a salad, pasta, potatoes, vegetables, and so on, and (3) casseroles can be made ahead of time and stored in the refrigerator. Actually, they taste better the next day and most are at their best in two.

Easy Oven Lasagne

I was skeptical when I tested this recipe. Would everything really get baked all together and would real lasagne result? Any lasagne I'd made before required boiling the lasagna noodles, browning the meat, and assembling the layers carefully. Here, hard, uncooked noodles are lain like boards on the bottom of a baking dish, followed by a deluge of sauce and water in which raw ground meat, dollops of ricotta, and clumps of shredded mozzarella are swimming alongside little flotillas of basil and oregano! The toaster oven, once again, performs its magic. Slowly, through the baking, everything gets not only cooked, but also bakes beautifully. The lasagna noodles are tender and very tasty, having absorbed the water and some of the marinara sauce, while the meat is well done, min-

gling delectably with the cheeses, oregano, and basil. All of the laborious procedures I once attributed to lasagne are banished forever. Try this lasagne in your toaster oven! Assemble and arrange everything as directed, then let your toaster oven do the rest while you prepare the Rosemary Bread (page 179) and the Spinach Salad (recipe follows).

6 uncooked lasagna noodles, broken in half

1 15-ounce jar marinara sauce

$\frac{1}{2}$ pound ground turkey or chicken breast

$\frac{1}{2}$ cup part-skim ricotta cheese

$\frac{1}{2}$ cup shredded part-skim mozzarella cheese

2 tablespoons chopped fresh oregano leaves or 1 teaspoon dried oregano

2 tablespoons chopped fresh basil leaves or 1 teaspoon dried basil

1 tablespoon garlic cloves, minced

$\frac{1}{4}$ cup grated Parmesan cheese

Salt and freshly ground black pepper to taste

PREHEAT the toaster oven to 375°F.

LAYER in a 1-quart $8\frac{1}{2} \times 8\frac{1}{2} \times 4$-inch ovenproof baking dish in this order: 6 lasagna noodle halves, $\frac{1}{2}$ jar of the marinara sauce, $\frac{1}{2}$ cup water, half of the ground meat, half of the ricotta and mozzarella cheeses, half of the oregano and basil leaves, and half of the minced garlic. Repeat the layer, starting with the noodles. Cover the dish with aluminum foil.

BAKE, covered, for 50 minutes, or until the noodles are tender. Uncover, sprinkle the top with Parmesan cheese and bake for another 10 minutes, or until the liquid is reduced and the top is browned.

Prep: 15 minutes

Total time: 1 hour and 15 minutes

Serves 4

Spinach Salad

4 cups spinach leaves, rinsed, drained, and pulled apart into small pieces

2 tablespoons chopped Vidalia onion

2 hard-boiled eggs, peeled and chopped

2 tablespoons minced pimiento, drained well

2 tablespoons raspberry wine vinegar

3 tablespoons olive oil

2 tablespoons grated Parmesan cheese

Salt and freshly ground black pepper

Continued

TOSS together the spinach, onion, eggs, and pimiento with the vinegar and oil. Sprinkle with the Parmesan cheese and season to taste with salt and pepper.

Total time: 10 minutes
Serves 4

Tarragon Beef Ragout

When the nights get chilly and you've spent a good part of Saturday raking leaves, it's time for Tarragon Beef Ragout. It's easy to prepare in one step and when you finish your hot bath the ragout will be ready. Serve this ragout with Marjoram New Potatoes (page 85) and drizzle the ragout sauce on the potatoes.

1 pound lean round steak, cut across the grain of the meat into thin strips, approximately $1/4 \times 2$ inches
$1/2$ cup dry red wine
1 small onion, chopped
2 carrots, peeled and thinly sliced
2 plum tomatoes, chopped
1 celery stalk, chopped

1 10-ounce package frozen peas
3 garlic gloves, minced
1 tablespoon Dijon mustard
$1/2$ teaspoon ground cumin
$1/2$ teaspoon dried tarragon
Salt and freshly ground black pepper to taste

PREHEAT the toaster oven to 375° F.
COMBINE all the ingredients with $1/2$ cup water in an $8^1/2 \times 8^1/2 \times 4$-inch ovenproof baking dish. Adjust the seasonings. Cover with aluminum foil.
BAKE, covered, for 45 minutes, or until the beef, onion, and celery are tender. Remove the cover.
BROIL 8 minutes to reduce the liquid and lightly brown the top.

Prep: 12 minutes
Total time: 1 hour and 5 minutes
Serves 6

Classic Beef Stew

This is a one-step recipe that showcases the ability of the toaster oven to bake to perfection a wonderful medley of ingredients that takes no time at all to assemble and combine. Simply mix everything together in a baking dish and let it bake for 50 minutes. Beer and bay leaves give this stew a wonderful aromatic flavor. Serve this stew with slices of warm Country Bread (page 183) and Blackberry Pie (page 212) for dessert. Creamed Horseradish (recipe follows) is a great condiment with this stew.

1 1/2 cups dark beer
4 tablespoons unbleached flour
2 cups (approximately 1 pound) lean top round steak, cut into 1-inch cubes
1 cup peeled and coarsely chopped carrots
1 cup peeled and coarsely chopped potatoes

1/2 cup coarsely chopped onion
1 cup fresh or frozen peas
2 plum tomatoes, chopped
3 garlic cloves, minced
3 bay leaves
1/4 teaspoon ground cumin
Salt and butcher's pepper to taste

PREHEAT the toaster oven to 400° F.

WHISK together the beer and flour in a 1-quart 8 1/2 × 8 1/2 × 4-inch ovenproof baking dish. Add all the other ingredients and seasonings and mix well, adjusting the seasonings to taste. Cover the dish with aluminum foil.

BAKE, covered, for 50 minutes, or until the meat is cooked and the vegetables are tender. Remove the bay leaves before serving.

Prep: 20 minutes
Total time: 1 hour and 10 minutes
Serves 4

Creamed Horseradish

3 tablespoons horseradish
1 cup low-fat or nonfat sour cream

Salt and freshly ground black pepper to taste

COMBINE the ingredients in a small bowl, mixing well, and serve.

Spicy Oven-Baked Chili

Often, ground meat that is labeled "lean" still has a relatively high fat content of 7 to 10 percent. Buy ground chicken breast or turkey breast, or, if you prefer, beef, ground sirloin, or ground round that has a fat content of 2 or 3 percent. The very short preparation time and elegant simplicity of this recipe is based on very lean meat being combined with all of the other chili ingredients. If you prefer a veggie chili, substitute your favorite vegetables for the meat (approximately 2 cups coarsely chopped). Whether with meat or veggies, this chili will satisfy even the most discriminating chili lover and . . . it's all done in your toaster oven! Serve this chili with Nacho Chips (page 43) and a salad of chopped chicory (recipe follows).

1 pound lean ground turkey or
   ground chicken breast or
   1 pound lean ground sirloin or
   round steak
1 15-ounce can black beans, drained
1 8-ounce can tomato sauce
3/4 cup chopped onion

1/4 cup dry white wine
1 cup tomato salsa
1 tablespoon garlic powder
1 tablespoon chili powder
1/8 teaspoon cayenne
2 teaspoons unsweetened cocoa
Salt and butcher's pepper to taste

PREHEAT the toaster oven to 375°F.

COMBINE all the ingredients in a 1-quart 8½ × 8½ × 4-inch ovenproof baking dish and mix well. Adjust the seasonings to taste. Cover with aluminum foil.

BAKE, covered, for 30 minutes.

Prep: 10 minutes
Total time: 40 minutes
Serves 6

Chopped Chicory Salad

4 cups chicory, rinsed, drained well,
   and chopped
2 tablespoons chopped fresh cilantro
3 scallions, thinly sliced
3 tablespoons pitted and chopped
   kalamata olives

2 tablespoons olive oil
1 tablespoon balsamic vinegar
Salt and freshly ground black pepper
   to taste

TOSS the chicory, cilantro, and scallions in a large bowl. Combine the oil, vinegar, and salt and pepper in a small bowl and toss with the greens.

Total time: 10 minutes
Serves 4

Herbal Summer Casserole

Is it possible for a casserole to be pretty? This medley of yellow squash, red plum tomatoes, orange carrots, and green bell peppers is a spectrum of summer colors and flavors as well, with celery seed, caraway seeds, roasted garlic, and freshly ground pepper for accent. Serve with crusty Italian bread and Oven-Crisped Chicken (page 101).

4 small yellow (summer) squashes, cut into ³/₄-inch slices
1 green bell pepper, seeded and chopped
1 tablespoon roasted garlic, mashed in 1 tablespoon olive oil
¹/₄ cup seasoned bread crumbs
¹/₄ cup grated Parmesan cheese
¹/₄ cup chopped fresh parsley
2 tablespoons chopped fresh cilantro

2 tablespoons chopped onion
2 plum tomatoes, chopped
2 carrots, peeled and cut into ¹/₄-inch slices
2 tablespoons fresh lemon juice
¹/₂ teaspoon caraway seeds
¹/₄ teaspoon celery seed
Salt and freshly ground black pepper to taste

PREHEAT the toaster oven to 400°F.
COMBINE all the ingredients in a 1-quart 8¹/₂ × 8¹/₂ × 4-inch ovenproof baking dish, mixing well. Cover the dish with aluminum foil.
BAKE, covered, for 45 minutes, or until the vegetables are tender.

Prep: 15 minutes
Total time: 1 hour
Serves 4

One-Step Classic Goulash

As a child growing up in Minnesota, I consumed a lot of Mom's goulash. I have adapted her recipe here, right down to the fresh tomatoes, which are peeled easily by placing them in boiling water for a minute. Remove with tongs and, when cool enough to handle, peel by pulling the skin away from the flesh with a sharp paring knife. Later on, when I lived in Boston, I found out that this dish was called American Chop Suey. Whatever you call it, it probably is on your comfort food list, as it is on mine. If you are not sure, try this recipe to find out. One bite should immediately take you back to pleasant meals of your childhood, when you were debt free and without a cell phone.

1 cup elbow macaroni
1 cup (8-ounce can) tomato sauce
1 cup very lean ground round or
    sirloin
1 cup peeled and chopped fresh
    tomato
½ cup finely chopped onion

1 teaspoon garlic powder
Salt and freshly ground black pepper

Topping:
1 cup homemade bread crumbs
1 tablespoon margarine

PREHEAT the toaster oven to 400° F.

COMBINE all the ingredients, except the topping, with 2 cups water in a 1-quart 8½ × 8½ × 4-inch ovenproof baking dish and mix well. Adjust the seasonings to taste. Cover with aluminum foil.

BAKE, covered, for 50 minutes, or until the macaroni is cooked, stirring after 25 minutes to distribute the liquid. Uncover, sprinkle with bread crumbs, and dot with margarine.

BROIL for 6 minutes, or until the topping is lightly browned.

Prep: 10 minutes
Total time: 1 hour and 6 minutes
Serves 4

Fillets en Casserole

Any thin fish fillet will do for this delicious casserole (flounder, tilapia, catfish, or scrod). We usually think of fish as broiled or baked in a pan. En casserole, the fillets stay moist and absorb the flavors of the sauce. Serve this casserole with Oven-Baked Rice (page 175) and a Simple Green Salad (recipe follows).

½ cup multigrain bread crumbs
4 6-ounce fish fillets

Sauce:
2 tablespoons white wine
1 teaspoon Worcestershire sauce
1 teaspoon lemon juice

1 tablespoon vegetable oil
1 teaspoon Dijon mustard
Salt and freshly ground black pepper
  to taste

2 tablespoons capers

PREHEAT the toaster oven to 400°F.
LAYER the bottom of an oiled or nonstick 8½ × 8½ × 2-inch square baking (cake) pan with the bread crumbs and place the fillets on the crumbs.
COMBINE the sauce ingredients, mixing well, and spoon over the fillets. Sprinkle with the capers.
BAKE, covered, for 20 minutes, or until the fish flakes easily with a fork.

Prep: 10 minutes
Total time: 30 minutes
Serves 4

Simple Green Salad

2 cups chopped escarole, drained well
2 cups chopped romaine, drained
  well
1 carrot, peeled and grated
3 radishes, stemmed and thinly
  sliced
2 tablespoons chopped fresh parsley

2 tablespoons wine vinegar
2 tablespoons olive oil
1 tablespoon toasted sesame oil
Salt and freshly ground black pepper
  to taste

Total time: 15 minutes
Makes approximately 3 cups

Baked Picnic Pinto Beans

These beer-baked beans can be made ahead of time, stored in a covered baking dish in the refrigerator, and heated in a microwave or toaster oven just before leaving for a picnic. Wrapped in a heavy towel, the baking dish and its contents will still be hot even if the picnic is several hours' drive away. Canned beans are low in fat and an excellent source of vitamins, minerals, and fiber. Keep a variety of canned and dried pinto, navy, kidney, black, and garbanzos (chickpeas) on hand.

1 tomato, peeled and finely chopped	1 tablespoon ketchup
2 15-ounce cans pinto beans, drained	2 tablespoons molasses
	1 teaspoon Dijon mustard
6 lean turkey bacon strips, cooked, drained, and crumbled	1 teaspoon Worcestershire sauce
	1 teaspoon garlic powder
1 cup good-quality dark beer or ale	Salt and butcher's pepper to taste
3 tablespoons finely chopped onion	

PREHEAT the toaster oven to 375°F.

PEEL the tomato by immersing it in boiling water for 1 minute. Remove with tongs and when cool enough to handle, pull the skin away with a sharp paring knife. Chop and place in a 1-quart $8\frac{1}{2} \times 8\frac{1}{2} \times 4$-inch ovenproof baking dish. Add all the other ingredients, stirring to mix well. Adjust the seasonings to taste. Cover with aluminum foil.

BAKE, covered, for 40 minutes.

Prep: 15 minutes
Total time: 55 minutes
Serves 4

Classic Tuna Casserole

The macaroni is cooked in the toaster oven, drained, and combined with the other ingredients, then baked for 35 minutes. Basically, one dish is used for everything. With fat only from dotting the bread crumb topping with a tablespoon of margarine, this is indeed a healthy version of the traditional high-fat (cream for the white sauce) or high-sodium (a can of mushroom soup) versions. It still satisfies my comfort food needs, however, and I'm sure you will find it satisfying, too.

1 cup elbow macaroni

2 6-ounce cans tuna packed in
water, drained well and crumbled

1 cup frozen peas

1 6-ounce can button mushrooms,
drained

1 tablespoon margarine

Salt and freshly ground black pepper

1 cup fat-free half-and-half

4 tablespoons unbleached flour

1 teaspoon garlic powder

1 cup multigrain bread crumbs

PREHEAT the toaster oven to 400°F.

COMBINE the macaroni and 3 cups water in a 1-quart 8½ × 8½ × 4-inch ovenproof
baking dish, stirring to blend well. Cover with aluminum foil.

BAKE, covered, for 35 minutes, or until the macaroni is tender. Remove from the
oven and drain well. Return to the baking dish and add the tuna, peas, and mushrooms. Add salt and pepper to taste.

WHISK together the half-and-half, flour, and garlic powder in a small bowl until
smooth. Add to the macaroni mixture and stir to blend well.

BAKE, covered, for 25 minutes. Remove from the oven, sprinkle the top with the
bread crumbs, and dot with the margarine. Bake, uncovered, for 10 minutes, or
until the top is browned.

Prep: 15 minutes
Total time: 1 hour and 20 minutes
Serves 4

Chicken Gumbo

*This quintessential gumbo casserole is my low-fat adaptation of a recipe in an old
Southern cookbook I bought at a tag sale. When you adjust the seasonings, you may want
to add more hot sauce or perhaps you would prefer a little more cayenne. The seasoning
is up to you! Serve over Oven-Baked Rice (page 175).*

2 skinless, boneless chicken breast
halves, cut into 1-inch cubes

½ cup dry red wine

1 small onion, finely chopped

1 celery stalk, finely chopped

2 plum tomatoes, chopped

1 bell pepper, chopped

1 tablespoon minced fresh garlic

2 okra pods, stemmed, seeded, and
finely chopped

1 bay leaf

½ teaspoon hot sauce

½ teaspoon dried thyme

Salt and freshly ground black pepper
to taste

Continued

PREHEAT the toaster oven to 400° F.

COMBINE all the ingredients in a 1-quart 8½ × 8½ × 4-inch ovenproof baking dish. Adjust the seasonings to taste. Cover with aluminum foil.

BAKE, covered, for 40 minutes, or until the onion, pepper, and celery are tender. Discard the bay leaf before serving.

Prep: 20 minutes
Total time: 1 hour
Serves 4

Cornucopia Casserole

A rainbow of colors and flavors, this festive vegetable casserole harmonizes well with Sesame Chicken Breasts (page 93) or Spice-Rubbed Split Game Hen (page 97).

1 celery stalk, chopped
2 tablespoons chopped Vidalia onion
½ bell pepper, chopped
1 carrot, peeled and chopped
1 small zucchini, chopped
½ cup green beans, cut into 1-inch pieces
½ cup frozen peas
½ cup frozen corn
½ cup frozen broccoli florets
½ cup frozen cauliflower florets
2 tablespoons vegetable oil
1 teaspoon ground cumin
1 teaspoon garlic powder
½ teaspoon paprika
Salt and freshly ground black pepper to taste
½ cup finely chopped pecans
3 tablespoons grated Parmesan cheese

PREHEAT the toaster oven to 400° F.

COMBINE all the ingredients, except the pecans and Parmesan cheese, in a 1-quart 8½ × 8½ × 4-inch ovenproof baking dish and adjust the seasonings to taste. Cover with aluminum foil.

BAKE, covered, for 35 minutes, or until the vegetables are tender. Uncover, stir to distribute the liquid, and adjust the seasonings again. Sprinkle the top with the pecans and Parmesan cheese.

BROIL for 10 minutes, or until the pecans are lightly browned.

Prep: 20 minutes
Total time: 1 hour and 5 minutes
Serves 4

Scalloped Corn Casserole

I confess that the scalloped corn casserole made by my Swedish grandmother was, and still is, a wonderful comfort food for me. Without sacrificing anything but the fat, I have duplicated her recipe, eliminating the $^1/_2$ cup butter, adding an extra egg, and using fat-free half-and-half thickened by unbleached flour instead of heavy cream. I find that much mileage can be gotten out of a tablespoon of margarine by dotting the bread crumbs with it, then browning the top. The flavor of the margarine penetrates the bread crumbs and percolates down through the corn casserole, giving everything a rich, but not frightfully fattening, flavor.

Casserole mixture:
2 15-ounce cans corn
1 red bell pepper, chopped
$^1/_4$ cup chopped scallions
$^1/_2$ cup fat-free half-and-half
2 tablespoons unbleached flour
2 eggs
$^1/_2$ teaspoon chili powder

1 teaspoon ground cumin
1 teaspoon garlic powder
Salt and freshly ground black pepper
  to taste

$^1/_4$ cup multigrain seasoned bread
  crumbs
1 tablespoon margarine

PREHEAT the toaster oven to 400° F.

COMBINE all the casserole mixture ingredients in a 1-quart $8^1/_2 \times 8^1/_2 \times 4$-inch oven-proof baking dish, mixing well. Adjust the seasonings to taste. Cover with aluminum foil.

BAKE, covered, for 30 minutes, or until the pepper and onions are tender. Remove from the oven and uncover. Sprinkle with the bread crumbs and dot with the margarine.

BROIL for 8 minutes, or until the bread crumb topping is lightly browned.

Prep: 15 minutes
Total time: 53 minutes
Serves 4

Light Quiche Lorraine

If you like quiche, try this recipe and dare to compare it with the traditional ingredients. I think you'll prefer this one!

Crust:
1 ½ cups bread crumbs
1 tablespoon olive oil

Filling:
4 eggs
½ cup plain nonfat yogurt
2 tablespoons finely chopped scallions

¼ cup shredded low-fat mozzarella
4 strips lean turkey bacon, broiled, blotted with paper towels, and chopped
Salt and freshly ground black pepper to taste

PREHEAT the toaster oven to 350° F.

COMBINE the bread crumbs, 1 tablespoon water, and the oil in a small bowl and transfer to a pie pan, pressing the mixture flat, starting at the center and working out to the sides. Chill for at least 5 minutes in the refrigerator.

COMBINE the filling ingredients and pour into the chilled bread crumb mixture in the pie pan.

BAKE for 40 minutes, or until the center is firm and springy to the touch.

Prep: 15 minutes
Total time: 50 minutes
Serves 4

Light Beef Stroganoff

Would it be possible to make a stroganoff that had all the rich, creamy taste and texture of a traditional stroganoff but none of the fat? Yes, and in creating this recipe, I simplified the steps. Browning the steak strips is done in the broiler, requiring only one turn with tongs midbroiling. Replacing the traditional heavy cream is skim milk, low-fat cream cheese, and fat-free half-and-half whisked together with flour. In the baking, all blends together beautifully—the sauce thickens, the meat becomes tender, and the flavors mingle. Whether you serve this with Oven-Baked Rice (page 175) or Classic Baked Potatoes (page 78), the lovely (and not fattening) sauce can be spooned over either.

Sauce:

1 cup skim milk

1 cup fat-free half-and-half

2 tablespoons reduced-fat cream
  cheese, at room temperature

4 tablespoons unbleached flour

2 pounds lean round or sirloin
  steak, cut into strips 2 inches long
  and $\frac{1}{2}$ inch thick

Browning mixture:

1 tablespoon soy sauce

2 tablespoons spicy brown mustard

1 tablespoon olive oil

2 teaspoons garlic powder

Salt and freshly ground black pepper
  to taste

WHISK together the sauce ingredients in a medium bowl until smooth. Set aside.

COMBINE the beef strips and browning mixture ingredients in an oiled or nonstick
$8\frac{1}{2} \times 8\frac{1}{2} \times 2$-inch square baking (cake) pan.

BROIL for 8 minutes, or until the strips are browned, turning with tongs after 4
minutes. Transfer to a 1-quart $8\frac{1}{2} \times 8\frac{1}{2} \times 4$-inch ovenproof baking dish. Add the
sauce and mix well. Adjust the seasonings to taste. Cover with aluminum foil.

BAKE, covered, for 40 minutes, or until the meat is tender.

Prep: 15 minutes
Total time: 55 minutes
Serves 4

Harvest Chicken and Rice Casserole

There is a festive look about this dish and a traditional flavor, which seems to be appropriate for harvest-time meals. The pilgrims would probably have been as thankful for this nutritious sustenance as we were after hiking in the foothills one crisp fall day. Accompanying this casserole, I serve Corn Bread (page 184) and Maple-Glazed Pumpkin Pie (page 217).

4 skinless, boneless chicken thighs,
  cut into 1-inch cubes

$\frac{1}{2}$ cup brown rice

4 scallions, chopped

1 plum tomato, chopped

1 cup frozen peas

1 cup frozen corn

1 cup peeled and chopped carrots

2 tablespoons chopped fresh parsley

1 teaspoon mustard seed

1 teaspoon dried dill weed

$\frac{1}{4}$ teaspoon celery seed

Salt and freshly ground black pepper
  to taste

$\frac{1}{2}$ cup finely chopped pecans

Continued

PREHEAT the toaster oven to 400° F.

COMBINE all the ingredients, except the pecans, with 2½ cups water in a 1-quart 8½ × 8½ × 4-inch ovenproof baking dish. Adjust the seasonings to taste. Cover with aluminum foil.

BAKE, covered, for 45 minutes, or until the rice is tender, stirring after 20 minutes to distribute the liquid. When done, uncover and sprinkle the top with the pecans.

BROIL for 7 minutes, or until the pecans are browned.

Prep: 15 minutes
Total time: 1 hour and 7 minutes
Serves 4

Zucchini Casserole

Fresh oregano and basil add depth of flavor to the zucchini, but if they are not readily available, try steeping 1 teaspoon dried oregano and 1 teaspoon dried basil in 2 tablespoons boiling water for 5 minutes. Drain through a tea strainer and add to the casserole ingredients. I've found that this steeping method will enliven the flavors of dried seasonings when fresh are not available.

4 small zucchini squashes, halved and quartered
2 plum tomatoes, quartered
1 8-ounce can tomato sauce
2 tablespoons chopped onion
2 garlic cloves, minced
1 tablespoon olive oil

1 tablespoon chopped fresh oregano
1 tablespoon chopped fresh basil
2 tablespoons pine nuts (pignoli)
Salt and freshly ground black pepper to taste
½ cup shredded low-fat mozzarella cheese

PREHEAT the toaster oven to 400° F.

COMBINE all the ingredients, except the mozzarella cheese, in a 1-quart 8½ × 8½ × 4-inch ovenproof baking dish. Cover with aluminum foil.

BAKE, covered, for 30 minutes, or until the zucchini is tender. Uncover and sprinkle the top with the cheese.

BROIL for 7 minutes, or until the cheese is melted and lightly browned.

Prep: 10 minutes
Total time: 47 minutes
Serves 4

Chicken Marengo

I remember having enjoyed Chicken Marengo in a restaurant in New York City many years ago. The name of the restaurant is long gone from my memory, but I can still visualize the pale blue tablecloths, little tin lamps with flickering candles on the tables, and this delectable dish! I have lightened the fat content of the ingredients, but did not compromise the wonderful combinations of flavors: the landscape of shrimp, chicken, tomato, wine, and tarragon basking in a sunlight of sliced hard-boiled eggs dappled with black olives and parsley. Poetry for the palate!

Chicken mixture:
2 skinless, boneless chicken breast
  halves, cut into 1 × 1-inch pieces
6 large shrimp, peeled, deveined,
  and cut into 1 × 1-inch pieces
2 plum tomatoes, chopped
1 tablespoon olive oil
$\frac{1}{2}$ cup dry white wine
3 garlic cloves, chopped
6 fresh mushrooms, rinsed quickly,
  patted dry, and thinly sliced

1 teaspoon dried tarragon
1 tablespoon chopped fresh parsley
Salt and freshly ground black pepper
  to taste
2 hard-boiled eggs, peeled and
  sliced
$\frac{1}{2}$ cup pitted and sliced black olives
2 tablespoons chopped fresh parsley

PREHEAT the toaster oven to 375° F.

COMBINE the chicken mixture ingredients in a 1-quart $8\frac{1}{2}$ × $8\frac{1}{2}$ × 4-inch oven-proof baking dish and adjust the seasonings to taste. Cover with aluminum foil.

BAKE, covered, for 30 minutes, or until the chicken and shrimp are tender.

GARNISH with slices of hard-boiled eggs, black olives, and parsley.

Prep: 15 minutes
Total time: 45 minutes
Serves 4

Lima Bean and Artichoke Casserole

The subtle vinegar of marinated artichokes lightens the lima beans, and the onions, carrots, and roasted peppers give this casserole a variation of flavors and textures. Serve chilled with salad greens or heated with fish, meat, or poultry.

1 15-ounce can lima beans, drained
1 6-ounce jar artichokes, marinated
  in olive oil (include the oil)
$\frac{1}{2}$ cup dry white wine
1 small onion, thinly sliced
2 medium carrots, thinly sliced
1 5-ounce can roasted peppers,
  drained and chopped

$\frac{1}{4}$ teaspoon paprika
$\frac{1}{2}$ teaspoon ground cumin
1 teaspoon curry powder
Salt and freshly ground black pepper
  to taste

PREHEAT the toaster oven to 350° F.

COMBINE all the ingredients in a 1-quart $8\frac{1}{2} \times 8\frac{1}{2} \times 4$-inch ovenproof baking dish, blending well. Adjust the seasonings to taste. Cover with aluminum foil.

BAKE, covered, for 40 minutes, or until the carrots and onion are tender.

Prep: 15 minutes
Total time: 55 minutes
Serves 4

Pork and Brown Rice Casserole

I adapted this recipe from one in a very old cookbook, the theme of which is "a good cook always gets her man." The recipes are traditionally hearty but high in fat content. For this recipe, I deleted the potatoes and added uncooked brown rice, substituted plum tomatoes and zucchini for the slab bacon, and omitted altogether the browning of the pork in pork fat. I also added some lovely spices: cumin, ginger, and bay leaves. After all the changes, this dish has garnered kudos from male and female dinner guests alike. The key here is to use very lean pork because everything is combined uncooked and baked to completion. The uncooked rice absorbs the liquid from the wine and tomato sauce, and all inherit the deep, rich flavor of the sauce and spices. As it's a meal in itself, very little needs to accompany this casserole. I like to serve it with Pepper Slaw (page 117) and slices of pumpernickel bread.

2 very lean 6-ounce boneless pork
  chops, cut into 1-inch cubes
$1/2$ cup brown rice
1 cup chunky tomato sauce
$1/2$ cup dry white wine
3 tablespoons finely chopped onion
2 small zucchini squashes, finely
  chopped

2 plum tomatoes, chopped
$1/2$ teaspoon ground cumin
$1/2$ teaspoon ground ginger
1 teaspoon garlic powder
2 bay leaves
Salt and freshly ground black pepper

PREHEAT the toaster oven to 400° F.

COMBINE all the ingredients in a 1-quart $8^1/_2 \times 8^1/_2 \times 4$-inch ovenproof baking dish.
Cover with aluminum foil.

BAKE, covered, for 45 minutes, or until the rice is cooked to your preference.
Discard the bay leaves before serving.

Prep: 15 minutes
Total time: 1 hour
Serves 4

Baked Tomato Casserole

Easy to prepare, this tomato casserole lends itself well to many ways of serving. It is great tossed with pasta, as a warm condiment for steak or chicken dishes, or as a dip for sliced Italian bread rounds that have been sprinkled with Parmesan cheese and toasted twice. I like the texture of unpeeled chopped tomatoes, but peeling them is a simple process and takes only a few minutes. Place the tomatoes in boiling water for a minute, remove them with tongs, and when they are cool enough to handle, gently pull the skin from the flesh with your fingers or with the aid of a sharp paring knife.

Casserole mixture:
1 medium onion, coarsely chopped
3 medium tomatoes, coarsely
  chopped
1 medium green pepper, coarsely
  chopped
2 garlic cloves, minced
$1/2$ teaspoon crushed oregano

$1/2$ teaspoon crushed basil
1 tablespoon extra virgin olive oil
2 tablespoons chopped fresh cilantro
Salt and freshly ground black pepper
4 tablespoons grated Parmesan
  cheese
$1/4$ cup multigrain bread crumbs

Continued

PREHEAT the toaster oven to 400°F.

COMBINE the casserole mixture ingredients in a 1-quart 8½ × 8½ × 4-inch oven-proof baking dish. Adjust the seasonings to taste and cover with aluminum foil.

BAKE, covered, for 35 minutes, or until the tomatoes and pepper are tender. Remove from the oven, uncover, and sprinkle with the bread crumbs and Parmesan cheese.

BROIL for 10 minutes, or until the topping is lightly browned.

Prep: 10 minutes
Total time: 55 minutes
Serves 4

Moussaka

Moussaka is essentially layer upon layer of wonderful textures and delightful flavors. The eggy, crusty topping should be well browned. In light and tart contrast with the dense, rich moussaka, I like to serve Marinated Cucumbers and Carrots (recipe follows). One needs little else to complete this meal, except maybe a glass of wine!

2 cups eggplant, peeled and cut into
   1-inch cubes

Beef mixture:
1 pound very lean ground beef
2 tablespoons finely chopped onion
4 tablespoons tomato paste
¼ cup dry red wine
2 tablespoons finely chopped fresh
   parsley
¼ teaspoon ground cinnamon
Salt and freshly ground black pepper
   to taste

Cheese mixture:
2 eggs, beaten
1 tablespoon unbleached flour
½ cup fat-free half-and-half
¼ teaspoon grated nutmeg
1 cup low-fat ricotta cheese

Bread crumb mixture:
1 cup multigrain bread crumbs
1 cup freshly grated Parmesan
   cheese

Olive oil

PREHEAT the toaster oven to 375°F.

DISSOLVE 1 tablespoon salt in 2 cups water. Add the eggplant cubes and let soak for 10 minutes. Rinse well, drain, and pat with paper towel to remove any excess moisture. Set aside.

COMBINE the beef mixture ingredients in a medium bowl and set aside.

WHISK together the cheese mixture ingredients in a medium bowl and set aside.

COMBINE the bread crumb mixture in a medium bowl and set aside.

LAYER half the eggplant cubes in a 1-quart $8^{1}/_{2} \times 8^{1}/_{2} \times 4$-inch ovenproof baking dish that has been brushed with olive oil.

SPRINKLE the eggplant with half the bread crumb mixture.

ADD a layer of half the beef mixture. Repeat the layering process, using up the remaining eggplant, beef, and bread crumb mixtures.

POUR the cheese mixture over the top.

BAKE, uncovered, for 50 minutes, or until the eggplant is tender and the top is golden.

Prep: 20 minutes
Total time: 1 hour and 10 minutes
Serves 6

Marinated Cucumbers and Carrots

Peel the cucumbers, scoop out the seeds with a teaspoon, then halve the cucumbers and slice crosswise into thin slices. Cut the peeled carrots diagonally into thin slices. A sharp knife will make the cutting easy.

2 cucumbers, peeled, seeded, and
  thinly sliced
2 carrots, peeled and thinly sliced
$^{1}/_{2}$ cup white vinegar
1 tablespoon sugar

$^{1}/_{4}$ teaspoon salt
$^{1}/_{2}$ teaspoon dill weed
Butcher's pepper to taste

COMBINE all the ingredients in a medium bowl and chill at least 1 hour in the refrigerator before serving.

Total time: 10 minutes
Makes approximately 2 cups

Chapter 12

Grains

A toaster oven can bake rice, lentils, couscous, barley, hominy grits, and kasha to perfection. During baking, the grains slowly absorb the liquid and then continue to cook to completion in 10 to 20 minutes after being removed from the oven. A glass or ceramic baking dish that retains heat well works best. Adding oil, herbs, and seasonings at this time enables the grains to absorb flavors slowly. In boiling, cooked grains are often drained of excess liquid that has nutrients and vitamins. But in baking, no nutrients and vitamins are lost and seasonings and flavors are amplified. Here are recipes for Oven-Baked Barley, Rosemary Lentils, Baked Parslied Cheese Grits, Coconut Rice Pudding, Kasha Loaf, and others that prove the broad capabilities of the toaster oven and showcase the wonderful flavors and textures of grains.

Gardener's Rice

The combination of rice and vegetables creates a colorful medley of flavors and textures. Rice and vegetables bake to near completion and the final cooking is done after baking by the heat conducted by the baking dish.

$\frac{1}{2}$ cup rice
2 tablespoons finely chopped scallions
2 small zucchini, finely chopped
1 bell pepper, finely chopped
1 small tomato, finely chopped
$\frac{1}{4}$ cup frozen peas

$\frac{1}{4}$ cup frozen corn
1 teaspoon ground cumin
1/2 teaspoon dried oregano or
  1 teaspoon chopped fresh oregano
Salt and freshly ground black pepper
  to taste

PREHEAT the toaster oven to 400° F.

COMBINE all the ingredients with 1¼ cups water in a 1-quart 8½ × 8½ × 4-inch ovenproof baking dish, stirring well to blend. Adjust the seasonings to taste. Cover with aluminum foil.

BAKE, covered, for 30 minutes, or until the rice and vegetables are almost cooked. Remove from the oven, uncover, and let stand for 10 minutes to complete the cooking. Fluff once more and adjust the seasonings before serving.

Prep: 10 minutes
Total time: 50 minutes
Serves 4

Moroccan Couscous

Couscous refers to the small, hard grains of wheat left after sieving. Like lentils, couscous can be served hot or cold with endless combinations of vegetables and meat. In Morocco, this dish is usually served in a mound on a platter with stewed meat in the center.

1 cup couscous
2 tablespoons finely chopped scallion
2 tablespoons finely chopped bell pepper
1 plum tomato, finely chopped
2 tablespoons chopped pitted black olives

1 tablespoon olive oil
¼ teaspoon ground cumin
¼ teaspoon ground cinnamon
¼ teaspoon turmeric
Pinch of cayenne
Salt and freshly ground black pepper to taste

PREHEAT the toaster oven to 400° F.

COMBINE all the ingredients with 1¼ cups water in a 1-quart 8½ × 8½ × 4-inch ovenproof baking dish. Adjust the seasonings to taste. Cover with aluminum foil.

BAKE, covered, for 12 minutes. Remove from the heat and fluff with a fork. Cover again and let stand for 10 minutes. Fluff once more before serving.

Prep: 20 minutes
Total time: 42 minutes
Serves 4

Oven-Baked Couscous

Served hot, couscous is an excellent side dish for meat, fish, poultry, or seafood, or it can be served as an entrée.

1 10-ounce package couscous
2 tablespoons olive oil
2 tablespoons canned chickpeas
2 tablespoons canned or frozen
  green peas

1 tablespoon chopped fresh parsley
3 scallions, chopped
Salt and pepper to taste

PREHEAT the toaster oven to 400°F.

MIX together all the ingredients with 2 cups water in a 1-quart $8\frac{1}{2} \times 8\frac{1}{2} \times 4$-inch ovenproof baking dish. Adjust the seasonings to taste. Cover with aluminum foil.

BAKE, covered, for 10 minutes, or until the couscous and vegetables are tender. Adjust the seasonings to taste and fluff with a fork before serving.

Prep: 8 minutes
Total time: 18 minutes
Serves 4

Oven-Baked Barley

Barley is a best-kept secret. Full of vitamins, nourishing, flavorful, and wonderfully textured, barley can be used in place of rice to add originality and interest to a meal. As a grain, it accepts seasonings and spices readily and responds well to toasting. To toast: Place $\frac{1}{3}$ cup barley in a baking pan and broil for 3 minutes, turning with a small spatula after 1 minute to brown the grains evenly. After baking, when the barley is almost cooked, add the seasonings and oil and allow the barley to sit covered for 10 minutes, baking to completion and absorbing the flavors of the oil and seasonings.

$\frac{1}{3}$ cup barley, toasted

Seasonings:
1 tablespoon sesame oil
1 tablespoon sesame seeds

$\frac{1}{4}$ teaspoon ground cumin
$\frac{1}{4}$ teaspoon turmeric
$\frac{1}{2}$ teaspoon garlic powder
Salt and freshly ground black pepper
  to taste

COMBINE the barley and 1¹/₂ cups water in a 1-quart 8¹/₂ × 8¹/₂ × 4-inch ovenproof baking dish. Cover with aluminum foil.

BAKE, covered, for 50 minutes, or until almost cooked, testing the grains after 30 minutes for softness.

ADD the oil and seasonings and fluff with a fork to combine. Cover and let the barley sit for 10 minutes to finish cooking and absorb the flavors of the seasonings. Fluff once more before serving.

Prep: 5 minutes
Total time: 1 hour and 5 minutes
Serves 2

Salad Lentils

Toss cold, baked lentils with celery, cucumber, fresh tomatoes, and spinach leaves for a simple and hearty salad.

¹/₄ cup lentils
1 tablespoon olive oil

Salad ingredients:
1 celery stalk, trimmed and chopped
1 plum tomato, chopped
1 cucumber, peeled, seeded, and chopped

1¹/₂ cups spinach leaves, pulled into small pieces
1 tablespoon balsamic vinegar
1 tablespoon olive oil
¹/₂ teaspoon dried oregano
1 tablespoon chopped scallions
2 tablespoons sliced pitted black olives
1 teaspoon minced roasted garlic

PREHEAT the toaster oven to 400° F.

COMBINE the lentils, 1¹/₄ cups water, and olive oil in a 1-quart 8¹/₂ × 8¹/₂ × 4-inch ovenproof baking dish. Cover with aluminum foil.

BAKE, covered, for 35 minutes, or until the lentils are tender. When cool, combine with all the salad ingredients in a serving bowl and toss well. Adjust the seasonings, chill, and serve.

Prep: 20 minutes
Total time: 55 minutes
Serves 4

Salad Couscous

Chilled couscous on a bed of fresh spinach or lettuce makes a tasty, nearly fat-free salad.

1 10-ounce package precooked couscous
2 tablespoons olive oil
Salt and freshly ground black pepper
1/4 cup chopped fresh tomatoes
2 tablespoons chopped fresh basil leaves

1 tablespoon sliced almonds
1/2 bell pepper, chopped
3 scallions, chopped
2 tablespoons lemon juice

PREHEAT the toaster oven to 400° F.

MIX together the couscous, 2 cups water, and olive oil in a 1-quart 8 1/2 × 8 1/2 × 4-inch ovenproof baking dish. Add salt and pepper to taste. Cover with aluminum foil.

BAKE, covered, for 10 minutes, or until the couscous is cooked. Remove from the oven, fluff with a fork and, when cool, add the tomatoes, basil leaves, almonds, pepper, scallions, and lemon juice. Adjust the seasonings to taste. Chill before serving.

Prep: 12 minutes
Total time: 22 minutes
Serves 4

Spanish Rice

The rice absorbs the water, wine, and the juice of the tomatoes and gains a great flavor. Onions, cilantro, bell pepper, and bay leaves add an herbal, aromatic taste and just a pinch of red pepper flakes brings a hint of spicy hotness.

3/4 cup rice
2 tablespoons dry white wine
3 tablespoons olive oil
1 15-ounce can whole tomatoes
1/4 cup thinly sliced onions

2 tablespoons chopped fresh cilantro
1/2 cup chopped bell pepper
2 bay leaves
Salt and a pinch of red pepper flakes to taste

PREHEAT the toaster oven to 375°F.

COMBINE all the ingredients with 1 cup water in a 1-quart $8\frac{1}{2} \times 8\frac{1}{2} \times 4$-inch oven-proof baking dish and adjust the seasonings. Cover with aluminum foil.

BAKE, covered, for 45 minutes, or until the rice is cooked, removing the cover after 30 minutes.

Prep: 10 minutes
Total time: 55 minutes
Serves 4

Oven-Baked Rice

Baking rice in an oven produces rice grains that are well cooked, separated, and full flavored because they absorb the water slowly through baking, not boiling. A glass or ceramic baking dish retains the heat and remains hot enough to complete the cooking process gently and efficiently. Rice has texture and absorbs the flavors of the seasonings, which have not been diminished by boiling or steaming.

$\frac{1}{4}$ cup regular rice (not parboiled or precooked)

Seasonings:
1 tablespoon olive oil
1 teaspoon dried parsley or 1 tablespoon chopped fresh parsley

1 teaspoon garlic powder or roasted garlic
Salt and freshly ground black pepper to taste

PREHEAT the toaster oven to 400°F.

COMBINE $1\frac{1}{4}$ cups water and the rice in a 1-quart $8\frac{1}{2} \times 8\frac{1}{2} \times 4$-inch ovenproof baking dish. Stir well to blend. Cover with aluminum foil.

BAKE, covered, for 30 minutes, or until the rice is almost cooked. Add the seasonings, fluff with a fork to combine the seasonings well, then let the rice sit, covered, for 10 minutes. Fluff once more before serving.

Prep: 8 minutes
Total time: 48 minutes
Serves 2

Rosemary Lentils

Lentils can be served hot as a side dish with chicken, meat, or fish. Stirring in 2 table-spoons each of low-fat buttermilk and tomato sauce before serving adds a rich, creamy flavor and brightens the rather somber, gray color of the lentils.

$\frac{1}{4}$ cup lentils
1 tablespoon mashed Roasted Garlic
(page 75)
1 rosemary sprig

1 bay leaf
Salt and freshly ground black pepper
2 tablespoons low-fat buttermilk
2 tablespoons tomato sauce

PREHEAT the toaster oven to 400° F.

COMBINE the lentils, $1\frac{1}{4}$ cups water, garlic, rosemary sprig, and bay leaf in a 1-quart $8\frac{1}{2} \times 8\frac{1}{2} \times 4$-inch ovenproof baking dish, stirring to blend well. Add the salt and pepper to taste. Cover with aluminum foil.

BAKE, covered, for 35 minutes, or until the lentils are tender. Remove the rosemary sprig and bay leaf and stir in the buttermilk and tomato sauce. Serve immediately.

Prep: 10 minutes
Total time: 45 minutes
Serves 2

Kasha Loaf

Kasha has a unique, nutlike, almost sweet flavor that harmonizes well with onions, gar-lic, and spices. Like lentils, it lends itself well to vegetarian dishes where a meaty texture and hearty taste is called for. Serve as a side dish with fish, meat, or poultry or sliced cold with a salad.

1 cup whole grain kasha
2 cups tomato sauce or 2 8-ounce
cans tomato sauce (add a small
amount of water to make 2 cups)
3 tablespoons minced onion or scallions

1 tablespoon minced garlic
1 cup multigrain bread crumbs
1 egg
1 teaspoon paprika
1 teaspoon chili powder
1 teaspoon sesame oil

PREHEAT the toaster oven to 400° F.

COMBINE all the ingredients in a bowl and transfer to an oiled or nonstick regular-size 4½ × 8½ × 2¼-inch loaf pan.

BAKE, uncovered, for 30 minutes, or until lightly browned.

> *Prep:* 10 minutes
> *Total time:* 40 minutes
> Serves 4

Kashaburgers

Most veggie burgers employ some kind of grain or combination of grains to produce a meatlike texture and taste. Where soy or rice is adequate but rather bland, kasha's flavor brings substance as well as texture. Double or triple this recipe and freeze the uncooked patties in resealable plastic bags to have on hand for quick lunches or suppers. No need to thaw the patties: Simply unwrap, place on the broiling rack, and broil for 30 minutes, or until cooked through and browned.

1 cup kasha	¼ teaspoon paprika
2 tablespoons minced onion or scallions	½ teaspoon chili powder
1 tablespoon minced garlic	¼ teaspoon sesame oil
½ cup multigrain bread crumbs	1 tablespoon vegetable oil
1 egg	Salt and freshly ground black pepper to taste

PREHEAT the toaster oven to 400° F.

COMBINE 2 cups water and the kasha in a 1-quart 8½ × 8½ × 4-inch ovenproof baking dish.

BAKE, uncovered, for 30 minutes, or until the grains are cooked. Remove from the oven and add all the other ingredients, stirring to mix well. When the mixture is cooled, shape into 4 to 6 patties and place on a rack with a broiling pan underneath.

BROIL for 20 minutes, turn with a spatula, then broil for another 10 minutes, or until browned.

> *Prep:* 10 minutes
> *Total time:* 1 hour
> Serves 4

Baked Parsleyed Cheese Grits

Great served with fried eggs and toast with ketchup, barbecue sauce, or hot pepper sauce on the side.

4 strips lean uncooked turkey
  bacon, cut in half
1 cup grits
2 cups skim or low-fat soy milk
1 egg

$\frac{1}{2}$ cup shredded Parmesan cheese
1 tablespoon chopped fresh parsley
$\frac{1}{2}$ teaspoon garlic powder
Salt and butcher's pepper to taste

PREHEAT the toaster oven to 350° F.

LAYER an $8\frac{1}{2} \times 8\frac{1}{2} \times 2$-inch square baking (cake) pan with the bacon strips.

COMBINE the remaining ingredients in a medium bowl and pour the mixture over the strips.

BAKE, uncovered, for 30 minutes, or until the grits are cooked. Cut into squares with a spatula and serve.

Prep: 10 minutes
Total time: 40 minutes
Serves 4

Chapter 13

Breads

Toaster ovens can easily bake bread. Why heat up your kitchen and big oven when a toaster oven will bake bread just as beautifully? Frequently, the satisfaction of baking bread is put off for that reason. Toaster ovens generate a third to half the heat of a large stove oven and most of today's models that are well insulated, especially those with cool-touch exteriors, reduce heat radiation further. This chapter offers a variety of bread recipes: yeast breads like Country Bread; quick breads, including Yogurt Bread, Banana Bread, Quick Fruit and Raisin Bread; as well as Popovers, Crepes, Onion and Cheese Buttermilk Biscuits, and more.

Rosemary Bread

The flavor of rosemary, garlic, olive oil, and Parmesan cheese changes a baguette or loaf of French bread into an elegant accompaniment for any meal. Lightly browned, it comes from the toaster oven tasting as if you'd just made the bread yourself! If fresh rosemary is not available, use 1 teaspoon dried rosemary leaves and steep it in 1 tablespoon boiling water. Drain through a tea strainer or on paper towels and mix into the spread.

Spread:
3 tablespoons olive oil
2 tablespoons margarine
1 teaspoon garlic
2 tablespoons grated Parmesan cheese
1 tablespoon finely chopped fresh
   rosemary leaves

$^{1}/_{2}$ teaspoon freshly ground black
   pepper
Salt to taste

1 French baguette, sliced 2 inches
   thick

Continued

PREHEAT the toaster oven to 350° F.

COMBINE the spread ingredients in a small bowl, blending well with a fork. Adjust the seasonings to taste.

SPREAD the mixture on both sides of the bread slices and wrap the loaf in aluminum foil.

BAKE for 10 minutes. Remove from the oven and peel back the foil, exposing the top of the bread loaf. Bake for another 5 minutes, or until the top is lightly browned.

Prep: 15 minutes
Total time: 30 minutes
Serves 6

Popovers

Use paper baking cups or oil the muffin pans generously. Preheat the muffin tin at 400° F. for a minute or two in the oven before filling the pans with batter. Popover batter should be at room temperature to work at its best, so set the cup of milk out ¹/₂ hour before you make the batter.

2 eggs	1 cup unbleached flour
1 cup skim milk	Salt to taste
2 tablespoons vegetable oil	

PREHEAT the toaster oven to 400° F.

BEAT all the ingredients in a medium bowl with an electric mixer at high speed until smooth. The batter should be the consistency of heavy cream.

FILL the pans of a 6-muffin tin three-quarters full.

BAKE for 20 minutes, then reduce the heat to 350° F. and bake for 10 minutes, or until golden brown.

Prep: 5 minutes
Total time: 35 minutes
Makes 6 to 9 popovers

Good Stuff Bread

I created this recipe by assembling all the good ingredients I thought should go into a tasty, healthy quick bread. Warm slices of this hearty bread, served in a basket covered with a linen napkin, are a delightful departure from the usual rolls or crusty bread. Toast a thick slice for breakfast or brunch—delicious spread with marmalade. Add your own special healthy ingredients to custom make this bread for yourself.

First mixture:
1 apple, peeled and grated
1 carrot, peeled and grated
1 cup unbleached flour
2 teaspoons baking powder
$\frac{1}{3}$ cup chopped walnuts
$\frac{1}{3}$ cup raisins
$\frac{1}{3}$ cup rolled oats
$\frac{1}{3}$ cup shredded sweetened coconut

Blending mixture:
1 banana
1 egg
1 cup low-fat buttermilk
2 tablespoons dark brown sugar
2 tablespoons vegetable oil
Salt to taste

PREHEAT the toaster oven to 375° F.

COMBINE all the first mixture ingredients in a medium bowl and stir to mix well. Set aside.

PROCESS all the blending mixture ingredients in a blender or food processor until the mixture is smooth. Add to the first mixture ingredients and stir to mix thoroughly. Transfer to an oiled or nonstick $8\frac{1}{2} \times 4\frac{1}{2} \times 2\frac{1}{4}$-inch regular size loaf pan.

BAKE for 40 minutes, or until a toothpick inserted in the center comes out clean and the top is well browned.

Prep: 15 minutes
Total time: 55 minutes
Makes 1 loaf

Quick Fruit and Raisin Bread

This bread makes a great holiday or housewarming gift! Use the small aluminum foil loaf pans available in the supermarket and gift wrap. Triple the recipe and send Quick Fruit and Raisin Bread to everyone on your list or store extras in the freezer for impromptu holiday get-togethers.

2 cups unbleached flour	$\frac{1}{4}$ cup chopped raisins
3 tablespoons margarine	$\frac{1}{2}$ cup chopped dried fruit
$\frac{3}{4}$ cup low-fat buttermilk	2 tablespoons chopped almonds
4 teaspoons baking powder	$\frac{1}{2}$ teaspoon grated nutmeg
1 egg, beaten	Salt to taste
2 tablespoons honey	

PREHEAT the toaster oven to 400° F.

COMBINE all the ingredients in a large bowl, stirring well. Pour the batter into an oiled or nonstick regular-size $8\frac{1}{2} \times 4\frac{1}{2} \times 2\frac{1}{4}$-inch loaf pan or 2 small-size $3\frac{1}{2} \times 7\frac{1}{2} \times 2\frac{1}{4}$-inch loaf pans.

BAKE for 35 minutes, or until a toothpick inserted in the center comes out clean.

Prep: 20 minutes
Total time: 55 minutes
Serves 6

Yogurt Bread

This remarkable bread has the taste and texture of a yeast bread with a quarter of the time in preparation. Also, it's fun to make! You get to knead it, but you don't have to wait for it to rise. Because this is essentially a white bread, additions of wheat germ, rolled oats, cornmeal, poppy seeds, sesame seeds, grated onions, or carrots produce wonderful variations on the theme. Add more yogurt to compensate for the extra dry ingredients.

3 cups unbleached flour	1 cup plain nonfat yogurt
4 teaspoons baking powder	$\frac{1}{4}$ cup vegetable oil
2 teaspoons sugar	1 egg, beaten, to brush the top
Salt to taste	

PREHEAT the toaster oven to 375°F.

COMBINE the flour, baking powder, sugar, and salt in a large bowl. Make a hole in the center and spoon in the yogurt and oil.

STIR the flour into the center. When the dough is well mixed, turn it out onto a lightly floured surface and knead for 8 minutes, until the dough is smooth and elastic. Place the dough in an oiled or nonstick regular-size $8^1/_2 \times 4^1/_2 \times 2^1/_4$-inch loaf pan. Brush the top with the beaten egg.

BAKE for 40 minutes, or until a toothpick inserted in the center comes out clean and the loaf is browned. Invert on a wire rack to cool.

Prep: 10 minutes
Total time: 50 minutes
Makes 1 loaf

Country Bread

Making a yeast bread is not as labor-intensive as it appears to be. Making the bread (the dough must be kneaded well, then placed in a warm place for an hour or so to rise) can be interspersed with doing other things. My grandmother always had dough rising in a bowl covered with a damp towel on the countertop, its yeasty fragrance permeating her kitchen. The promise of rolls or bread to be baked later was, and still is, a primal comfort for me, like a glowing fireplace on a cold winter evening or hot bowls of soup and candle light on a midwinter afternoon.

Yeast mixture:
$1^1/_4$-ounce package active dry yeast
$^1/_4$ cup skim milk, at room temperature
1 teaspoon brown sugar

Flour mixture:
$^3/_4$ cup tepid water
$2^1/_2$ cups unbleached flour

1 egg
2 teaspoons granulated sugar
2 tablespoons vegetable oil
2 tablespoons wheat germ
Salt to taste

Vegetable oil
1 egg, beaten, to brush the top

COMBINE the yeast mixture ingredients in a large bowl and let stand for 10 minutes, or until the yeast is dissolved and foamy.

Continued

ADD the flour mixture ingredients to the yeast mixture, blending well. Turn out the mixture on a lightly floured surface.

KNEAD the dough for 6 minutes, or until smooth and elastic. Return the dough to the large bowl, cover with a clean damp towel, and put in a warm place for 1 hour, or until doubled in size.

PUNCH down the dough and turn out onto a lightly floured surface. Knead for 2 minutes, then place the dough in an oiled or nonstick regular size $8\frac{1}{2} \times 4\frac{1}{2} \times 2\frac{1}{4}$-inch loaf pan. Brush the loaf with vegetable oil, cover the pan with a damp towel, and place in a warm place for 1 hour, or until doubled in size. Brush the loaf with the beaten egg.

PREHEAT the toaster oven to 375°F.

BAKE for 30 minutes, or until a toothpick inserted in the middle comes out clean and the top is browned. Sharply tap the pan to loosen the loaf, invert, and place on a rack to cool.

Prep: 20 minutes
Total time: 50 minutes (rising: 2 hours)
Makes 1 loaf

Corn Bread

Simple to make, corn bread is great for breakfast, drizzled with maple syrup, or served as an accompaniment to Oven-Crisped Chicken (page 101).

1 cup cornmeal	1 egg, beaten
$\frac{3}{4}$ cup unbleached flour	1 cup skim milk
2 tablespoons sugar	2 tablespoons vegetable oil
4 teaspoons baking powder	Salt to taste

PREHEAT the toaster oven to 425°F.

COMBINE all the ingredients in a medium bowl and mix just to blend. The batter will be slightly lumpy. Pour into an oiled or nonstick regular-size $8\frac{1}{2} \times 4\frac{1}{2} \times 2\frac{1}{4}$-inch loaf pan.

BAKE for 20 minutes, or until a toothpick inserted in the center comes out clean.

Prep: 10 minutes
Total time: 30 minutes
Serves 6

Crepes

Very thin crepes are made easily in the toaster oven broiler. The batter will puff while cooking and care must be taken not to allow the crepes to brown and crisp if they are to be rolled or folded. Wear oven mitts to protect the tops of your hands when placing the pan in the toaster oven and removing it.

$\frac{1}{2}$ cup unbleached flour	2 teaspoons vegetable oil
$\frac{3}{4}$ cup skim milk	Salt to taste
1 egg	

WHISK together all the ingredients in a small bowl until smooth. Set aside.

PREHEAT an oiled or nonstick $9\frac{3}{4}$-inch round pie pan by placing it under the broiler for 2 minutes, or until the pan is heated but not smoking. Remove from the oven and spoon 2 tablespoons crepe batter into the pan, tilting the pan to spread the batter evenly into a circle. Return to the broiler.

BROIL for 4 minutes, or until the crepe is cooked but not browned. Remove the pan from the oven and invert onto paper towels to cool and drain. Repeat the procedure with the remaining batter.

Prep: 8 minutes
Total time: 35 minutes
Serves 6

Zucchini Bread

Zucchini Bread is great with soups or salads, and because it is not sweet, it compliments meat, fish, and poultry entrées. For lunch or brunch, toast slices of Zucchini Bread, top with Yogurt Cheese Spread (page 32), and sprinkle with chopped fresh parsley, basil, or oregano leaves.

1 cup grated zucchini	1 egg
2 tablespoons grated onion	2 tablespoons vegetable oil
2 tablespoons grated Parmesan cheese	$1\frac{1}{2}$ cups unbleached flour
$\frac{1}{2}$ cup skim milk	1 tablespoon baking powder
	Salt to taste

Continued

PREHEAT the toaster oven to 375°F.

STIR together all the ingredients in a medium bowl until smooth. Pour the batter into an oiled or nonstick regular-size $8\frac{1}{2} \times 4\frac{1}{2} \times 2\frac{1}{4}$-inch loaf pan.

BAKE for 30 minutes, or until a toothpick inserted in the center comes out clean.

Prep: 15 minutes
Total time: 45 minutes
Serves 6

Onion and Cheese Buttermilk Biscuits

These biscuits are essentially baking powder biscuits enhanced by the additions of Parmesan cheese, fresh parsley, and onion. They are particularly good with Oven-Crisped Chicken (page 101). An irresistible "down-home" combination!

2 cups unbleached flour
3 tablespoons margarine, at room temperature
$\frac{3}{4}$ cup low-fat buttermilk
4 teaspoons baking powder

1 teaspoon garlic powder
$\frac{1}{4}$ cup grated Parmesan cheese
3 tablespoons finely chopped onion
2 tablespoons chopped fresh parsley
Salt to taste

PREHEAT the toaster oven to 400°F.

BLEND all the ingredients in a medium bowl with a fork, then press together to form a dough ball.

KNEAD the dough on a lightly floured surface just until smooth.

ROLL the dough to $\frac{1}{2}$-inch thickness and cut with a round 3-inch cookie cutter. Place on an oiled or nonstick $6\frac{1}{2} \times 10$-inch baking sheet or in an oiled or non-stick $8\frac{1}{2} \times 8\frac{1}{2} \times 2$-inch square baking (cake) pan.

BAKE for 15 minutes, or until lightly browned.

Prep: 12 minutes
Total time: 27 minutes
Serves 4

Garlic Basil Bread

If you don't have time to make bread, here is a way to make a loaf of French bread especially good. Serve as an appetizer, with pasta, or as an accompaniment to fish and seafood dishes.

Mixture:
3 tablespoons olive oil
2 garlic cloves
¼ cup pine nuts (pignoli)
½ cup fresh basil leaves

2 plum tomatoes, chopped
Salt to taste

1 French baguette, cut diagonally
  into 1-inch slices

PREHEAT the toaster oven to 400° F.

PROCESS the mixture ingredients in a blender or food processor until smooth.

SPREAD the mixture on both sides of each bread slice, reassemble into a loaf, and wrap in aluminum foil.

BAKE for 12 minutes, or until the bread is thoroughly heated. Peel back the aluminum foil to expose the top of the bread.

BAKE again for 5 minutes, or until the top is lightly browned.

Prep: 9 minutes
Total time: 27 minutes
Serves 6

Banana Bread

Banana bread, warm from the oven, makes a healthy breakfast, and the mild sweetness of bananas takes the place of jam or marmalade. Here's my own recipe for banana bread with a trail mix of sunflower seeds, raisins, pecans, and walnuts. Substitute chopped nuts or chopped dried fruit for the trail mix, if you prefer. On the grocery shelves these days are great dried fruit medleys that are a tasty alternative to nuts.

2 ripe bananas
1 egg
½ cup milk
2 tablespoons honey
2 tablespoons vegetable oil

¾ cup chopped trail mix
1 cup unbleached flour
1 teaspoon baking powder
Pinch of salt

Continued

PREHEAT the toaster oven to 400°F.

PROCESS the bananas, egg, milk, honey, and oil in a blender or food processor until smooth. Pour into a mixing bowl.

ADD the flour and trail mix, stirring to mix well. Add the baking powder and salt and stir just enough to blend. Pour the mixture into an oiled or nonstick regular-size $8^{1}/_{2} \times 4^{1}/_{2} \times 2^{1}/_{4}$-inch loaf pan.

BAKE for 40 minutes, or until a knife inserted in the center comes out clean.

Prep: 10 minutes
Total time: 50 minutes
Serves 6

Chapter 14

Fruit

The toaster oven showcases the jewel-like beauty of fruit. Baking and broiling concentrate the natural sugars and juices in fruit and berries, so a minimum of white sugar and flavorings are required to bring out their delicate flavors. When the meal is sumptuous and the conclusion needs to be sweet and light, these recipes are excellent candidates. All you need is your toaster oven to perform the magic. Some of these luscious recipes include shortcake, crisps, baked apples, brandied and flamed cherries and bananas, glazed pears, curried fruit, raspberry pie, apple meringue, and apple pudding. Simple but elegant, the recipes' average total preparation time is 30 minutes. In addition, there are several recipes for low-fat, light, flaky, and flavorful piecrusts. Where a cake or pastry would be too heavy for dessert, fruit is the answer: light, sweet, seductive!

Broiled Bananas

One of my favorites, this dessert can be made in minutes. Overripe bananas are particularly good candidates and the addition of lemon juice and honey gives the bananas a wonderful caramelized texture and slightly tart flavor. Just a tablespoon of margarine goes a long way in making this simple dessert taste wickedly rich.

Sauce:
1 tablespoon margarine
2 tablespoons honey
2 tablespoons lemon juice
Pinch of salt (optional)

2 bananas, peeled, halved and quartered
Creamy Yogurt Sauce (page 197) or fat-free half-and-half

Continued

PLACE the sauce ingredients in an oiled or nonstick $8\frac{1}{2} \times 8\frac{1}{2} \times 2$-inch square baking (cake) pan.

BROIL for 5 minutes, or until the mixture begins to bubble. Remove the pan carefully from the oven using oven mitts and stir to blend. Add the bananas and spoon the sauce over them.

BROIL for 5 minutes, or until the bananas are tender and golden in color.

PLACE 4 banana quarters each in 2 dessert dishes and spoon equal portions of the sauce over them. Serve with Creamy Yogurt Sauce or drizzle with fat-free half-and-half.

Prep: 10 minutes
Total time: 20 minutes
Serves 2

Strawberry Shortcake with Buttermilk Biscuits

When I checked out commercial shortcake shells in the supermarket, full of fat, sodium, and a plethora of seven-syllable chemicals, I decided to make my own. Buttermilk biscuits are easy to make—light and flaky on the inside and crusty on the outside, absolutely the perfect match for fresh strawberries. The flavor may take you back to sultry summer days when you were a kid running through the sprinkler to cool off.

1 quart fresh strawberries, rinsed and sliced
2 tablespoons sugar
1 tablespoon lemon juice

$\frac{1}{2}$ teaspoon baking soda
Salt to taste
$\frac{1}{4}$ cup margarine
1 cup low-fat buttermilk
Vegetable oil

Buttermilk biscuit mix:
2 cups unbleached flour
2 teaspoons baking powder

Nonfat whipped topping

PREHEAT the toaster oven to 400° F.

COMBINE the strawberries, sugar, and lemon juice in a large bowl, mixing well to blend. Set aside.

COMBINE the flour, baking powder, baking soda, and salt in a large bowl. Add the margarine, cutting it into the flour with a knife or pastry cutter. Add just enough buttermilk so that the dough will hold together when pinched.

TURN the dough out onto a lightly floured surface and knead 5 or 6 times. Drop the dough from a tablespoon onto an oiled or nonstick $6\frac{1}{2} \times 10$-inch baking sheet. Make 8 mounds $1\frac{1}{2}$ inches across and flatten the tops with a spoon.

BAKE for 15 minutes, or until the biscuits are lightly browned. Cool. Spoon on the fresh strawberries. Top with nonfat whipped topping and serve.

Prep: 10 minutes
Total time: 25 minutes
Serves 8

Berry Crisp

Prepare this lovely dessert ahead and serve hot or cold. Any berries can be used for this recipe—fresh or frozen. Frozen fruit mixtures (use 2 cups) work well also. These medleys, available in the frozen section of the supermarket, usually contain sliced peaches, grapes, strawberries, kiwi, and pears. Because the pieces of fruit are larger than berries, they will take longer to bake.

2 16-ounce packages frozen berries
  or 4 cups fresh berries
2 tablespoons lemon juice
$\frac{1}{2}$ cup rolled oats
1 tablespoon margarine, at room
  temperature

2 tablespoons wheat germ
$\frac{1}{4}$ cup honey
1 teaspoon vanilla extract
Salt to taste

PREHEAT the toaster oven to 400° F.

COMBINE the berries or fruit and lemon juice in a 1-quart-size $8\frac{1}{2} \times 8\frac{1}{2} \times 4$-inch ovenproof baking dish, tossing well to mix. Set aside.

COMBINE the rolled oats, margarine, wheat germ, honey, vanilla, and salt in a small bowl and stir with a fork until the mixture is crumbly. Sprinkle evenly on top of the berries.

BAKE, covered, for 20 minutes, or until the berries are bubbling. Remove from the oven and uncover.

BROIL for 5 minutes, or until the topping is lightly browned.

Prep: 10 minutes
Total time: 35 minutes
Serves 4

Apple Maple Pudding

I modified this traditional recipe by increasing the amount of raisins and nuts, and deleting altogether the beef suet. Brown the top by finishing with broiling.

Pudding mixture:
2 eggs
½ cup brown sugar
4 tablespoons maple syrup
3 tablespoons unbleached flour
1 teaspoon baking powder

1 teaspoon vanilla extract

¼ cup chopped raisins
¼ cup chopped walnuts
2 medium apples, peeled and
   chopped

PREHEAT the toaster oven to 350° F.

COMBINE the pudding mixture ingredients in a medium bowl, beating the eggs, sugar, and maple syrup together first, then adding the flour, baking powder, and vanilla. Add the raisins, nuts, and apples and mix thoroughly. Pour into an oiled or nonstick 8½ × 8½ × 2-inch square baking (cake) pan.

BAKE for 20 minutes, or until a toothpick inserted in the center comes out clean.

BROIL for 5 minutes, or until the top is lightly browned.

Prep: 18 minutes
Total time: 38 minutes
Serves 4

Cherries Jubilee

Flaming fruit desserts are exciting to serve and their rich flavors cannot be duplicated. As a dessert for four or six dinner guests, it can be prepared beforehand, reheated, ignited, and flamed at the table (reheat the cherries for several minutes under the broiler before flaming).

1 15-ounce can cherries, pitted and
   drained, with 2 tablespoons juice
   reserved
1 tablespoon orange juice
1 tablespoon sugar

1 tablespoon cornstarch
¼ cup warmed Kirsch or Cognac
Vanilla yogurt or fat-free half-and-
   half

COMBINE the reserved juice, orange juice, sugar, and cornstarch in a shallow baking pan, blending well.

BROIL for 5 minutes, or until the juice clarifies and thickens slightly. Add the cherries and heat, broiling for 5 minutes more and stirring to blend. Remove from the oven and transfer to a flameproof serving dish.

SPOON the Kirsch over the cherries and ignite. Top with vanilla yogurt or drizzle with warm fat-free half-and-half and serve.

Prep: 10 minutes
Total time: 20 minutes
Serves 4

Strawberry Pie

This pie is so simple to make (the crust is a snap!). This gives you time to make the glaze that turns the strawberries into jewels—a glaze that can be done easily in the toaster oven. Depending on how you feel about hiding the lovely glazed strawberries, you can cover them with nonfat whipped topping or vanilla frozen yogurt and still call this dessert nothing short of spectacular.

2 16-ounce packages frozen sliced strawberries or 1 quart fresh strawberries, washed, stemmed, and sliced
1/4 cup sugar
2 tablespoons lemon juice
2 tablespoons cornstarch
1 single Oatmeal Piecrust, baked (recipe follows)
Strawberry Pie Glaze (recipe follows)

PREHEAT the toaster oven to 350°F.

COMBINE the strawberries, sugar, lemon juice, and cornstarch in a medium bowl, mixing well. Fill the piecrust shell with the strawberries, spreading evenly.

BAKE for 25 minutes, or until the strawberries are tender. Glaze with Strawberry Pie Glaze.

Prep: 8 minutes
Total time: 33 minutes
Serves 6

Strawberry Pie Glaze

$\frac{1}{2}$ cup apple juice   1 teaspoon lemon or lime juice
2 tablespoons sugar

COMBINE all the ingredients in an oiled or nonstick $8\frac{1}{2} \times 8\frac{1}{2} \times 2$-inch square baking (cake) pan.

BROIL for 6 minutes, or until the sugar is melted. Carefully remove from the oven using oven mitts, stir to blend, then broil again for 6 minutes, or until the liquid is reduced and clear. Remove from the oven and brush the strawberries immediately with the glaze. Chill before serving.

Total time: 15 minutes
Makes $\frac{3}{4}$ cup

Oatmeal Piecrust

2 cups quick-cooking rolled oats $\frac{1}{2}$ cup confectioners' sugar
3 tablespoons margarine   Salt to taste
1 tablespoon vegetable oil

PREHEAT the toaster oven to 350° F.

COMBINE all the ingredients with a fork in a medium bowl, blending well and adding a little water if the mixture is too crumbly.

PRESS the mixture into a $9\frac{3}{4}$-inch round pie pan. The crust must be even in thickness.

BAKE for 20 minutes, or until the crust is lightly browned. Cool before filling.

Prep: 8 minutes
Total time: 28 minutes
Makes 1 piecrust

Baked Macs

The aroma of baking apples takes me back to the kitchens of my grandmothers. My Swedish grandmother made apple pies and applesauce, while my German grandmother made apple cake and apple strudel. Any kind of apple will produce delicious results, but I think McIntoshes have the best flavor. To core an apple without slicing it, use a potato peeler or melon ball scoop to carefully carve out the center from the top of the apple, leaving the bottom intact. Serving a Baked Mac with Maple Yogurt Sauce (recipe follows), vanilla frozen yogurt, or fat-free whipped topping still keeps it a low-calorie dessert, so go ahead and add a sprinkling of chopped pecans and cinnamon, too!

2 tablespoons rolled oats
2 tablespoons applesauce
1 tablespoon honey
1 teaspoon ground cinnamon
Pinch of ground allspice
Pinch of salt

2 McIntosh apples, cored
Maple Yogurt Sauce (recipe follows)

PREHEAT the toaster oven to 375°F.

MIX together the oatmeal, applesauce, honey, and seasonings in a small bowl. Spoon the mixture into the cavities of the apples and place the apples in an oiled or non-stick $8^{1}/_{2} \times 8^{1}/_{2} \times 2$-inch square baking (cake) pan.

BAKE the apples for 30 minutes, or until tender. Serve chilled or warm with Maple Yogurt Sauce.

Prep: 5 minutes
Total time: 35 minutes
Serves 2

Maple Yogurt Sauce

$^{3}/_{4}$ cup low-fat yogurt
$^{1}/_{4}$ cup maple syrup

$^{1}/_{4}$ cup finely ground pecans
Ground cinnamon

COMBINE the yogurt and maple syrup in a small bowl and stir to blend well. Drizzle over individual Baked Macs and sprinkle with finely ground pecans and cinnamon.

Total time: 5 minutes
Makes 1 cup

Baked Meringue Apples

Many wonderful packaged dried fruit combinations are available in the supermarket these days. The apples' mincemeatlike flavor harmonizes beautifully with the light, crusty cap of meringue. I have baked the apples ahead of time, then whipped up the meringue and baked them again to completion hours before serving. The apples and meringue will keep well, and having them sit an hour or two only enhances all of their wonderful flavors.

Filling:
4 tablespoons chopped dried fruit
2 tablespoons chopped walnuts
1 tablespoon brown sugar
1 teaspoon ground cinnamon
1 tablespoon lemon juice

4 Granny Smith apples, peeled and
   cored
$1/2$ cup dry white wine

Meringue:
2 egg whites
2 tablespoons granulated sugar

PREHEAT the toaster oven to 375°F.

COMBINE the filling ingredients in a small bowl and fill the apple cavities in equal portions. Place the apples in an oiled or nonstick $8^{1}/_{2} \times 8^{1}/_{2} \times 2$-inch square baking (cake) pan and pour the wine over them.

BAKE for 50 minutes, or until the apples are tender. Cool.

BEAT the egg whites and sugar together in a small bowl until stiff and top the apples with the meringue.

BAKE at 350°F. for 10 minutes, or until the meringue is lightly browned.

Prep: 17 minutes
Total time: 1 hour and 17 minutes
Serves 4

Orange-Glazed Pears

With a pleasing golden color, these glazed pears have a caramelized flavor but are less sweet and sticky. I prepare this dessert ahead of time, spoon the pears and lovely sauce into individual dessert dishes, and refrigerate until I'm ready to serve, topped with nonfat whipped topping. Serve warm, drizzled with Creamy Yogurt Sauce (recipe follows), or chilled and topped with a spoonful of vanilla frozen yogurt and a sprinkle of grated nutmeg.

2 ripe pears

1 tablespoon lemon juice

1 tablespoon margarine

Pinch of salt

Glaze:

2 tablespoons sugar

3 tablespoons orange juice

PREPARE the pears: peel, cut in half, remove the seeds and fibrous centers with a teaspoon, quarter and brush the pear pieces with the lemon juice, and set aside.

COMBINE the glaze ingredients in an oiled or nonstick $8^{1}/_{2} \times 8^{1}/_{2} \times 2$-inch square baking (cake) pan.

BROIL for 4 minutes, or until the margarine is melted. Remove from the oven, stir to blend, add the pear quarters, and spoon the glaze mixture over the pears to coat well.

BROIL for 15 minutes, or until the glaze has thickened and the pears are tender and golden in color. Serve warm or chilled.

Prep: 8 minutes

Total time: 27 minutes

Serves 4

Creamy Yogurt Sauce

1 cup plain nonfat yogurt

1 tablespoon low-fat cream cheese

$^{1}/_{4}$ cup confectioners' sugar

$^{1}/_{2}$ cup fat-free half-and-half

1 teaspoon vanilla extract

COMBINE all the ingredients in a mixing bowl and beat with an electric mixer until smooth.

Total time: 5 minutes

Makes approximately 2 cups

Autumn Berry Dessert

For this quick and easy dessert, you can broil the berries ahead of time, transfer them in equal portions to small ovenproof dessert dishes, then reheat them prior to serving by broiling for a minute or two. They should be served warm, not hot, or there's a chance the yogurt will separate and become curds.

½ cup nonfat sour cream	1 16-ounce package frozen sliced
½ cup nonfat plain yogurt	strawberries or 2 cups sliced fresh
3 tablespoons brown sugar	strawberries
1 16-ounce package frozen blue-	4 tablespoons ground walnuts or
berries or 2 cups fresh blueberries,	pecans
rinsed well and drained	Grated lemon zest

BEAT together the sour cream, yogurt, and brown sugar in a small bowl with an electric mixer until smooth. Set aside.

COMBINE the berries in an oiled or nonstick 8½ × 8½ × 2-inch square baking (cake) pan.

BROIL for 5 minutes, or until bubbling. Fill 4 individual 1-cup-size ovenproof dishes with equal portions of the berries and top with the yogurt/sour cream mixture. Serve immediately or reheat by broiling for 1 or 2 minutes prior to serving. Sprinkle each serving with a tablespoon of ground walnuts or a pinch of lemon zest.

Prep: 6 minutes
Total time: 11 minutes
Serves 4

Baked Grapefruit

I am not much of a morning person. Cold crunchy cereal and cheerfully chirping birds do not inspire me to start the day with gusto. When I have the time, I like to sip a cup of coffee and then ease into something warm, soft, and sweet: a muffin, coffeecake, or . . . baked grapefruit. Slathered with currant jelly (or just about any other kind of jelly, for that matter) and baked for 20 minutes, grapefruit becomes mellow and soft, with a subtle, fruity flavor. You'd probably never heat up your big oven to bake a grape-

fruit in the morning, but it's so easy in the toaster oven! Sprinkling the grapefruit with raisins and nuts prior to broiling adds a toasty flavor and an interesting texture without making it blatantly crunchy.

1 grapefruit, cut in half
2 tablespoons currant jelly
2 tablespoons ground almonds, walnuts, or pecans

2 tablespoons chopped raisins

PREHEAT the toaster oven to 350°F.

SECTION the grapefruit halves with a serrated knife. Place them in an oiled or non-stick $8\frac{1}{2} \times 8\frac{1}{2} \times 2$-inch square baking (cake) pan. Spread 1 tablespoon currant jelly on each half and sprinkle each with 1 tablespoon ground nuts and 1 table-spoon chopped raisins.

BAKE for 20 minutes, or until the grapefruit is lightly browned.

Prep: 5 minutes
Total time: 25 minutes
Serves 4

Apple Incredibles

My daughter and I crafted this recipe several years ago when we were housebound after Boston had been blanketed by a record-breaking snowfall. We surveyed the pantry and came up with some apples, raisins, and pecans. We began making an apple cake and decided muffins would be nice in her school lunch box. My daughter was quite sure the apple slices, inserted into the muffins, would cook properly and be absolutely delicious sprinkled with the raisins and pecans. She was right.

Muffin mixture:
2 cups unbleached flour
1 teaspoon baking powder
$\frac{1}{4}$ cup brown sugar
$\frac{1}{2}$ teaspoon salt
$\frac{1}{4}$ cup margarine, at room temperature
$\frac{1}{2}$ cup skim milk
1 egg, beaten

2 tablespoons finely chopped
raisins
2 tablespoons finely chopped
pecans

1 apple, peeled, cored, and thinly
sliced

Continued

PREHEAT the toaster oven to 400° F.

COMBINE the muffin mixture ingredients in a large bowl, stirring just to blend. Fill the pans of an oiled or nonstick 6-muffin tin with the batter. Insert the apple slices vertically into the batter, standing and pushing them all the way down to the bottom of the pan.

BAKE for 25 minutes, or until the apples are tender and the muffins are lightly browned.

Prep: 10 minutes
Total time: 35 minutes
Makes 6 muffins

Baked Curried Fruit

Serve curried fruit in small baking dishes with a Sesame Wafer (recipe follows) in the bottom, spooning the curried fruit on top of the baked wafer, then drizzling with Yogurt Sauce (page 197). There are many intricate flavors, all orchestrated into one unusual and delicious dessert!

Curry mixture:
2 tablespoons dry white wine
1 teaspoon lemon juice
$\frac{1}{4}$ teaspoon ground allspice
$\frac{1}{4}$ teaspoon ground ginger
$\frac{1}{4}$ teaspoon ground cardamom
$\frac{1}{4}$ teaspoon turmeric
$\frac{1}{4}$ teaspoon ground cumin
$\frac{1}{4}$ teaspoon ground coriander

Pinch of grated nutmeg
Pinch of cayenne
2 tablespoons honey
1 teaspoon soy sauce

1 16-ounce can pear halves, drained
1 8-ounce can pineapple chunks, drained
1 16-ounce can peach halves

PREHEAT the toaster oven to 350° F.

COMBINE the curry mixture ingredients in a 1-quart $8\frac{1}{2} \times 8\frac{1}{2} \times 4$-inch ovenproof baking dish and add the fruit, mixing well.

BAKE, uncovered, for 25 minutes, or until bubbling and the sauce is thickened. Cool and serve on a sesame wafer with Creamy Yogurt Sauce.

Prep: 10 minutes
Total time: 35 minutes
Serves 4 to 6

Sesame Wafers

$^1/_2$ cup sesame seeds
1 tablespoon unbleached flour
1 tablespoon margarine, at room
   temperature

1 teaspoon dark brown sugar

PREHEAT the toaster oven to 400° F.

COMBINE the sesame seeds, flour, margarine, and sugar in a small bowl, mixing well. Sprinkle equal portions into 4 individual 1-cup-size ovenproof dishes and press to cover the bottom evenly.

BAKE for 6 minutes, or until lightly browned.

Prep: 6 minutes
Total time: 12 minutes
Serves 4

Chapter 15

Desserts

There is a certain tension to the concoction of those sweet things we end a meal with. It is a tension between the seduction of creating something very rich and sweet and the knowledge that it is probably not what the doctor ordered. The recipes in this chapter are proof that a dessert can be rich tasting and delicious, yet easy on the arteries. These simple yet elegant recipes attest to the myriad abilities of the toaster oven to create desserts that will please the most discriminating sweet tooth and dessert-loving palate. The dessert recipes include Strawberry Blueberry Cobbler, Green Grape Meringues, Chocolate and Vanilla Swirled Pudding, Maple-Glazed Pumpkin Pie, Orange-Glazed Brownies, Lemon Torte, and many, many more.

Cranapple Crisp

A new twist for apple crisp—tart and sweet, this dessert is so simple and so good! There's plenty of topping, but not a whole lot of fat.

2 apples, peeled, cored, and diced
3 cups chopped fresh or thawed
   frozen cranberries
1/4 cup brown sugar

Topping:
1/2 cup instant rolled oats
1 cup multigrain bread crumbs

1/4 cup wheat germ
1 tablespoon margarine
1 tablespoon vegetable oil
1/2 cup brown sugar
1 teaspoon ground cinnamon
1/4 teaspoon grated nutmeg
Salt to taste

PREHEAT the toaster oven to 350°F.

COMBINE the cranberries, apples, and sugar in a large bowl, mixing well. Transfer to an oiled or nonstick $8\frac{1}{2} \times 8\frac{1}{2} \times 2$-inch square baking (cake) pan. Set aside.

COMBINE the topping ingredients in a medium bowl, stirring with a fork until crumbly. Sprinkle evenly on top of the cranberry/apple mixture.

BAKE for 35 minutes, or until the top is golden brown.

> *Prep:* 20 minutes
> *Total time:* 55 minutes
> Serves 6

Coconut Rice Pudding

Is rice pudding a comfort food for you? It is for me, and interwoven with my tender rice pudding memories of childhood are, no doubt, thousands of calories consumed in my age of innocence! Why not keep the comfort part and let the fat and calories go? With that in mind, I created this recipe, which satisfies my ancient rice pudding needs without taking me into another dress size. Use regular rice, not precooked or parboiled, for best results.

$\frac{1}{2}$ cup short-grain brown rice

Pudding mixture:
1 egg, beaten
1 tablespoon cornstarch
$\frac{1}{2}$ cup fat-free half-and-half
$\frac{1}{2}$ cup chopped raisins

1 teaspoon vanilla extract
$\frac{1}{2}$ teaspoon ground cinnamon
$\frac{1}{2}$ teaspoon grated nutmeg
Salt to taste

$\frac{1}{4}$ cup shredded sweetened coconut
Fat-free whipped topping

PREHEAT the toaster oven to 400°F.

COMBINE the rice and $1\frac{1}{2}$ cups water in a 1-quart $8\frac{1}{2} \times 8\frac{1}{2} \times 4$-inch ovenproof baking dish. Cover with aluminum foil.

BAKE, covered, for 45 minutes, or until the rice is tender. Remove from the oven and add the pudding mixture ingredients, mixing well.

BAKE, uncovered, for 10 minutes, or until the top is lightly browned. Sprinkle the top with coconut and chill before serving. Top with fat-free whipped topping.

> *Prep:* 10 minutes
> *Total time:* 1 hour and 5 minutes
> Serves 6

Heavenly Chocolate Cupcakes

Melting the chocolate and margarine is done easily in the toaster oven broiler. Paper baking cups will make removing the cupcakes from the tins very easy. If you don't use baking cups, oil the tins well to prevent sticking.

2 squares semisweet chocolate
2 tablespoons margarine
1 cup unbleached flour
2 teaspoons baking powder
Salt to taste

$3/4$ cup brown sugar
$1/2$ cup skim milk
1 egg, beaten
$1/2$ cup chopped pecans
$1/2$ teaspoon vanilla extract

MELT the chocolate and margarine in an oiled or nonstick $8^1/_2 \times 8^1/_2 \times 2$-inch square baking (cake) pan under the broiler for 5 minutes, or until about half melted. Remove from the oven and stir until completely melted and blended.

COMBINE the flour, baking powder, salt, and sugar in a medium bowl, mixing well. Add the melted chocolate/margarine mixture, then the milk and egg. Stir to blend well, then stir in the pecans and vanilla. Fill paper baking cups or well-oiled tins in a 6-muffin pan three-quarters full with batter.

BAKE at 350°F. for 25 minutes, or until a toothpick inserted in the center comes out clean.

Prep: 10 minutes
Total time: 40 minutes
Makes 6 cupcakes

Green Grape Meringues

A delectable trilogy of green grapes, meringue, and bitter chocolate shavings topped with vanilla frozen yogurt and nonfat whipped topping—what could be a lovelier end to a meal?

1 cup sugar
3 egg whites, beaten until stiff
$1/2$ teaspoon lemon juice
Vanilla frozen yogurt

1 cup sliced fresh green grapes
2 squares unsweetened baking
  chocolate, shaved
Nonfat whipped topping

PREHEAT the toaster oven to 250°F.

ADD the sugar slowly to the egg white mixture and continue to beat. Add the lemon juice. With a tablespoon, drop on an oiled or nonstick 6½ × 10-inch baking sheet to make a mound of meringue approximately 2 inches across. Make a slight depression in the center of each one.

BAKE for 40 minutes, or until crusty and browned. Cool and fill each meringue shell with a scoop of vanilla frozen yogurt. Top with equal portions of green grapes, chocolate shavings, and nonfat whipped topping. The meringues may be stored in an airtight container until ready to use.

Prep: 15 minutes
Total time: 55 minutes
Serves 4

Little Swedish Coffee Cakes

This recipe is an adaptation of the little cakes my Swedish grandmother used to make. These little coffee cakes are rich tasting minus the butter.

Cake batter:
1 cup unbleached flour
1 teaspoon baking powder
½ cup sugar
½ cup finely ground pecans
¾ cup low-fat buttermilk
1 tablespoon vegetable oil

1 egg, lightly beaten
1 teaspoon vanilla extract
Salt to taste

Sifted confectioners' sugar
Canola oil for brushing pan

PREHEAT the toaster oven to 350°F.

COMBINE the cake batter ingredients in a bowl, mixing well. Pour the batter into an oiled or nonstick 8½ × 8½ × 2-inch square baking (cake) pan.

BAKE for 30 minutes, or until a toothpick inserted in the center comes out clean. Run a knife around the edge of the pan, invert, and place on a rack to cool. Sprinkle the top with sifted confectioners' sugar and cut into small squares.

Prep: 10 minutes
Total time: 40 minutes
Serves 6

Currant Carrot Cake

Currants add extra texture and flavor to this traditional favorite. A friend from North Dakota had an aunt who was fond of saying, "If you have an old banana, make banana bread. If you have an old carrot, make carrot cake. If you have an old man, get a new one." There is no limit to the resourcefulness of prairie women!

1 cup unbleached flour
1 teaspoon baking powder
1 teaspoon baking soda
½ cup evaporated skim milk
½ cup brown sugar
2 tablespoons vegetable oil
1 egg

1 cup grated carrots
½ cup chopped currants
¼ cup finely chopped pecans
Salt to taste

Yogurt Cream Icing (recipe follows)

PREHEAT the toaster oven to 350° F.
COMBINE all the ingredients in a medium bowl, stirring well to mix thoroughly.
SPREAD the batter in an oiled or nonstick 8½ × 8½ × 2-inch square baking (cake) pan.
BAKE for 30 minutes, or until a toothpick inserted in the center comes out clean. Cool on a wire rack. Ice with Yogurt Cream Icing.

Prep: 12 minutes
Total time: 42 minutes
Serves 6

Yogurt Cream Icing

2 tablespoons plain yogurt
1 teaspoon vanilla extract
1 tablespoon reduced-fat cream cheese

1½ cups confectioners' sugar, sifted
Salt

STIR together the icing ingredients in a small bowl, then beat with an electric mixer until smooth. Add more confectioners' sugar or yogurt until the icing is the consistency of very thick cream.

Total time: 5 minutes
Makes 1 cup

Cinnamon Sugar Rolls

Low in fat, phyllo pastry makes excellent layered crusts and pastries. With this in mind, I created a light pastry that makes a great dessert when just a little bit of something sweet is needed with coffee or tea.

½ cup margarine   10 sheets phyllo pastry, thawed

Filling mixture:
1 tablespoon ground cinnamon
½ cup brown sugar
½ cup finely chopped walnuts

BROIL the margarine in an oiled or nonstick 8½ × 8½ × 2-inch square baking (cake) pan for 3 minutes, or until almost melted. Remove from the oven and stir until melted (the pan will be hot and the margarine will continue to melt). Set aside.

COMBINE the filling mixture in a small bowl, mixing well.

LAY a sheet of phyllo pastry on a clean flat surface. Brush with the melted margarine, sprinkle with a heaping tablespoon of the filling mixture, and spread evenly to cover the sheet of pastry. Repeat the brushing and sprinkling procedure for each sheet, layering one on top of the other until all 10 sheets are done. Use up any remaining filling mixture on the last sheet. Starting at the 9-inch (long) edge, slowly roll all of the sheets up like a jelly roll. With a sharp knife, cut the roll into 1¼-inch slices. Place the slices on an oiled or nonstick baking sheet or baking pan.

BAKE at 350° F. for 10 minutes, or until golden brown.

Prep: 20 minutes
Total time: 30 minutes
Makes approximately 8 rolls

Pear Praline Pie

Just a dollop of nonfat whipped topping is all you need to showcase this exquisite dessert. This recipe has all of the seductiveness of pecan pie, with none of the fat.

Pie filling:
5 pears, peeled, cored, and sliced, or 3 cups sliced canned pears, well drained
$\frac{1}{2}$ cup dark brown sugar
$\frac{1}{4}$ cup unbleached flour
$\frac{1}{2}$ teaspoon ground ginger
1 teaspoon lemon juice
Salt to taste

1 Apple Juice Piecrust, baked (page 218)

Praline topping:
$\frac{1}{2}$ cup brown sugar
$\frac{1}{2}$ cup chopped pecans
$\frac{1}{2}$ cup unbleached flour
2 tablespoons margarine

PREHEAT the toaster oven to 400° F.

COMBINE the pie filling ingredients in a large bowl, mixing well. Spoon the filling into the piecrust shell.

COMBINE the praline topping ingredients in a small bowl, mixing with a fork until crumbly. Sprinkle evenly on top of the pear mixture.

BAKE for 40 minutes, or until the pears are tender and the topping is browned.

Prep: 15 minutes
Total time: 55 minutes
Serves 10

Chocolate and Vanilla Swirled Pudding

Artful swirls of light and dark pattern this smooth-textured pudding. Low in fat and high in flavor, this pudding can be appreciated by the eye as well as the palate! If you prefer not to hide it with a whipped topping, a shaving of semisweet chocolate on top adds more texture, pattern, and chocolate!

1 square semisweet chocolate
$1\frac{1}{2}$ cups fat-free half-and-half
1 tablespoon sugar

2 egg yolks
$\frac{1}{2}$ teaspoon vanilla extract
Fat-free whipped topping

MELT the chocolate in an oiled or nonstick $8^{1}/_{2} \times 8^{1}/_{2} \times 2$-inch square baking (cake) pan under the broiler for approximately 5 minutes, removing the pan from the oven before the chocolate is completely melted. Stir until melted and smooth. Set aside.

WHISK together the half-and-half, sugar, egg yolks, and vanilla in a medium bowl. Divide into two portions and add the melted chocolate to one, stirring to blend well.

FILL four 1-cup-size ovenproof dishes with equal portions of the vanilla mixture, then top with equal portions of the chocolate mixture. With a skewer or toothpick, stir the pudding in little circles to create a swirling pattern of light and dark.

BAKE at 350° F. for 25 minutes, or until the pudding is firm. Chill before serving. Top with fat-free whipped topping.

Prep: 10 minutes
Total time: 35 minutes
Serves 4

Coconut Cake

Rich tasting, moist, and light, this cake is delicious iced with Creamy Frosting and sprinkled with sweetened flaked coconut. Place the mandarin oranges in the coconut-sprinkled frosting and chill the cake for at least 2 hours in the refrigerator before serving.

2 cups unbleached flour
2 teaspoons baking powder
1 cup skim or low-fat soy milk
2 tablespoons vegetable oil
1 teaspoon vanilla extract

1 egg, beaten
$^{3}/_{4}$ cup sugar
Salt to taste

Creamy Frosting (recipe follows)

PREHEAT the toaster oven to 350° F.
COMBINE all the ingredients in a large bowl, mixing well.
POUR the cake batter into an oiled or nonstick $8^{1}/_{2} \times 8^{1}/_{2} \times 2$-inch square baking (cake) pan.
BAKE for 25 minutes, or until a toothpick inserted in the center comes out clean. Ice with Creamy Frosting and sprinkle with coconut.

Prep: 12 minutes
Total time: 37 minutes
Serves 6

Creamy Frosting

1 1/2 cups confectioners' sugar, sifted
3 tablespoons margarine
1 tablespoon fat-free half-and-half or
  skim milk
1/2 teaspoon vanilla extract

Salt to taste
1/2 cup sweetened flaked coconut
1 5-ounce can mandarin oranges,
  drained well

COMBINE all the ingredients except the flaked coconut and mandarin oranges
(reserve for sprinkling and decorating later) in a medium bowl.

BEAT with an electric mixer at high speed until light and fluffy. Add more confectioners' sugar if the frosting is too liquid or more fat-free half-and-half if the frosting is
too stiff. It should be about the consistency of room-temperature peanut butter.

Prep: 8 minutes
Total time: 8 minutes
Makes approximately 1 cup

Orange-Glazed Brownies

*Melting the chocolate and margarine and making the glaze is done easily in the toaster
oven broiler. The orange and chocolate combination takes these brownies to another level
and the slightly tart glaze makes them an excellent low-fat partner for a topping of
vanilla yogurt or orange sherbet. Piercing the top with a fork or toothpick allows the
orange glaze to seep down into the dark rich cake.*

3 squares unsweetened chocolate
3 tablespoons margarine
1 cup sugar
1/2 cup orange juice
2 eggs
1 1/2 cups unbleached flour

1 teaspoon baking powder
Salt to taste
1 tablespoon grated orange zest

Orange Glaze (recipe follows)

BROIL the chocolate and margarine in an oiled or nonstick 8 1/2 × 8 1/2 × 2-inch
square baking (cake) pan for 3 minutes, or until almost melted. Remove from the
oven and stir until completely melted. Transfer the chocolate/margarine mixture
to a medium bowl.

BEAT in the sugar, orange juice, and eggs with an electric mixer. Stir in the flour, baking powder, salt, and orange zest and mix until well blended. Pour into the oiled or nonstick square cake pan.

BAKE at 350°F. for 30 minutes, or until a toothpick inserted in the center comes out clean. Make holes over the entire top by piercing with a fork or toothpick. Paint with Orange Glaze and cut into squares.

Prep: 13 minutes
Total time: 43 minutes
Makes 12 squares

Orange Glaze

1 cup orange juice
½ cup sugar

COMBINE the orange juice and sugar in a small bowl and mix well. Transfer the mixture to a baking pan.

BROIL for 10 minutes, stirring after 5 minutes, or until the sugar is dissolved and the liquid is reduced. Drizzle on top of brownies and cool. Cut into squares and serve with scoops of vanilla frozen yogurt or orange sherbet.

Prep: 2 minutes
Total time: 12 minutes
Makes 1 cup

Scones

The buttery taste characteristic of scones is still here in this low-fat version. True to their calling, scones are delicious with coffee or tea. Once baked, they store well in the refrigerator or an airtight container, ready to serve when friends drop in.

Scone mixture:
1 cup unbleached flour
1 teaspoon baking powder
¼ cup brown sugar
2 tablespoons vegetable oil
¼ cup low-fat buttermilk
½ teaspoon vanilla extract

Topping mixture:
1 tablespoon granulated sugar
1 tablespoon margarine
1 teaspoon ground cinnamon

Continued

PREHEAT the toaster oven to 425° F.

COMBINE the scone mixture ingredients in a medium bowl, cutting to blend with 2 butter knives or a pastry blender. Add a little more buttermilk, if necessary, so that the dough is moist enough to stay together when pinched.

KNEAD the dough on a lightly floured surface for 2 minutes, then place the dough in an oiled or nonstick 9¾-inch round cake pan and pat down to spread out evenly to the edges of the pan. Cut into 8 wedges.

COMBINE the topping mixture in a small bowl, mixing well, and sprinkle evenly on the dough.

BAKE for 20 minutes, or until golden brown.

Prep: 12 minutes
Total time: 32 minutes
Makes 8 wedges

Blackberry Pie

Even if you are totally full after a sumptuous meal, there is always room for a wedge of blackberry pie. A light graham cracker crust, a nonfat fruit filling, and a meringue topping make this dessert delicious, lovely to look at, and nearly fat free.

Filling:
2 16-ounce bags frozen blackberries, thawed, or 2 cups fresh blackberries, washed and well drained
1 4-ounce jar baby food prunes
2 tablespoons cornstarch
¼ cup brown sugar

1 tablespoon lemon juice
Salt to taste

1 Graham Cracker Crust, baked (recipe follows)

Meringue Topping (recipe follows)

PREHEAT the toaster oven to 350° F.

COMBINE the filling ingredients in a large bowl, mixing well. Spoon the filling into the baked Graham Cracker Crust and spread evenly.

BAKE for 30 minutes. When cool, top with the Meringue Topping.

Prep: 4 minutes
Total time: 34 minutes
Serves 6

Meringue Topping

3 egg whites
1 cup sugar

BEAT the egg whites and sugar together in a medium bowl until the mixture is stiff. Spread on top of the pie.
BAKE at 375°F. for 12 minutes, or until the meringue topping is browned.

Prep: 3 minutes
Total time: 15 minutes
Makes 1 cup

Graham Cracker Crust

This is a quick crust with a rich, buttery taste, and it uses just 1 tablespoon of margarine! The baked crust will store for up to one week in the refrigerator. An easy but elegant dessert like Blackberry Pie is even easier when the baked piecrust is made ahead of time.

1⅓ cups reduced-fat graham
cracker crumbs
2 tablespoons brown sugar
1 teaspoon ground cinnamon
Salt to taste
1 tablespoon margarine
2 tablespoons vegetable oil

PROCESS the graham crackers in a food processor or blender to produce finely ground crumbs. Add the sugar, cinnamon, and salt and blend by stirring. Set aside.
HEAT the margarine and oil under a broiler for 4 minutes, or until the margarine is almost melted. Remove from the oven and stir until the margarine is completely melted. Add the graham cracker crumbs and mix thoroughly.
PRESS the mixture into a 9¾-inch pie pan, spreading it out evenly from the middle and up the sides of the pan.
BAKE at 350°F. for 10 minutes, or until lightly browned. Cool before filling.

Prep: 7 minutes
Total time: 21 minutes
Makes 1 piecrust

Blueberry Cookies

The dough is purple and the cookies bake to a lovely violet color. The blueberries remain juicy and biting into one is pure heaven! Use a toaster oven baking sheet or a baking pan, all the better if it's nonstick.

1 egg
1 tablespoon margarine, at room
  temperature
$1/3$ cup sugar
$1\frac{1}{4}$ cups unbleached flour
Salt to taste

1 teaspoon baking powder
1 10-ounce package frozen blueberries, well drained, or $1\frac{1}{2}$ cups
  fresh blueberries, rinsed and
  drained

PREHEAT the toaster oven to 400° F.

BEAT together the egg, margarine, and sugar in a medium bowl with an electric mixer until smooth. Add the flour, salt, and baking powder, mixing thoroughly. Gently stir in the blueberries just to blend. Do not overmix.

DROP by teaspoonfuls on an oiled or nonstick $6\frac{1}{2} \times 10$-inch baking sheet or an oiled or nonstick $8\frac{1}{2} \times 8\frac{1}{2} \times 2$-inch square baking (cake) pan.

BAKE for 12 minutes, or until the cookies are golden brown.

Prep: 15 minutes
Total time: 27 minutes
Makes 3 dozen

Spice Cake

Baby food fruit and applesauce are excellent substitutes for oil or margarine in many baking recipes, giving moisture and texture to a cake without increasing the fat content. Simple and quick to make, this cake bakes in only 25 minutes. It is delicious frosted or served with a dollop of fat-free whipped topping. Why use a commercial cake mix with all the chemical ingredients, fat, and sodium when, in the same amount of prep time, you can make a healthy, homemade spice cake for dessert?

1 cup applesauce or 2 4-ounce jars
  baby food prunes
$1/4$ cup skim milk or low-fat soy milk

1 tablespoon vegetable oil
$1/2$ cup brown sugar
1 egg

1 1/2 cups unbleached flour
1 teaspoon baking powder
1/2 teaspoon baking soda
1/4 teaspoon grated nutmeg
1/2 teaspoon ground cinnamon

1/2 teaspoon grated orange zest
Salt to taste

Creamy Frosting (page 210)

PREHEAT the toaster oven to 350°F.

STIR together the applesauce, milk, oil, sugar, and egg in a small bowl. Set aside.

COMBINE the flour, baking powder, nutmeg, cinnamon, orange zest, and salt in a medium bowl. Add the applesauce mixture and stir to mix well. Pour the batter into an oiled or nonstick 8 1/2 × 8 1/2 × 2-inch square baking (cake) pan.

BAKE for 25 minutes, or until a toothpick inserted in the center comes out clean. Frost with Creamy Frosting.

Prep: 12 minutes
Total time: 37 minutes
Serves 6

Orange Strawberry Flan

Caramelize the sugar in the broiler of the toaster oven. A garnish of sliced strawberries and fresh mint leaves completes this sweet and delectable dessert.

1/4 cup sugar
1/2 cup concentrated orange juice
1 12-ounce can low-fat evaporated milk
3 egg yolks

1 cup frozen strawberries, thawed and sliced, or 1 cup fresh strawberries, washed, stemmed, and sliced
4 fresh mint sprigs

PREHEAT the toaster oven to 375°F.

PLACE the sugar in a baking pan and broil for 4 minutes, or until the sugar melts. Remove from the oven, stir briefly, and pour equal portions of the caramelized sugar into four 1-cup-size ovenproof dishes. Set aside.

BLEND the orange juice, evaporated milk, and egg yolks in a food processor or blender until smooth. Transfer the mixture to a medium bowl and fold in the sliced strawberries. Pour the mixture in equal portions into the four dishes.

BAKE for 45 minutes, or until a knife inserted in the center comes out clean. Chill

Continued

for several hours. The flan may be loosened by running a knife around the edge and inverted on individual plates or served in the dishes. Garnish with fresh mint sprigs.

Prep: 9 minutes
Total time: 54 minutes
Serves 4

Lemon Torte

The size and accessibility of a toaster oven makes crafting this recipe fascinating and fun. This lovely little lemony torte can be baked ahead of time and keeps well, frosted or unfrosted, in the refrigerator until time for dessert. Note: *Because of frequent placing and removing of the cake pan, care must be taken to wear oven mitts.*

First mixture:
¼ cup margarine, at room temperature
½ teaspoon grated lemon zest
3 egg yolks
¼ cup sugar
⅓ cup unbleached flour
3 tablespoons cornstarch

Second mixture:
3 egg whites
2 tablespoons sugar

Cream Cheese Frosting (recipe follows)

BEAT together the first mixture ingredients in a medium bowl with an electric mixer until the mixture is smooth. Set aside. Clean the electric mixer beaters.
BEAT the second mixture together: Beat the egg whites into soft peaks in a medium bowl, gradually adding the sugar, and continue beating until the peaks are stiff. Fold the first mixture into the second mixture to make the torte batter.
POUR ½ cup torte batter into a small oiled or nonstick 3½ × 7½ × 2¼-inch loaf pan.
BROIL for 1 or 2 minutes, or until lightly browned. Remove from the oven.
POUR and spread evenly another ½ cup batter on top of the first layer. Broil again for 1 or 2 minutes, or until lightly browned. Repeat the process until all the batter is used up. When cool, run a knife around the sides to loosen and invert onto a plate. Chill. Frost with Cream Cheese Frosting and serve chilled.

Prep: 20 minutes
Total time: 36 minutes
Serves 6

Cream Cheese Frosting

1 cup confectioners' sugar
1 tablespoon fat-free half-and-half
2 tablespoons reduced-fat cream
  cheese

1 teaspoon lemon juice

BEAT the frosting ingredients in a medium bowl with an electric mixer until light and fluffy, adding more confectioners' sugar if the mixture is too liquid or more cream cheese if the mixture is too stiff. It should have the consistency of room-temperature peanut butter.

Prep: 10 minutes
Total time: 10 minutes
Makes 1 cup frosting

Maple-Glazed Pumpkin Pie

This pumpkin pie is delicious any time of year. I created a glaze that glosses the top of the pie with a dark brown lacquer of sugar. The toaster oven broiler easily makes the glaze. Serve sweet-varnished wedges with a drizzle of warm fat-free half-and-half and a sprinkle of grated nutmeg.

Filling:
1 15-ounce can pumpkin pie filling
1 12-ounce can low-fat evaporated
  milk
1 egg
3 tablespoons maple syrup
$\frac{1}{2}$ teaspoon grated nutmeg
$\frac{1}{2}$ teaspoon ground ginger
1 teaspoon ground cinnamon
Salt to taste

1 Apple Juice Piecrust, baked
  (recipe follows)

Dark glaze:
3 tablespoons maple syrup
2 tablespoons dark brown sugar

PREHEAT the toaster oven to 400°F.
COMBINE all the filling ingredients in a large bowl and beat with an electric mixer until smooth. Pour into the piecrust shell.

Continued

BAKE for 40 minutes, or until a knife inserted in the center comes out clean.

COMBINE the dark glaze ingredients in a baking pan.

BROIL for 5 minutes, or until bubbling. Remove from the oven and stir to dissolve the sugar. Broil again for 3 minutes, or until the liquid is thickened and the sugar is dissolved. Spoon on top of the cooled pumpkin pie, spreading evenly, then chill for at least 1 hour before serving.

Prep: 15 minutes
Total time: 13 minutes
Serves 10

Apple Juice Piecrust

An error-free crust, ideal for pumpkin, fruit, or berry pies. Add a pinch of nutmeg to the dough when making a crust for pumpkin pie.

1¼ cups unbleached flour
¼ cup margarine
¼ cup apple juice

Pinch of grated nutmeg
Salt to taste

PREHEAT the toaster oven to 350°F.

CUT together the flour and margarine with a knife or pastry cutter until the mixture is crumbly. Add the apple juice, nutmeg, and salt and cut again to blend. Turn the dough out onto a lightly floured surface and knead for 2 minutes. Roll out into a circle large enough to fit a 9¾-inch pie pan. Pierce in several places to prevent bubbling and press the tines of a fork around the rim to decorate the crust edge.

BAKE for 10 minutes, or until lightly browned.

Prep: 10 minutes
Total time: 20 minutes
Makes 1 piecrust

Coconut Drop Cookies

I had my first coconut cookie (also known in some circles as macaroons) when I was eight and I've been hooked ever since. Is it the moist texture? The sweet and oh-so-endearing coconut taste? Or is it the lightly browned tops that look like little snowy mountains? In any case, they may be the easiest and most rewarding cookies in the world to make. And baking them in a toaster oven makes them even easier!

1 14-ounce package shredded and
   sweetened coconut
2 eggs
1 tablespoon margarine

$^{3}/_{4}$ cup unbleached flour
1 teaspoon baking powder
Salt to taste

PREHEAT the toaster oven to 250° F.

COMBINE all the ingredients in a medium bowl, mixing well. Drop in small portions with a teaspoon onto an oiled or nonstick 6$^{1}/_{2}$ × 10-inch baking sheet or an oiled or nonstick 8$^{1}/_{2}$ × 8$^{1}/_{2}$ × 2-inch square baking (cake) pan.

BAKE for 10 minutes, or until golden brown.

Prep: 9 minutes
Total time: 21 minutes
Makes 2 dozen

Almost Sinless Pear Banana Bread Pudding

I had two very ripe pears, several slices of leftover toast, and one banana. Eureka! This pudding has a great texture and wonderful flavor. Reconsider old-fashioned bread pudding. You really can't taste the bread; it blends with the other ingredients and produces a wonderful, textured pudding that tastes full and rich, but has very little fat content. This pudding is definitely a comfort food candidate!

1 cup peeled and sliced fresh pears
   or 1 cup sliced canned pears, well
   drained
1 banana
1 cup skim milk
1 egg

2 tablespoons light brown sugar
$^{1}/_{4}$ teaspoon salt
$^{1}/_{2}$ teaspoon ground cinnamon
2 cups toast, cut into 1 × 1-inch
   cubes or pieces

Continued

PREHEAT the toaster oven to 400° F.

BLEND the pears, banana, milk, egg, sugar, salt, and cinnamon in a food processor or blender until smooth. Transfer to an $8\frac{1}{2} \times 8\frac{1}{2} \times 4$-inch ovenproof baking dish. Add the toast and mix well.

BAKE for 40 minutes, or until the center is firm and lightly browned. Cool and top with whipped cream, ice cream, nuts, or fresh or canned berries.

> *Prep:* 10 minutes
> *Total time:* 50 minutes
> Serves 4

Baked Custard

My Swedish grandmother made wonderful custard. Dark-crusted on top, with a hint of nutmeg, I remember it hot from the oven and swimming in a pool of heavy cream. In adapting the recipe to a low-fat version, I wondered if I could retain the warm richness of this wonderful comfort food. I succeeded! Upon tasting, I was transported back in time to Grandma's cozy little house in Minneapolis, snowflakes drifting lazily down from the dark gray sky and a pale yellow sun of custard glowing in a baking dish.

2 eggs	Fat-free half-and-half
$\frac{1}{4}$ cup sugar	
1 cup low-fat evaporated milk	
$\frac{1}{2}$ teaspoon vanilla extract	
Pinch of grated nutmeg	

PREHEAT the toaster oven to 350° F.

BEAT together the eggs, sugar, milk, vanilla, and nutmeg in a small bowl with an electric mixer at medium speed. Pour equal portions of the custard mixture into 2 oiled 1-cup-size ovenproof dishes.

BAKE for 45 minutes, or until a toothpick inserted in the center comes out clean. Serve drizzled with warm fat-free half-and-half.

> *Prep:* 8 minutes
> *Total time:* 53 minutes
> Serves 2

Pineapple Tartlets

This is a very sweet, light dessert and a pleasant end to a summer meal. Keep the phyllo pastry in the freezer and, half an hour before preparation, set the phyllo pastry box out at room temperature to defrost slightly. Peel off the six sheets you will need and return the box to the freezer. Baking time is only 15 minutes!

Vegetable oil
6 sheets phyllo pastry
1 8-ounce can crushed pineapple, drained
3 tablespoons low-fat cottage cheese
2 tablespoons orange or pineapple marmalade

6 teaspoons concentrated thawed frozen orange juice
Vanilla frozen yogurt or nonfat whipped topping

PREHEAT the toaster oven to 350° F.

BRUSH the pans of a 6-muffin tin with vegetable oil. Lay a phyllo sheet on a clean, flat surface and brush with oil. Fold the sheet into quarters to fit the muffin pan. Repeat the process for the remaining phyllo sheets and pans.

BAKE for 5 minutes, or until lightly browned. Remove from the oven and cool.

COMBINE the pineapple, cottage cheese, and marmalade in a small bowl, mixing well. Fill the phyllo shells (in the pans) with equal portions of the mixture. Drizzle 1 teaspoon orange juice concentrate over each.

BAKE at 400° F. for 15 minutes, or until the filling is cooked. Cool and remove the tartlets carefully from the muffin pans to dessert dishes. Top with vanilla frozen yogurt or nonfat whipped topping.

Prep: 15 minutes
Total time: 35 minutes
Serves 4

Strawberry Blueberry Cobbler

This luscious cobbler is simple, easy, and delicious. Preparation takes 10 minutes; the toaster oven does the rest. In 40 minutes you have a beautiful dessert, ready to serve and warm from the oven.

Berry filling:
1 10-ounce package frozen blueberries, thawed, or 1½ cups fresh blueberries
1 10-ounce package frozen strawberries, thawed, or 1½ cups fresh strawberries
½ cup strawberry preserves
¼ cup unbleached flour
1 teaspoon lemon juice

Topping:
¼ cup unbleached flour
2 tablespoons margarine
1 tablespoon fat-free half-and-half
½ teaspoon baking powder
1 tablespoon sugar

PREHEAT the toaster oven to 400° F.

COMBINE the berry filling ingredients in a large bowl, mixing well. Transfer to an oiled or nonstick 8½ × 8½ × 2-inch square baking (cake) pan. Set aside.

COMBINE the topping ingredients in a small bowl, blending with a fork until the mixture is crumbly. Sprinkle the mixture evenly over the berries.

BAKE for 30 minutes, or until the top is lightly browned.

Prep: 10 minutes
Total time: 40 minutes
Serves 6

Index